Get the eBooks FREE!

(PDF, ePub, and Kindle all included)

We believe that once you buy a book from us, you should be able to read it in any format we have available. To get electronic versions of this book at no additional cost to you, purchase and then register this book at the Manning website following the instructions inside this insert.

That's it!
Thanks from Manning!

SOA Patterns

ARNON ROTEM-GAL-OZ

MANNING

SHELTER ISLAND

For online information and ordering of this and other Manning books, please visit
www.manning.com. The publisher offers discounts on this book when ordered in quantity.
For more information, please contact

> Special Sales Department
> Manning Publications Co.
> 20 Baldwin Road
> PO Box 261
> Shelter Island, NY 11964
> Email: orders@manning.com

 Manning Publications Co.
20 Baldwin Road
PO Box 261
Shelter Island, NY 11964

Development editor:	Cynthia Kane
Copyeditor:	Andy Carroll
Technical Proofreader:	Karsten Strøbæk
Proofreader:	Elizabeth Martin
Typesetter:	Dottie Marsico
Cover designer:	Marija Tudor

ISBN 9781933988269
Printed in the United States of America
3 4 5 6 7 8 9 10 – MAL – 17 16 15 14 13

To Aya, Tohar, Neder, and Yarom
You make my life rock!

brief contents

contents

ix

foreword

Building distributed yet integrated systems remains a difficult problem to solve. First, it requires a solid understanding of the individual components to be connected. Next, we have to connect these components in a way that balances loose coupling against system-wide requirements, such as latency and security. Last but not least, the resulting system has to be monitored and managed. Over time, a number of approaches have set out to solve these challenges: distributed components, EAI messaging, and, more recently, service-oriented architectures (SOA). While these approaches and tools have been a tremendous help, there is still no easy step-by-step recipe for balancing potentially opposing requirements into a coherent solution.

This is why design patterns are such a critical resource for building successful SOA solutions. Patterns encode knowledge and experience in a way that can be applied in a variety of contexts and technologies. They are not a one-size-fits-all silver bullet, but they do present forces and counterforces that steer us toward a reusable, well-balanced solution. At the same time, they form an important vocabulary that allows us to communicate our design decisions succinctly and precisely.

Arnon has harvested design decisions from years of building SOA solutions and has encoded his knowledge and experience in this book. He presents a conceptual framework of an SOA, which serves as the roadmap through various aspects of SOA design. For each aspect, he shares actionable guidance and examples from real-world project experience. At the end, he pulls all the pieces together in a real-world case study.

Rather than compiling a tome of every possible pattern that could be relevant to an SOA, Arnon selected and documented a core set of patterns and arranged them in a logical fashion. He discusses the trade-offs and design decisions involved in applying each pattern in detail, down to actual code examples. Like most tools, SOA patterns can be used, but also abused or overused. That's why Arnon takes care to warn us of the temptation to SOA-ify every architectural nail with our newfound "SOA hammer."

When Bobby Woolf and I wrote *Enterprise Integration Patterns*, Web Services had just entered the technology arena, and there was little knowledge and experience on how to turn individual services into a full-fledged service-oriented architecture. So, we decided to focus on messaging patterns first, with the hope of covering service patterns in the future. Alas, we never managed to complete that formidable task, so we are doubly thankful to Arnon—not only did he document the significant body of knowledge on SOA, he also filled in an important gap that we had left. Well done.

GREGOR HOHPE
COAUTHOR OF
ENTERPRISE INTEGRATION PATTERNS

preface

In 1996, I led development in a small startup. I had worked on multiuser systems before, but this was the first big distributed system I wrote. I found out the hard way that it isn't a simple task—a lot can and does go wrong, and simplified assumptions you make at the onset will come back to haunt you.

I learned my lesson, and I've been developing distributed systems ever since. Over the years, I discovered service-oriented architecture (SOA), and I found that, with its emphasis on interfaces and flexibility, it's a really good way to build distributed systems and it brings a lot of benefits. As I spent a few years working on many projects, I saw that a lot of people misuse SOA, that a lot don't understand it, and that good advice is hard to find. I decided to write a book—the year was 2006.

It is now 2012 and the book is finally finished. Any author will tell you that writing a book is hard, and it takes more time than initially thought. This is all true, but that's not my excuse. I finished the first third of the book reasonably on schedule, but then I joined another startup, which consumed every shred of free time I had for almost four years. On the upside, I gained more experience and I went over what I had written and updated the technology mapping sections, so you're essentially getting a second edition now. Also, the startup that prevented me from completing this book stars as the case study for chapter 9, so it did contribute something to the book as well.

Why patterns? That has to do with the first startup where I worked. As we worked on the development of the user interface (UI), I had this innovative idea—we should separate the UI logic from the UI controls and from the data-access code. This would give us more flexibility and better testability. It was only later that I learned that my "innovation" had been developed in the 1970s. It also had a name, and it was also more refined and solved the problem better—it was the Model-View-Controller (MVC) pattern. This discovery of documented architectural solutions and the time they can save in development sparked my interest in software patterns.

I really like the fact that patterns present a problem in context and don't presume the solution is always correct. I think that's a great way to present a topic, and it also let me break the book into independent bits, which makes the book usable as a reference and not something you need to read cover to cover.

One point about this book that's relatively unique is that I wrote about *architectural* patterns and not design patterns. I think it is beneficial to provide guidance at the architectural level and to understand the impact it has on the system as a whole, and not focus solely on the local effect as design patterns do. This is especially important when we're talking about SOA, because SOA is about the overall system more than it is about individual components. Another important benefit of focusing on architecture is that architecture transcends technology. The technology mapping section for each pattern shows just some examples of where each pattern can be used; you can apply the ideas using the technology of your choice.

This book summarizes my experience writing distributed systems in general, and SOA systems specifically. I hope you find it useful.

acknowledgments

Writing a book takes a major effort, and even though my name is on the cover, there are a lot of people without whom this wouldn't have happened. I'd like to thank David Stommer—the first person who said he would buy the book, back when I had the crazy idea to write it. A thank you is also due to Roy Osherove for introducing my SOA patterns idea to Manning.

A huge thanks goes to the Manning team for keeping the faith and pushing me forward. Specifically, I'd like to thank Michael Stephens, who not only contacted me with the offer to start this project but also kept nagging me to finish it. I'd like to thank Cynthia Kane, my development editor, for her patience and help in making the narrative more compelling. Also a huge thank you to Andy Carroll, my copyeditor, for taking my blubber and turning it into succinct English, and to Elizabeth Martin, my proofreader. Another thank you goes to Olivia Booth for organizing the reviews. And while he's not a Manning member, I'd also like to thank Eric Bruno who unfortunately couldn't join me as a coauthor but who did a lot of housekeeping and helped organize the book.

More thanks go to the following reviewers for providing feedback and helping make this book better: Antti Koivisto, Barry Polley, Clarence Scates, Dan Dobrin, Darren Neimke, Dave Crane, Eddy Vluggen, Eric Bowman, Eric Farr, Glenn Stokol, Gregor Hohpe, Kunal Mittal, Pat Dennis, Rick Wagner, Robert Trausmuth, Robin Anil, Roy Prins, Srikanth Vadlamani, Stephen Friend, Tijs Rademakers, and Udi Dahan.

Special thanks to Gregor Hohpe for contributing the foreword to my book and to Karsten Strøbæk for reviewing the manuscript and for his technical proofread of the book just before it went into production.

I'd especially like to thank my wife, Aya, for pushing me to man up and finish the book, and for spending nights alone while I wrote it.

Last but not least, I would like to thank all the MEAP readers, who, even though the book took ages to complete, kept on buying more and more copies and helped motivate me to complete it.

about this book

Service-oriented architecture has been around for years now. The hype surrounding it in the past has finally waned, and we are now free to do real work and build real systems using it.

Do not mistake the lack of hype for a lack of relevance. If anything, SOA is more relevant than ever, as it's practically the only good way to build cloud-based solutions (something I'll discuss in chapter 10). Additionally, the SOA landscape has become more complicated over the years because SOA is now living side-by-side (or is integrated) with other architectures like event-driven architecture, REST, and big data (discussed in chapters 5 and 10).

SOA-related technologies are more mature now, but technology alone is not enough without proper architecture. That's the main point behind this book: solving the architectural challenges of distributed systems in general and of SOA specifically by using architectural solutions expressed as patterns and antipatterns.

Roadmap

Part 1 of this book focuses on SOA patterns. It looks at ways to solve SOA challenges by using contextual solutions:

- Chapter 1 introduces SOA, its components, their relations, and the benefits of SOA. The chapter also introduces the concept of patterns and the pattern structure used in the book.
- Chapter 2 introduces some of the fundamental building blocks for building services.

- Chapter 3 tackles the core challenges of SOA, namely performance, scalability, and availability. These aspects are hard to get right because SOA adds latency by its very nature (because there are more components and distribution).
- Chapter 4 takes a look at different aspects of security and the management of services. Security is often a neglected part of any solution, and when we're talking about SOA, which is composed of many services, this can prove to be a grave mistake.
- Chapter 5 covers the common interaction patterns for services, from the simple request/reply interaction to more advanced options.
- Chapter 6 looks at patterns for integrating services and service consumers, especially UIs that are not services in themselves.
- Chapter 7 takes a look at patterns that handle the composition and integration of services.

Part 2 focuses on different aspects of SOA in the real world:

- Chapter 8 introduces SOA antipatterns. These are some of the things that can go wrong when you implement SOA, and this chapter discusses how to redesign or refactor the solutions to solve the problems.
- Chapter 9 demonstrates, via a case study, how the different patterns can work together to create a greater whole—a complete system.
- Chapter 10 takes a look at additional architectures and technologies and how they work with SOA. Specifically, the chapter covers the REST architectural style, cloud computing, and big data.

SOA Patterns can be read cover to cover, but the discussion of each individual pattern and antipattern pretty much stands on its own and can be read for reference when you face a specific challenge. To help with that, the book includes an appendix that maps quality attribute scenarios back to individual patterns and helps identify patterns that are relevant to problems you face.

Who should read this book?

This is a book about service-oriented architecture, so it will appeal to anyone tasked with building a system based on these principles. It is also about building distributed systems in general, and I believe a lot of the patterns will appeal to a wide audience.

As its main concern is with software architecture, the book is naturally targeted at software architects. I'd like to think it's also relevant for a wider audience, including developers who are tasked with building services and managers who want to understand the range of possible solutions.

The technology mapping sections of the book contain code excerpts mainly in C# and Java, but these are just examples and the designs are applicable in other languages. I've applied some of the patterns in projects that used Ruby and Scala and still found them relevant.

Code conventions

All the code in the examples used in this book is presented in a `monospaced font like this`. For longer lines of code, a wrapping character may be used to keep the code technically correct while conforming to the limitations of a printed page.

Annotations accompany many of the code listings and numbered cueballs are used if longer explanations are needed. Longer listings of code examples appear under clear listing headers; shorter listings appear between lines of text.

Author Online

Purchase of *SOA Patterns* includes free access to a private web forum run by Manning Publications where you can make comments about the book, ask technical questions, and receive help from the author and from other users. To access the forum and sub-scribe to it, point your web browser to www.manning.com/SOAPatterns. This page provides information on how to get on the forum once you're registered, what kind of help is available, and the rules of conduct on the forum.

Manning's commitment to our readers is to provide a venue where a meaningful dialog between individual readers and between readers and the author can take place. It's not a commitment to any specific amount of participation on the part of the author, whose contribution to the AO remains voluntary (and unpaid). We suggest you try ask the author some challenging questions lest his interest stray!

The Author Online forum and the archives of previous discussions will be accessi-ble from the publisher's website as long as the book is in print.

about the author

With more than 20 years of experience in software, Arnon Rotem-Gal-Oz has spent the last 15 years as an architecture and system designer of large distributed systems, including business intelligence (BI) and analytics systems, C4ISR systems, and customer care and billing systems. He has experience with a variety of technologies (Java, .NET, Scala, Hadoop, NoSQL, CEP, and others) on diverse platforms (Linux, Windows, Solaris, iOS, AS/400). Arnon currently works as the director of architecture for Nice Systems developing big data and SOA systems. Prior to that, Arnon worked as VP R&D in a couple of startups in the cloud and internet industries. Arnon blogs at http://arnon.me.

about the cover illustration

The figure on the cover of *SOA Patterns* is a "Capidji Bachi," a personal officer of the Ottoman sultan, in ceremonial dress. The illustration is taken from a collection of costumes of the Ottoman Empire published on January 1, 1802, by William Miller of Old Bond Street, London. The title page is missing from the collection and we have been unable to track it down to date. The book's table of contents identifies the figures in both English and French, and each illustration bears the names of two artists who worked on it, both of whom would no doubt be surprised to find their art gracing the front cover of a computer programming book...two hundred years later.

The collection was purchased by a Manning editor at an antiquarian flea market in the "Garage" on West 26th Street in Manhattan. The seller was an American based in Ankara, Turkey, and the transaction took place just as he was packing up his stand for the day. The Manning editor did not have on his person the substantial amount of cash that was required for the purchase and a credit card and check were both politely turned down. With the seller flying back to Ankara that evening the situation was getting hopeless. What was the solution? It turned out to be nothing more than an old-fashioned verbal agreement sealed with a handshake. The seller simply proposed that the money be transferred to him by wire and the editor walked out with the bank information on a piece of paper and the portfolio of images under his arm. Needless to say, we transferred the funds the next day, and we remain grateful and impressed by this unknown person's trust in one of us. It recalls something that might have happened a long time ago.

The pictures from the Ottoman collection, like the other illustrations that appear on our covers, bring to life the richness and variety of dress customs of two centuries ago. They recall the sense of isolation and distance of that period—and of every other historic period except our own hyperkinetic present. Dress codes have changed since then and the diversity by region, so rich at the time, has faded away. It is now often hard to tell the inhabitant of one continent from another. Perhaps, trying to view it optimistically, we have traded a cultural and visual diversity for a more varied personal life. Or a more varied and interesting intellectual and technical life.

We at Manning celebrate the inventiveness, the initiative, and, yes, the fun of the computer business with book covers based on the rich diversity of regional life of two centuries ago, brought back to life by the pictures from this collection.

Part 1

SOA patterns

This is a book about service-oriented architecture (SOA) and about solving the challenges involved in implementing it. We'll discuss that in two parts. Part 1, the first seven chapters, discusses SOA and a range of architectural patterns, demonstrating them in numerous examples; part 2, chapters 8–10, looks at how it all works in real life.

Chapter 1 introduces SOA and its components (services, consumers, messages, endpoints, contracts, and policies) as well as the patterns approach. The subsequent chapters detail the different patterns.

Chapter 2 takes a look at foundation patterns—basic patterns that are needed to get started with implementing services. Chapter 3 covers patterns related to performance, scalability, and availability. Chapter 4 looks at what's needed to secure services and monitor their overall wellness. Chapter 5 details message exchange patterns, starting with the basic request/reply model and ending with long-running interactions. Chapter 6 covers patterns related to how consumers interact with services. Chapter 7 examines service composition patterns that show how you can go from a bunch of services to a system.

The patterns presented in the book are architectural patterns, and the architecture is driven by quality attributes (also known as nonfunctional requirements or "illities"). The discussion of each pattern also has a quality attributes section detailing sample scenarios. Appendix A provides a cross reference from quality attributes to the patterns and can be used to quickly look up relevant patterns.

Solving SOA pains with patterns

In this chapter
- What is software architecture
- What SOA is and isn't
- Pattern structure

How do you write a book on service-oriented architecture (SOA) patterns? As I pondered this question, it led to many others. Should I explain the context for SOA, or explain the background that's needed to understand what SOA is? Should I mention distributed systems? Should I discuss when an SOA is needed, and when it isn't? After much thought, it became apparent to me: a book on SOA patterns should be a practitioner's book. If you're faced with the challenge of designing and building an SOA-based system, this book is for you.

You might not even agree with an SOA-based approach, but are forced into using it based on someone else's decision. Alternatively, you may think that SOA is the greatest thing since sliced bread. Either way, the fact that you're here, reading this, means you recognize that building an enterprise-class SOA-based system is challenging. There are indeed challenges, and they cut across many areas, such as security, availability, service composition, reporting, business intelligence, and performance.

To be clear, I won't be lecturing you on the merits of some wondrous solution set I've devised. True to the profession of the architect, my goal is to act as a mentor. I intend to provide you with patterns that will help you make the right decisions for the particular challenges and requirements you'll face in *your* SOA projects, and enable you to succeed.

Before we begin our journey into the world of SOA patterns, there are three things we need to discuss:

- *What is software architecture?* The "A" in SOA stands for *architecture,* so we need to define this clearly.
- *What is a SOA?* This is an important question because SOA is an overhyped and overloaded term. We need to clearly define the term that sets the foundation for this book.
- *How will each pattern be presented in the book?* I've used a consistent structure to explain each of the patterns in this book. We'll take a quick look at this structure so you know what to expect in the discussion of each pattern.

Let's get started with the first question—what is software architecture?

1.1   *Defining software architecture*

There are many opinions as to what *software architecture* is. One of the more accepted ones is IEEE's description of software architecture as the "fundamental concepts or properties of a system in its environment embodied in its elements, relationships, and in the principles of its design and evolution" (IEEE 42010). My definition agrees with this one, but is a bit more descriptive:

> **DEFINITION**   Software architecture is the collection of fundamental decisions about a software product or solution designed to meet the project's quality attributes (the architectural requirements). The architecture includes the main components, their main attributes, and their collaborations (their interactions and behavior) to meet the quality attributes. Architecture can, and usually should, be expressed in several levels of abstraction, where the number of levels depends on the project's size and complexity.

Looking at this definition, we can draw some conclusions about software architecture:

- *Architecture occurs early.* It should represent the set of earliest design decisions that are both hardest to change and most critical to get right.
- *Architecture is an attribute of every system.* Whether or not its design was intentional, every system has an architecture.
- *Architecture breaks a system into components and sets boundaries.* It doesn't need to describe all the components, but the architecture usually deals with the major components of the solution and their interfaces.
- *Architecture is about relationships and component interactions.* We're interested in the behaviors of the individual components as they can be discerned from

other components interacting with them. The architecture doesn't have to describe the complete characteristics of the components; it mainly deals with their interfaces and other interactions.

- *Architecture explains the rationale behind the choices.* It's important to understand the reasoning as well as the implications of the decisions made in the architecture because their impact on the project is large. Also, it can be beneficial to understand what alternatives were weighed and abandoned. This may be important for future reference, if and when things need to be reconsidered, and for anyone new to the project who needs to understand the situation.
- *There isn't a single structure that is the architecture.* We need to look at the architecture from different directions or viewpoints to fully understand it. One diagram, or even a handful, isn't enough to be considered an architecture.

For a software system's architecture to be intentional, rather than accidental, it should be communicated. Architecture is communicated from multiple viewpoints to cater to the needs of the stakeholders. The Software Engineering Institute (SEI) defines an architectural style as a description of component types and their topology, together with a set of constraints on how they can be used.

1.2 *Service-oriented architecture*

The term *SOA* was first used in 1996 when Roy Schulte and Yeffim V. Natiz from Gartner defined it as "a style of multitier computing that helps organizations share logic and data among multiple applications and usage modes."[1] Now, SOA is finally at the forefront of IT architectures and systems. But on the uphill and rocky road to stardom, SOA has become a loaded term filled with misconceptions and hype. As in the game of "telephone," the definition of SOA has morphed as it was passed along in informal conversations. For the purposes of this book (and my view of SOA), we'll use the following definition:

> **DEFINITION** *Service-oriented architecture* (SOA) is an architectural style for building systems based on interactions of loosely coupled, coarse-grained, and autonomous components called *services*. Each service exposes processes and behavior through *contracts*, which are composed of *messages* at discoverable addresses called *endpoints*. A service's behavior is governed by policies that are external to the service itself. The contracts and messages are used by external components called *service consumers*.

Let's take a look at common misconceptions about SOA and see why they're not SOA. Then we'll come back and expand on this definition, and SOA's benefits both architecturally and business-wise.

---

[1] Roy W. Schulte and Yefim V. Natis, SPA-401-068: "'Service Oriented' Architectures, Part 1" (report for Gartner, 1996).

1.2.1 *What SOA is, and is not*

Many popular terms go through what Martin Fowler calls "semantic diffusion."[2] As a term becomes more popular, people try to make it stick to whatever they're doing. Additionally, the hype, or buzz, that a new term receives generates a lot of discussion around it. If the people using the term don't understand it completely, or if they're using the term in hopes that its popularity rubs off on their product, the results are misconceptions and inaccurate descriptions.

For instance, in the late 1980s, object-oriented programming (OOP) was the hot new topic. As a result, developers referred to everything in their design, and their code, as *objects* simply because they wanted to say they were using object-oriented design and development techniques. The truth was, because the methodology was so new and the hype was so great, their descriptions were, in most cases, inaccurate. It took several years for OOP to take root and for the development world to agree upon what it truly was.

One can argue that we're at the same stage with SOA; it has garnered many misconceptions and incomplete definitions. Table 1.1 outlines the most prevalent misconceptions and explains why they are, in fact, misconceptions.

Table 1.1   Common misconceptions about SOA

Misconception	Why it's not SOA
SOA is a way to align IT and the business team.	That's not true. Better IT and business alignment is something we want to achieve using SOA, but it isn't what SOA is. Nevertheless, the loosely coupled systems that result from a good SOA solution enable the agility needed to truly align IT and the business team.
SOA is an application that has a "web service" interface.	This isn't necessarily true. To begin with, we can implement SOA with other technologies. A nice example is the Open Services Gateway initiative (OSGi), which defines a Java-based service platform (see www.osgi.org). Furthermore, by exposing a method as a web service, we can create procedural-like RPCs, which is far from the SOA concepts and direction (see also the Nanoservice antipattern in chapter 8).
SOA is a set of technologies (SOAP, REST, WS-I, and so on).	This is a general case of the previous misconception. Although some technologies are identified with SOA, or fit in well with SOA, SOA is an architectural approach. Remember, SOA is technology-independent.
SOA is a reuse strategy.	This is not always true. Reuse certainly sounds like a tempting reason to use SOA, but the larger the granularity of a component, the harder it is to reuse it. Nevertheless, SOA will allow your services to evolve over time and adapt, so that you don't need to start from scratch every time.
SOA is an off-the-shelf solution.	SOA isn't a product you can buy—it's a way to architect distributed systems. Perhaps you can resell the resulting service, but that's only a convenient artifact of a good design.

---

[2]   Martin Fowler, "Semantic Diffusion," http://martinfowler.com/bliki/SemanticDiffusion.html.

Now that we've looked at some misconceptions, let's reexamine the SOA definition provided earlier. SOA is an architectural style. This means that SOA defines components, relationships, and constraints about each component's usage and interactions. As mentioned in the definition, the SOA style defines the following components: service, endpoint, message, contract, policy, and service consumer. SOA also defines certain interactions that the components can have. Figure 1.1 illustrates SOA's components and their relationships:

Let's take a deeper look at each of the six components of SOA.

SERVICE

The central pillar of SOA is the *service*. Merriam-Webster's dictionary has eleven different definitions for the word service; the most appropriate here is "a facility supplying some public demand."[3]

In my opinion, a service should provide a distinct business function, and it should be a coarse-grained piece of logic. Additionally, a service should implement all of the functionality promised by the contracts it exposes. One of the characteristics of services is *service autonomy*, which means the service should be mainly self-sufficient.

CONTRACT

The collection of all the messages supported by the service is known as the service's *contract*. The contract can be unilateral, meaning it provides a closed set of messages that flow in one direction. Alternatively, a contract might be bilateral, with the service exchanging messages with a predefined group of components. A service's contract is analogous to the interface of an object in object-oriented design.

ENDPOINT

An *endpoint* is a universal resource identifier (URI), such as an address or a specific place, where the service can be found. A specific contract can be exposed at a specific endpoint.

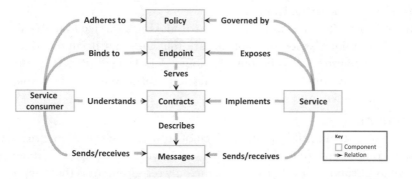

Figure 1.1 Apart from the obvious component (the service), SOA has several other components, such as the contract that the service implements, endpoints where the service can be contacted, messages that are moved back and forth between the service and its consumers, policies that the service adheres to, and consumers that interact with the service.

---

[3] Merriam-Webster, "service," http://www.merriam-webster.com/dictionary/service.

MESSAGE

The unit of communication in SOA is the *message*. Messages can come in many different forms, such as these:

- HTTP GET messages (in the representational state transfer (REST) style)
- Simple Object Access Protocol (SOAP) messages
- Java Message Services (JMS) messages
- Simple Mail Transfer Protocol (SMTP) messages

The difference between a message and other forms of communication, such as a remote procedure call (RPC), is subtle. An RPC often requires the caller to have intimate knowledge of the other system's implementation details. With messaging, this isn't the case. Messages have both a header and a body (the *payload*). The header is usually generic and can be understood by infrastructure and framework components without knowing implementation details. This reduces dependencies and coupling. The existence of the header allows for infrastructure components to route reply messages (for example, the routing of messages in the Saga pattern in chapter 5) or implement security transparently (see the Service Firewall pattern in chapter 4).

Messages are a very important part of SOA, and they've been thoroughly covered by other books, such as *Enterprise Integration Patterns* by Gregor Hohpe and Bobby Woolf (Addison-Wesley Professional, 2004). Nonetheless, this book also explores some messaging patterns where the SOA perspective enhances the more generic perspective used in Hohpe and Woolf's book. As an example, see the Request/Reply pattern in chapter 5.

POLICY

One important differentiator between SOA and object-oriented design (or even component-oriented design) is the existence of *policies*. Just as an interface or contract separates specifications from implementations, policies separate dynamic specifications from static or semantic specifications.

A policy defines the terms and conditions for making a service available for service consumers. The unique aspects of policies are that they can be updated at runtime and they're externalized from the business logic. A policy specifies dynamic properties, such as security (encryption, authentication, authorization), auditing, service-level agreements (SLAs), and so on.

SERVICE CONSUMER

A service is only meaningful if another piece of software uses it. *Service consumers* are the software components that interact with a service via messaging. Consumers can be either client applications or other services; the only requirement is that they adhere to an SOA contract themselves.

1.2.2 *SOA architectural benefits*

By definition, SOA brings many architectural benefits to a distributed software system. Many quality attributes are addressed, such as these:

- *Reusability*—This isn't reusability in the sense of "write once integrate any-where," but rather in the sense that you "don't throw everything out when you need different functionality."
- *Adaptability*—Isolating the internal structure of a service from the rest of the world lets you make changes more easily. You only need to adhere to the contracts you publish.
- *Maintainability*—Services can be maintained by dedicated, smaller teams and can be tested this way as well. Robert L. Glass has said, "software maintenance is a solution, not a problem".[4] SOA greatly helps make this a reality.

These benefits exist because SOA removes the dependency issues related to point-to-point integration.

Many enterprises have grown isolated systems to solve particular business needs. These are sometimes referred to as *stovepipe systems*. As time passes and business needs change, there's often a need to share data between systems. Each time such a need is identified, a new relationship is formed between these systems. The result, as seen in figure 1.2, is an integration mess that becomes very hard to maintain and evolve over time.

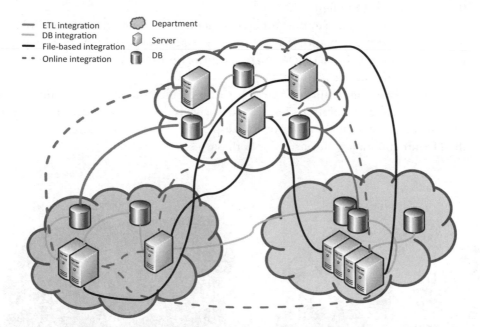

Figure 1.2   Typical integration spaghetti in enterprise systems. Each department builds its own systems, and as people use the systems, they find they need information from other systems. Point-to-point integration emerges.

---

[4]   Robert L. Glass, *Software Conflict 2.0: The Art and Science of Software Engineering* (Developer.* Books, 2006), 61–65.

The diagram shows four types of point-to-point integrations:

- *ETL (extract, transform, load)*—Database-to-database integration or other ETL-based integration
- *Online integration*—Application-to-application integration based on HTTP or TCP
- *File-based integration*—Application-to-application integration based on the filesystems and the exchange of files (such as comma-delimited files)
- *Direct database connection*—Application-to-database integration

NOTE   The preceding list isn't exhaustive. There are additional relationships such as replication, message-based relationships, and others that aren't expressed in figure 1.2.

In a well-defined SOA, the interfaces aren't designed to be point-to-point but are instead more generalized to serve many anonymous consumers. SOA eliminates this spaghetti and introduces more disciplined communication. Fewer connectors means less maintenance and fewer assumptions. Fewer connectors also result in increased flexibility, as shown in figure 1.3.

For enterprises that support a heterogeneous environment, with multiple operating systems (OSs) and platforms, SOA provides standards-based contracts that are platform-independent. In fact, SOA enables transparent interoperability among services and applications across platforms.

Policy-based communications also greatly enhance the maintainability and adaptability of SOA-based solutions because key aspects, like security and monitoring, are configurable. This moves some of the responsibility from the development team to the IT staff and makes life easier for both parties.

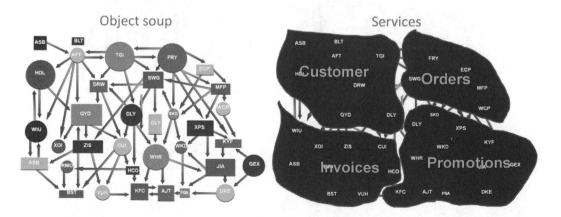

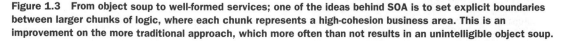

Figure 1.3   From object soup to well-formed services; one of the ideas behind SOA is to set explicit boundaries between larger chunks of logic, where each chunk represents a high-cohesion business area. This is an improvement on the more traditional approach, which more often than not results in an unintelligible object soup.

We can take all of these architectural benefits and translate them to business benefits, as discussed in the next section.

1.2.3 SOA for the enterprise

There are a lot of business-oriented aspects of SOA as well. SOA is described as a way to "increase the alignment of IT and the business." Essentially, increased alignment means that IT can adapt more easily to the changing business processes, and thus increase your business's agility.

To avoid overloading the term SOA, I'd like to refer to these aspects of SOA as "SOA initiatives." Table 1.2 points out some of these business benefits.

Table 1.2 SOA technical benefits and the business benefits they provide

SOA characteristic	Business benefit
Easier maintenance and replacement of components	Easier replacement of existing business components Better adaptability to accommodate changing business processes Faster time to market for new business functionality
Standards-based service interfaces (contracts)	Reduced effort to connect new systems Easier partner integration Enables automation of business process
Service autonomy	Reduced downtime and lower operational costs
Externalized policies	Ability to set service-level agreements Easier integration

In general, it's best to take an incremental approach to adopting SOA—your business can't afford to halt and wait for an SOA initiative to finish. You need to plan for SOA-like highway intersections; detours need to be created to enable business to continue while the new system is being developed.

Many SOA books cover the business aspects of the SOA initiatives, and this book isn't one of them. This book's scope is the software architecture aspects of SOA and technological implications of these aspects, not business analysis and related methods. One of the best ways to express these software architecture concerns and provide a better understanding of the architectural solutions is through the use of patterns (best practices) and antipatterns (lessons learned and mistakes to avoid).

1.3 Solving SOA challenges with patterns

Given all its benefits, why would anyone choose *not* to build with SOA? The truth is, building with SOA isn't easy. Even though SOA is designed to face the challenges of distributed systems design, there are still many issues you need to take care of and solve when you design viable solutions.

One set of problems is the quality attributes not inherently addressed by SOA, like availability, security, scalability, performance, and so on. Real projects have to deal with requirements like *five-nines availability* (99.999 percent uptime), which is no more than about five minutes of downtime per year.

Another set of problems has to do with the challenges of designing and building SOA. How do you gain a centralized view of business data in an architectural style that encourages encapsulation and privacy? What does it mean to aggregate services? How do you tie your services to a UI?

It would be nice if there were a few best practices already defined that could tell us how to cope with all of these issues. The truth is that there are no silver bullets in software design and development. Every system has its own set of prerequisites, hidden costs, one-off requirements, and special case exceptions. This is exactly why the use of patterns is so appealing as a medium to convey solutions. Patterns aren't defined to be perfect solutions. Instead, they give the context for where the solution works. To achieve this, patterns describe both the solution *and* the problem they solve, and any caveats associated with that solution.

The following section explains the pattern structure used in this book and demonstrates how to apply the patterns to your own set of design challenges.

1.3.1   *Pattern structure*

Patterns in this book mostly take after what is called the *Alexandrian form*, which is named after the style Christopher Alexander and his coauthors used in their book, *A Pattern Language*.[5] In this form, pattern descriptions are narrative with a few headings for readability, and they serve as a vocabulary for both designers and architects.

To start, each pattern has a descriptive name that's easy to remember and recall. The name is followed by a short narrative passage to introduce the problem, which is the first subsection. The other subsections in the pattern's description are solution, technology mapping, and quality attributes.

Let's examine the pattern form, and each of the subsections, in more detail now.

PROBLEM

The problem section, as its name implies, details the problem the pattern aims to solve. It includes a problem statement that summarizes the essence of the problem. More complex problems have an additional passage, prior to the problem statement, that details the problem's context. For instance, some patterns contain an example to help illustrate the problem.

Following the problem statement, the section often continues with a discussion of other related options—often a discussion of alternative solutions and why they fail to solve this particular problem (though these alternative solutions may still be applicable in other circumstances).

---

[5]   Christopher Alexander, Sara Ishikawa, and Murray Silverstein, *A Pattern Language: Towns, Buildings, Construction* (Oxford University Press, 1977).

SOLUTION

The solution begins with a solution statement that summarizes the essence of the solution. A diagram that serves as a visual representation of the solution's components and their relationships follows the solution statement.

The same diagram conventions are used for all the patterns, with different visualizations for the SOA components (see figure 1.1) and other neutral players. The figures include component relationships, other pattern components, attributes, and the functionality of the pattern's components. Take a look at figure 1.4.

Without getting into the details of the roles of the different components, in this diagram you can see that edge and endpoint are neutral components that aren't part of the pattern. The dispatcher and service instance components are part of the pattern. Each of the pattern's parts has one or more roles and attributes. In this case, you can see that the dispatcher is responsible for the distribution (of messages) and that the service instance is responsible for (running) the service business logic. The dispatcher and service instance are part of the pattern, while the innermost rectangles designate roles or attributes of the pattern's components (for instance, the dispatcher distributes messages). The arrows are used to show interactions and relationships. Requests and replies are passed back and forth between the dispatcher and service instance, for example.

The pattern description then continues with more details regarding the solution, such as how the solution addresses outside forces, and so on. There may be a discussion of the implications or consequences of applying the pattern as well as the relationship to other patterns and examples.

TECHNOLOGY MAPPING

The technology mapping section of the pattern description deals with technology implications. Although a system's architecture can be technology independent, a set of technologies must be chosen to build the system. Therefore, as a practicing architect, you often need to map parts of the architecture to specific technologies.

For SOA, there are many relevant technologies, such as the WS-* protocol stack, REST-based web services, dedicated products, EDBs, and many others. The technology

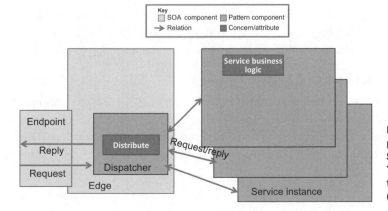

Figure 1.4 Sample pattern diagram: the Service Instance pattern. The endpoint and edge are two neutral components (not part of the pattern).

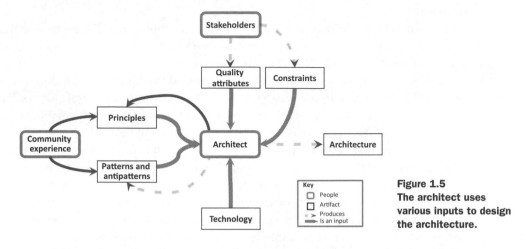

Figure 1.5
The architect uses various inputs to design the architecture.

mapping section of each pattern talks about the relevant technologies that can be used to implement the pattern or where the pattern is implemented.

QUALITY ATTRIBUTES

The final section of the pattern description has to do with identifying applicable patterns for your solution. If patterns are the solutions, then quality attributes are the requirements. The quality attributes section of each pattern talks about the architectural benefits of the pattern and provides sample scenarios that can be used to identify the pattern as relevant.

In figure 1.5, you can see the various inputs the architect can use before a solution is designed.

First and foremost, you work with the constraints and requirements gathered from the stakeholders. These include requirements for performance, security, scalability, and interoperability. You can augment these inputs by drawing on personal and community experience to add principles, patterns, and antipatterns. There are also the possibilities and constraints imposed by available technologies. Finally, you must analyze, prioritize, and balance all of these inputs to produce a final architecture to suit the problem.

Appendix A includes a cross-reference from quality attributes back to pattern names (and the chapters they're discussed in), and it provides some more background on quality attributes and quality attribute scenarios.

1.3.2   *From isolated patterns to a pattern language*

Each pattern on its own provides useful information and describes a good practice. As mentioned, patterns have relationships to other patterns—sometimes another pattern is an alternative, and sometimes patterns can complement one another. There is usually value in documenting these relationships, and this structural organization is called a "pattern language."

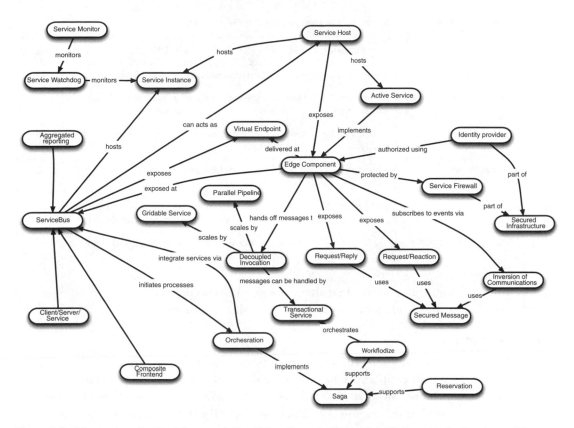

Figure 1.6 Like any good pattern language, the SOA patterns in this book build upon each other to provide a big-picture solution.

Evolving patterns into a pattern language that shows the patterns' relationships helps enable us to recognize related problems, and allows the architect to navigate the patterns in a logical way. In a sense, you can think of a pattern language as a logical and intuitive "mind map" of the patterns that lets you take different paths through the design process. As a result, patterns often open your mind to the bigger-picture problems that need to be solved, and provide an overview perspective you may not have had before (see figure 1.6).

Table 1.3 shows how the patterns in this book are categorized, and in which chapters they are discussed. Note that as you progress from chapter to chapter, you'll be moving outward. The first two pattern chapters (chapters 2 and 3) mostly deal with the internal structure of services. Chapter 4 focuses on the service interface, chapters 5 and 6 focus on the service consumer and its interaction with the service, and chapter 7 focuses on SOA as whole.

When you encounter a problem in your SOA implementation, you can use both the pattern diagram in figure 1.6 and the pattern categories in table 1.3 as roadmaps

Table 1.3 Pattern categories and the chapters they're discussed in

Category	Subcategory	Description	Chapter
Service structure	Foundation patterns	Common service building blocks	2
	Performance, availability, and scalability	Patterns to solve scalability, availability, and performance challenges	3
	Security and manageability	Patterns for securing and managing services	4
Integration	Message exchange patterns	Patterns for communication between services	5
	Consumer interaction	Interaction patterns for when the consumers are user clients or other services	6
Service composition		Patterns for making services work together and share information	7

to help you locate patterns that should be useful. The patterns diagram can also help you find related patterns to create more complete solutions.

1.4　Summary

We've now laid the foundation you need to understand the SOA patterns in this book and their overall context. We began with a definition of SOA and patterns in general, and we considered how patterns can be used to provide solutions to SOA challenges. We also looked at the technical and business benefits of SOA. The second part of this chapter explained what patterns are, the structure of the patterns as they'll be discussed in this book, and how to locate the patterns discussed in the book.

This chapter covered a lot of issues very briefly in order to create a common vocabulary for our discussion of SOA patterns. If you're interested in learning more about the issues discussed in this chapter, look at one or more of the resources listed in the further reading section.

Chapter 2 is our first pattern chapter, in which we'll take a look at some of the basic patterns used to build services.

1.5　Further reading

DISTRIBUTED SYSTEMS

Chris Britton, *IT Architectures and Middleware: Strategies for Building Large, Integrated Systems* (Addison-Wesley Professional, 2004).

Provides a good look at the history of distributed systems and the inherent difficulties that they inflict. It's a very thorough book—the only problem is that it ends just before the SOA era.

FALLACIES OF DISTRIBUTED COMPUTING

Arnon Rotem-Gal-Oz, "Fallacies of Distributed Computing Explained," www.rgoarchitects .com/ Files/fallacies.pdf.

SOA is an architectural style for distributed systems. Most other styles don't have a distributed mindshare and so, unlike SOA, they disagree with the fallacies. This paper, which I wrote, explains how the fallacies are still relevant today.

SOA

Dirk Krafzig, Karl Banke, and Dirk Slama, *Enterprise SOA: Service-Oriented Architecture Best Practices* (Prentice Hall, 2004).

This is one of the best books on SOA, and it provides a very good introduction to the subject.

Eric A. Marks and Michael Bell, *Service-Oriented Architecture: A Planning and Implementation Guide for Business and Technology* (Wiley, 2006).

Marks and Bell take a look at the business perspectives of SOA and provide a completely different (and complementary) look at SOA, as compared to this book.

Foundation
structural patterns

2

In this chapter

- Patterns dealing with services
- Lightweight containers and DI
- Poison messages

Congratulations, you're in charge of building your first service—now what? The first thing to do, before getting into advanced topics such as making your service secure and scalable, is to take care of the basics. Where will you deploy your service? How do you ensure your service's reliability? How do you enable anonymous access? And so on.

In chapter 1 we talked about SOA basics: creating autonomous components that publish and accept messages defined by contracts, delivered at endpoints, and governed by policies to service consumers. In contrast, this chapter deals with some foundation patterns—those that solve some of the more common issues related to all services. These are the patterns you're most likely to use, even if you have modest requirements for your services. Because they deal with fundamental issues, the patterns in this chapter are relevant to implementing the services themselves (see figure 2.1).

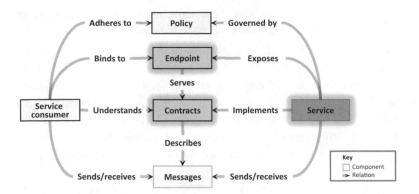

Figure 2.1   SOA defines six different components. This chapter has patterns that deal with services, which are the essence of SOA.

In this chapter, we'll discuss five patterns:

- *Service Host*—Make your services adaptable to different configurations easily and save yourself the repetitive and mundane tasks of setting listeners, wiring components, and so on
- *Active Service*—Increase service autonomy and handle temporal concerns
- *Transactional Service*—Handle messages reliably
- *Workflodize*—Increase the service's adaptability to changing business processes
- *Edge Component*—Allow the service's business aspects, technological concerns, and other cross-cutting concerns to evolve at their own pace, independently of one another

Enough introduction already. Let's look at the first pattern, which describes the platform where your services will run.

2.1   Service Host pattern

The first pattern we'll talk about, Service Host, is one of the most basic patterns, if not *the* most basic one. Service Host deals with the environment where service instances run. Let's start by looking at why we need this pattern.

PROBLEM

Pick a service, any service (don't tell me what it is). Wait, I think I see something … you have some code that sets up listeners for incoming messages or requests. You also have code to wire up components, and more code that initializes and activates that service. You probably also have some code to configure your service. Am I right? Chances are you have most of these pieces of code somewhere in your service.

The problem is you can end up with a lot of this code duplicated throughout the services you've built, or will build. When building services, there are quite a few basic tasks that are repetitive and common.

? **How can you easily configure services and avoid duplicating mundane tasks, such as setting listeners and wiring components, for each service?**

The first option, and one that's chosen all too often, is to rewrite the wiring and the rest of the repetitive code for each and every service. Obviously, this isn't a good choice because it wastes time and can be error-prone. The duplicated-effort problem is even worse when you consider maintaining a lot of similar code. If you make an enhancement or fix a bug in this configuration code in one service, you'll need to copy that fix to each other service that contains similar code. This isn't an efficient use of your time, and it requires an inordinate amount of testing to ensure you didn't miss anything.

A more reasonable solution is to create a library of common tasks and have each service work with a copy of it. A library helps, because the code is only written once, but you're still left with coding the wiring that's needed to utilize all of the library's functionality.

Another option is to use inheritance—create a base class that implements the common functionality, and have each service subclass it. But inheritance can be problematic, especially if the service functionality doesn't fit within a single class. Additionally, inheritance will prevent you from using techniques like dependency injection to replace behavior or components. Not to mention that this is the wrong use of inheritance; inheritance should indicate an "is a" relationship.

Nevertheless, inheritance comes close to solving the problem, as you only write the code once, and customization occurs where the services differ. If you want to get the same behavior without using inheritance, you can do that by using a framework—a service host.

SOLUTION

✓ **Create a common service host component or framework that acts as a container for services. This container should be configurable and will perform the wiring and setup of services.**

The Service Host, illustrated in figure 2.2, is a framework or a complete component that performs some or all of the following functions:

- *Lifecycle*—Takes care of instantiating services, recycling services on fault, in-place upgrades, and so on
- *Configuration*—Reads and applies configuration to hosted services, including configuration for security, contract policies, and ports
- *Wiring*—Performs runtime setup of component wiring such as binding a listener on a service's endpoint
- *Administration*—Lets an administrator control the lifecycle of a hosted service and may also include monitoring capabilities (this is an additional layer on top of lifecycle responsibility)
- *Environment*—Provides auxiliary services like logging, cache, database libraries (ODBC/JDBC), scheduler, and so on

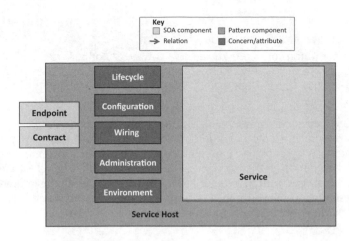

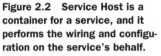

Figure 2.2   Service Host is a container for a service, and it performs the wiring and configuration on the service's behalf.

All of these tasks are supporting capabilities that are needed by services. As you saw in the problem introduction, you're likely to encounter these functions in more than one service.

The Service Host is a framework, which means it contains functionality and data flow, and it calls back into your code to extend the flow according to your service's needs. This callback principle is known as *Inversion of Control* (IoC), which is in wide use today in other object-oriented frameworks such as Spring, Hibernate, and Struts.

The Service Host pattern has several benefits when compared with the other options mentioned previously. One benefit already mentioned: as a framework, the Service Host performs the work and only calls your code to fine-tune the behavior rather than leaving this orchestration to you. Another benefit is that it better addresses the *Open Closed Principle* (OCP). OCP states that a class should be open to extension but closed for modification, which is exactly what a framework gives you.

A Service Host implementation may host more than one service—the number of services hosted depends on the scale of a deployed solution. I've seen this pattern successfully applied where a large solution had to be scaled down to run on a single computer. But more often than not, the Service Host pattern is used to build services that span more than one computer, appearing as one aggregated service.

You can roll your own Service Host implementation, but it's usually provided by technology vendors. We'll look into this in more detail next.

TECHNOLOGY MAPPING

The Service Host is a fundamental SOA structural pattern and, as such, it's supported by most available technologies.

The most basic option is to build your own Service Host. This is an option if you have modest or uncommon requirements. I did this when I needed stateful services on the .NET platform and couldn't find something suitable from Microsoft. If you're implementing the Service Host pattern yourself, you should take a look at lightweight containers, such as Spring or PicoContainer, to help you out with wiring and instantiation. In most cases there are plenty of better options from technology vendors.

Lightweight containers and Dependency Injection

Spring and a few other frameworks are known as lightweight containers. They allow you to decrease coupling and increase the testability of your solutions. They perform this magic through the use of the Dependency Injection pattern, which is a non-SOA pattern.

Dependency Injection occurs when a class lets a third-party component, which acts as an assembler, provide the entire implementation for the interfaces it depends upon. Using Dependency Injection, a class no longer depends on a specific implementation, but rather depends on the interface or abstract class. This helps with testability, as you can supply stubs or mocks for the class to simulate its environment. It also helps with flexibility, as you can easily change the implementation of the dependencies without affecting your code, as long as they keep their contracts.

Figure 2.3 shows Microsoft's implementation of the Service Host pattern, called App-Fabric. You can see that AppFabric (the service host) provides added value on top of hosting the services. You also get the means to control the lifecycle of the hosted services, monitor them, and so on.

AppFabric is a relatively new addition to Microsoft's server stack. The Java world, on the other hand, has a relatively long tradition of application servers, most of which, like

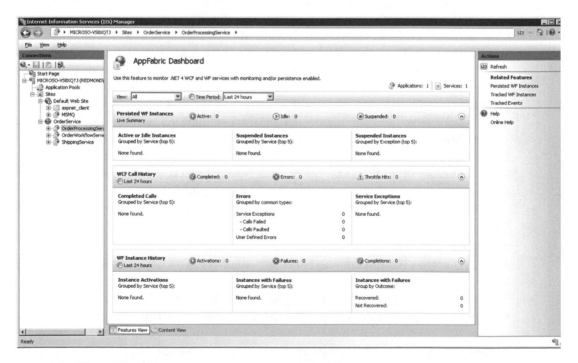

Figure 2.3   Microsoft's AppFabric is an example of an implementation of the Service Host pattern. Here you can see the AppFabric's Dashboard, showing that this instance has one service installed, as well as several statistics related to the service (like the number of calls, count of errors, and so on).

Service Host

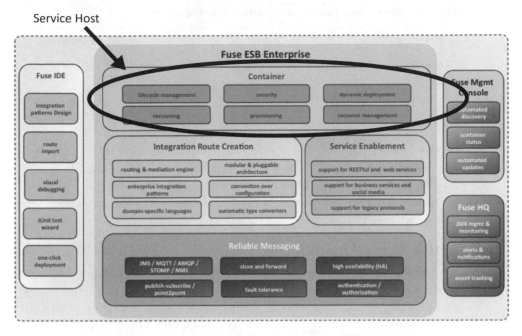

**Figure 2.4   An enterprise service bus (ESB) with Service Host capabilities
(© 2012 FuseSource Corp., modified with permission)**

WebSphere and WebLogic, can double as service hosts. Most application servers support both JAX-WS (SOAP-based web services) and JAX-RS (REST-based web services).

In addition to application servers, some Java enterprise service buses (ESBs) provide service host capabilities (see also the discussion of the Service Bus pattern in chapter 7). Figure 2.4 shows the components of Fuse ESB, an open source ESB based on Apache ServiceMix. In the circled area you can see the provisioning, deployment, and admin capabilities (based on Apache Felix—an OSGi implementation).

As you've seen, the Service Host pattern is basic but effective, and it's in wide use today. See the further reading section at the end of this chapter for links to resources that expand on the technologies mentioned in this section.

QUALITY ATTRIBUTES

The main reason to use the Service Host pattern is reusability. A nice side effect of reusability is the increased reliability you get as a result, because all of your services leverage a well-tested framework.

The other quality attribute this pattern provides is portability, which is enhanced by the separation of concerns effect of the pattern, as demonstrated in the scale-down example mentioned previously. Another facet of portability is the ability to deploy the same service code in different environments—a result of configuring the service context in markup.

Table 2.1 summarizes these attributes with two sample scenarios.

Table 2.1   Service Host pattern quality attributes and scenarios

Quality attribute	Concrete attribute	Sample scenario
Reusability	Development time	During development, you can set up the environment for a new service within minutes.
Portability	Installation	During installation, switching from one environment to another should take little to no time.

Service Host implementations, as you've seen, aren't unlike web servers in many ways. Like websites, services are passive by nature; a service will remain idle until a request arrives, at which time the service performs its work to generate a response.

That's not always the best option. Sometimes a service needs to be active rather than passive. Let's look at the Active Service pattern to learn why and how.

2.2   *Active Service pattern*

Recapping what I explained in chapter 1 and earlier in this chapter: It's important for services to be autonomous because autonomy decreases coupling between services and provides greater flexibility for the overall solution. This also means that there are few dependencies between the services, as they only know each other by contract. It also means that the teams working on different services can be working independently. Each team focuses on its own service, and there are no interdependencies with other service implementations or their development teams.

The most valuable (as in business value) aspect of service autonomy mentioned so far is that the services should be as self-sufficient as possible. Let's look at an example.

PROBLEM

Imagine a journal subscription agency, such as EBSCO or Blackwell, that needs to create a proposal for a potential customer. From the SOA perspective, you can have a Proposals service that will need, among other things, to produce a pro forma invoice, which is a document that precedes the actual business transaction. In this scenario, to produce the pro forma invoice, the service must know both the discounts offered to the customer and the discounts the subscription agency receives from its own vendors (the journals' publishers). With this data, the service can calculate whether the proposal is profitable. Figure 2.5 shows a simple diagram for such a flow.

The Proposals service must wait for the services it depends on to respond before it can send its own response. If either of the services it depends on fails, the Proposals service will be effectively unavailable. No amount of time, effort, or money spent in making the Proposals service resilient and fault tolerant will resolve such an outage because the Proposals service is coupled too tightly to the other services. It might be acceptable to have this coupling between the Proposals and the Customers services, as they're both internal and under your control. But the dependency on the external vendor's services is more risky—the internal Proposals service isn't autonomous.

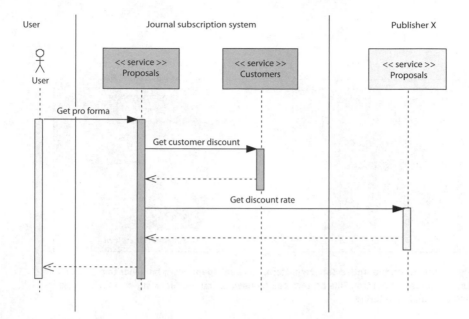

Figure 2.5 The Proposals service needs to get data from both internal and external services.

How can you increase service autonomy and handle temporal concerns?

As the preceding example demonstrates, a passive service that only reacts to requests is problematic. The service might not be able to fulfill its contract (or its SLA) if other services don't behave as intended. Even when the external services are available, a large load of requests can fail due to network congestion.

One option is for the service to cache previous results, but this is only a partial solution. It doesn't take care of data freshness, so data in the cache can become too stale. Nor does it take care of cache misses, which will require external service calls anyway. Depending on the variety of requests, the number of calls may not be negligible.

Even if a cache solved your online requests problem, you still need to be able to solve other recurring or one-time events that are tied to time (which I'll refer to as "temporal events"). Such events would include producing monthly bills, or publishing stock figures, or generating any other recurring report.

A solution that can solve all these issues is to make your service do some work on its own accord. You need an active service.

SOLUTION

Make the service an active service by implementing at least one active class, either on the edge, within the service, or both. Let the active class take care of temporal concerns and autonomy issues.

The Active Service pattern, illustrated in figure 2.6, gets its name from the object-oriented concept of *active classes*. Active classes, as defined in the official UML specification, represent objects that may execute their own behavior without requiring

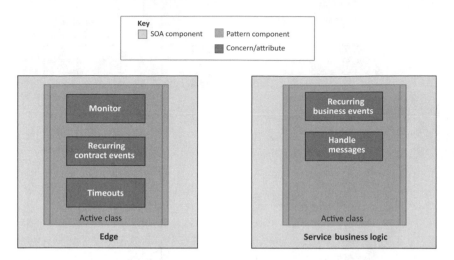

Figure 2.6   With the Active Service pattern, you add independent behavior to a service in its own thread of control. This pattern can be used to handle recurring events, such as timeouts and monitoring.

method invocation. The Active Service pattern implements the active class concept at the service level. As a result, the service creates worker threads to handle cyclic events, such as monthly billing, report generation, and so on. A service can use this pattern, become active, and monitor its own health, handling timeouts in addition to handling requests (the Service Watchdog and Decoupled Invocation patterns in chapter 3 utilize this approach).

How can the Active Service pattern help you solve the problems discussed earlier? Sometimes the best defense is *no* offense—instead of trying to solve the problem, you

Caching and the denormalization problem

If you have a database background, you may read the suggestion to actively fetch and cache data from remote services and identify this as a potential data denormalization problem. What happens when the external data changes and the services go out of synch with the rest of the system?

First, like any other cache, the items in the cache should have a time to live or some other measure to ensure their freshness. Second, you should strive to make the data in the cache immutable, such as by adding versioning so that snapshots of the data are correct for the creation time of each version. If you store the current balance of a bank account in a cache, it can easily go out of sync with the real balance, but if you store "the 8:00 a.m. balance for May 28, 2012," that data will remain correct for that time, regardless of the current balance. Lastly, you should strive to cache data that changes infrequently, if possible.

In any event, the owner of the data is the other service, and you should keep that in mind when coding a service that uses cached data.

can avoid the situation entirely. Instead of calling out to external services with each request to the service, you can actively fetch data from other services and refresh the caches according to an independent schedule. This effectively decouples requests to the service from the connectivity and health of the external services you depend on. Similarly, you can proactively publish your own state changes (see the Inversion of Communication pattern in chapter 5).

A periodically scheduled thread (one that performs its work according to a timer) can take care of most of the temporal events mentioned in the discussion of the problem, such as producing regular reports. A thread in the edge component is a good way to deal with contract-related temporal issues, such as timeout events (section 2.5 discusses the Edge Component pattern). A thread within the service can take care of purely business-related concerns, such as sending monthly bill notices, or handling an incoming messages queue (see the Decoupled Invocation pattern in chapter 3).

Let's reexamine the situation shown in figure 2.5 and see how you could redesign it using the Active Service pattern. Figure 2.5 shows a flow for a Proposals service that gets data from both an internal and an external service to produce a pro forma invoice. Consider figure 2.7, where the Proposals service actively goes to fetch data on a regular basis and caches the results. When a request to produce a pro forma invoice arrives, the Proposals service can immediately calculate the discount and return a reply. Using the Active Service pattern, the Proposals service is decoupled in time

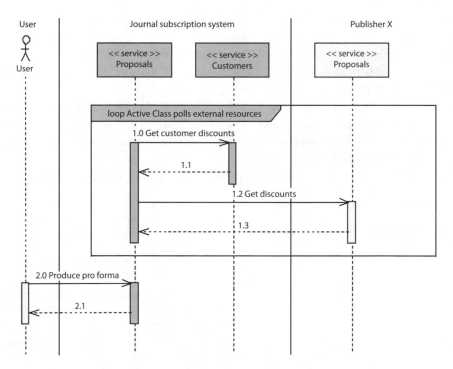

Figure 2.7   The Proposals service actively polls the other services for the information it needs. The proposal service can then respond to pro-forma requests (2.0 in the diagram) immediately, and without dependency on any other services' availability.

from the services it depends upon to complete its work. Furthermore, you can see in the request to get discounts (1.2 in figure 2.7) that the Proposals service gets all the discounts in bulk, so the contract of the external Proposals service can be simpler and less specific. This is also good for the publishers, as they can have more generic and reusable services as well.

> **NOTE**   An alternate solution to this problem is to use the Inversion of Communications pattern (see chapter 5).

Implementing the Active Service pattern is rather simple, as I'll explain in the next section.

TECHNOLOGY MAPPING

The idea behind the Active Service pattern is to have an active thread within the service, or in the edge component (the Edge Component pattern is discussed in section 2.5) that will provide some specific functionality. As a result, the Active Service pattern relies on the threading capabilities of your implementation language or platform.

It's important to decide exactly what you want to do with this thread in terms of external service call frequency and data caching strategy, but these are general programming considerations and not in the scope of this book.

Let's take a look at a few scenarios that use this pattern.

QUALITY ATTRIBUTES

The Active Service pattern helps satisfy several quality attributes, as you'll see shortly. But the Active Service pattern is also a prerequisite for many other patterns, such as Decoupled Invocation and Service Watchdog (both discussed in chapter 3), as mentioned previously. These patterns further help to handle many quality attributes including reliability and availability.

By itself, Active Service helps reduce overall latency because data is always available for the service to use in its response. As a result, application deadlines are met more often. Service availability is also increased, as services become more immune to failures of the services they depend upon.

Table 2.2 lists sample scenarios where the Active Service pattern can help.

Table 2.2   Active Service pattern quality attributes and scenarios

Quality attribute	Concrete attribute	Sample scenario
Performance	Latency	Evaluating the profitability of an offer suffers no delay from external service calls.
Performance	Deadline	Under load and normal conditions, the system can continue to update stock prices from an external service at regular intervals.
Availability	Uptime	Even disconnected from the WAN, the service can still produce internal results.

Moving forward, we need to consider how you can handle messages once you get them either at the Edge component or within the service. The Transactional Service pattern solves this problem, and it helps increase reliability.

2.3   *Transactional Service pattern*

In the previous section's discussion of the Active Service pattern, you saw that a service may need to call other services to perform its own responsibilities. Figure 2.8 illustrates such a scenario in an e-commerce system.

Here, a frontend component talks to an Ordering service (see the Client/Server/Service pattern in chapter 6 for more details on this type of configuration). The Ordering service registers the order request, sends the order to suppliers, and notifies a Billing service. When the order processing is complete, the service sends a confirmation to the e-commerce frontend application (the service consumer in this example).

This scenario looks simple and clean, but what happens when or if something goes wrong? Let's take a look at this case.

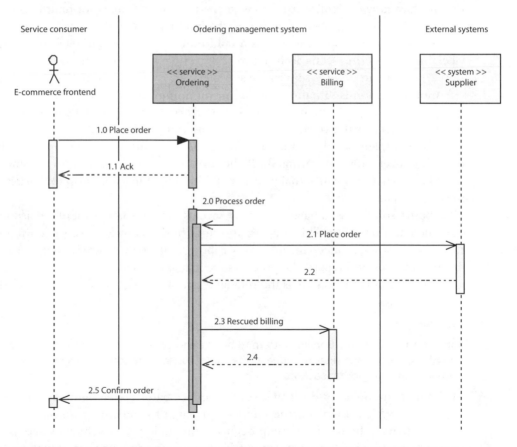

Figure 2.8   The frontend sends an order to an Ordering service that then orders the part from a supplier and asks a billing service to bill the customer.

PROBLEM

What might happen if the Ordering service crashed between acknowledging receipt of the order and processing it (for instance, between steps 1.1 and 2.0 in figure 2.8)? Or what would happen if the service failed just before requesting the Billing service to process the order, just before step 2.3?

In both of these cases, the order would be lost. Even worse, in the second scenario the system has already placed an order with the suppliers.

The handling of messages in services is filled with situations just like these. Fortunately, things work most of the time, but as Murphy has it, your service is bound to fail eventually. Therefore, we must answer this question:

? **How can a service handle requests reliably?**

One solution to the reliability problem is to push the responsibility to the service consumer. Consider the scenario where the service consumer doesn't get the order confirmation in step 2.5—the consumer must assume that the order failed. But this approach isn't very robust, and it decreases the service's autonomy, as the service doesn't have any control over its consumers; they may or may not handle problems. Additionally, this approach only solves the problems that the service consumer is exposed to. What happens if there's a failure in the internal interactions of the service? In the ordering scenario in figure 2.8, trouble will arise if the system fails after step 2.1, where an order is sent to the supplier. Clearly, this solution isn't thorough.

Another option is to handle messages synchronously. But synchronous operation can prove to be problematic in terms of performance, especially when the service needs to interact with external services, systems, or resources. Each step in the process needs to complete serially before a reply can be sent. More importantly, this solution doesn't entirely solve the problem. If the service fails at any point, for instance, you can't know what problem actually occurred. The only thing you know for sure is that a message was lost.

A better solution is to have the service save its state in some form of persistent storage, such as a database. This is a step in the right direction, but you need to ensure that the persistence mechanism is also robust. You need to know that the storage device can track and record the process state if a failure occurs.

To solve this issue, as well as the reliability problem in general, you need to define a *transactional* service.

SOLUTION

✓ Apply the Transactional Service pattern to handle the entire message flow, so that everything from receiving a request message to sending out a response is contained in a single transaction.

The main component of the Transactional Service pattern (see figure 2.9) is the message pump, which listens on the endpoint or edge for incoming messages. When a message arrives, the message pump begins a transaction, reads the message, passes it to other components to process, sends the appropriate response, and finally commits

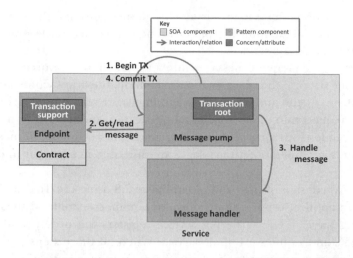

Figure 2.9 **The Transactional Service pattern creates a transaction envelope: it opens a transaction, reads the request, handles the message, sends the response, and closes the transaction.**

the transaction. You'll also need compensation logic for the case where the transaction aborts due to an error.

The advantage of using a transactional programming model is that it ensures that requests are processed completely or not at all. This guarantees that data integrity is maintained, and that no requests are ever lost. If request processing fails at any step, all processing up until that point is rolled back and the request is placed back into the incoming request queue (unless it's a problematic message that should be handled separately—see the discussion on poison message). Due to the properties of transactions—atomicity, consistency, isolation, and durability, known as the ACID properties—you're guaranteed that all of the messages and related suboperations are processed to completion.

In most cases, one tradeoff with the Transactional Service pattern is performance. Transaction processing can delay request processing due to the additional preparation, the IO needed for durability, lock management, and additional record keeping needed in case of a failure. One option when implementing the Transactional Service

ACID transactions

A transaction is a complete unit of work that demonstrates the following ACID properties or qualities:

- *Atomic*—Each step in a transaction occurs as one atomic unit. Either all the actions complete successfully, or none complete.
- *Consistent*—Each resource is left in a consistent state, whether the transaction fails or succeeds.
- *Isolated*—External observers (that don't participate in the transaction) never see the interim states. They see only the states before and after the transaction.
- *Durable*—Changes made in the transaction are saved in persistent storage so that they're available after a system restart.

pattern is to use a transactional message transport for all messages that flow between the services. This makes implementing the pattern much easier, as you leverage the qualities built into such a message service.

Another option is to place request messages into a transactional resource, such as an enterprise queuing system, and then manually commit the transaction after a response is sent. In this case, the initial message handling isn't transactional (it occurs before you place the request into the transactional queue), so you need to be able to cope with duplicate requests arriving at different times if the acknowledge message back to the consumer is lost (idempotent messages are discussed in a sidebar in chapter 4, section 4.1.2).

Figure 2.10 shows a redesign of the example in figure 2.8 using the Transactional Service pattern. To recap, the scenario illustrates an e-commerce frontend that connects to an Ordering service. The Ordering service registers the order, sends the order out to suppliers, and notifies a Billing service. When all those steps are complete, it sends a confirmation message to the e-commerce frontend application.

In this redesign using the Transactional Service pattern, the actions taken by the ordering service itself (steps 2.0 to 2.5 in figure 2.10) occur within the same transaction. If any step in this order process fails, any of the other steps already completed will be rolled back as though they never took place.

> **NOTE** A subtle issue here is what might happen if the Ordering service were to crash somewhere between steps 1.0 and 1.2.

Using a single transaction will work if the Billing process only produces an invoice. It won't work if the Billing service also needs to process a credit card, which requires an additional confirmation to continue. When a single transaction isn't enough, the process needs to be broken into smaller transactions, and the whole process becomes what's known as a long-running operation (see the Saga pattern in chapter 5). Additionally, request processing may need to be broken into smaller transactions if the service itself is distributed across multiple computers, or even geographically.

When applying the Transactional Service pattern, the transaction you make begins within the server, when the request is received. That's a distinct and important difference from the other option of initializing the transactions from within the service consumer when the request is made. Although transactions that span services and consumers can help with reliability and consistency when the service consumer fails, they also increase coupling in the system. When you extend a transaction beyond a service boundary and hold internal resources for anything beyond the service trust boundary, you introduce security and performance risks. We'll examine this in more detail in our discussion of the Transactional Integration antipattern in chapter 8.

Our next step is to look at what's needed to implement a transactional service.

TECHNOLOGY MAPPING

Implementing the Transactional Service pattern can be easy if the message transport is transaction-aware. Examples can be found in most ESB software (such as WebSphere

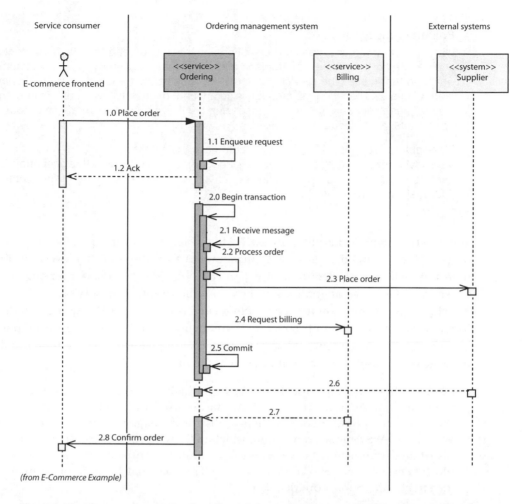

Figure 2.10   **The e-commerce flow from figure 2.8 redesigned to use the Transactional Service pattern.**

ESB and Apache ServiceMix), messaging-oriented middleware such as Microsoft Message Queue (built into .NET), any JMS implementation (such as WebSphere MQ or ActiveMQ), or even SQL Server's Service Broker. The process is for the service to read a message from the ESB or messaging middleware, process it, send new messages to outgoing destination queues, and then commit the transaction to indicate success. If any of the individual components fails, the entire transaction is rolled back.

Often you can implement the internal service transaction as a simple transaction, but you may need to start a distributed transaction if you need to access two or more internal resources in the same transaction. Suppose you want to perform a database update and remove a message from a queue, but both actions need to be successful, or both should fail. A distributed transaction, sometimes referred to as a two-phase commit (2PC) transaction, coordinates more than one resource. It can coordinate the queuing system's transaction engine with the database so that state changes are saved

> **Poison messages**
>
> When you read a message in a transactional manner, you need to be able to identify and handle *poison messages*. A poison message is a message that's faulty in some way, and that makes the service crash or always abort the transaction when it's handled. Within a transaction the problem is compounded, because with each failure, the message is requeued. Once the processing service recovers, it reads the request again, fails, and repeats the cycle.
>
> Most enterprise messaging products automatically detect and discard poison messages (via what is called a dead-message queue) to help you avoid this scenario. You need to make sure this case is handled for you, or at least be aware of the problem and deal with it yourself.

after each message is handled. In .NET 2.0 and later, you can open a `Transaction-Scope` object (defined in `System.Transactions`) to transparently move to a distributed transaction if needed. Similarly, Java code can use the transaction engine built into a Java EE-compliant application server or other transaction service.

A technology specification that may seem related is WS-ReliableMessaging. But despite its name, the protocol is only concerned with delivering messages safely from point to point (effectively making it act like TCP for the HTTP protocol). There is no durability promise or any transactional trait imbued in the protocol.

> **NOTE**   Other related protocols are WS-Coordination and its related specifications, WS-AtomicTransaction, and WS-BusinessActivity. We'll look into WS-BusinessActivity in more detail when we discuss the Saga pattern in chapter 5. We'll avoid WS-AtomicTransaction, which defines a protocol to orchestrate a distributed transaction between services, because it introduces a lot of coupling between services. (You can see the Transactional Integration antipattern in chapter 8 for more details.)

As usual, we'll end by looking at some of the motivations for using the Transactional Service pattern.

QUALITY ATTRIBUTES

The semantics that the Transactional Service pattern introduces can simplify both coding and testing. No longer do you need to write explicit error-handling code for each step of service processing. Most importantly, it greatly enhances the reliability and robustness of the service. The code becomes simpler, and you can focus on writing business logic, not error-handing code.

Table 2.3 presents two examples of successfully using the Transactional Service pattern.

Another pattern that can reduce the amount of code that needs to be written is the Workflodize pattern.

Table 2.3   Transactional Service pattern quality attributes and scenarios

Quality attribute	Concrete attribute	Sample scenario
Reliability	Data loss	A message acknowledged by the system won't be lost
Testability	Test coverage	For all critical requirements, achieves 100 percent test coverage

2.4   *Workflodize pattern*

I was once involved in building a sales support system for a mobile operator. It will probably not come as a surprise when I say that the competition between mobile operators is *quite* fierce. This operator created new usage plans and bundles several times a week to meet both internal goals and customers' requirements. Considerable time and effort was required to adjust the billing system to the new plans, but marketing requirements often pushed the development teams into fire-fighting mode to implement the changes in record time.

Changing business needs is something that's common to many, if not all, modern businesses. The degree of intensity may vary from system to system, but we've all experienced it at one point or other. We need to find a way to enable our services to efficiently cope with these changing processes.

PROBLEM

How can you increase a service's adaptability to changing business processes?

The most obvious option is to wait for the change requests, then develop the code and update the services. This approach poses at least two problems. First, you need a full development cycle to make the change happen. Second, code changes require testing, which translates to even longer time to market. In the mobile project mentioned previously, implementing changes to a plan, or adding a new plan, took three or more weeks, which was clearly too long for the business people involved.

Implementing well-built and correct logic is a daunting and error-prone task, but business requires quick changes. There must be an acceptable solution.

SOLUTION

Introduce a workflow engine within the service to handle the volatile and changing processes and orchestrate the stable logic.

The Workflodize pattern, as depicted in figure 2.11, is based on adding a workflow engine to the service to drive business processes. The workflow engine hosts workflow instances. The nominal case is one workflow per request type. Workflows can also become quite complex, handling long-running processes with several entry points, where requests and responses arrive from external services.

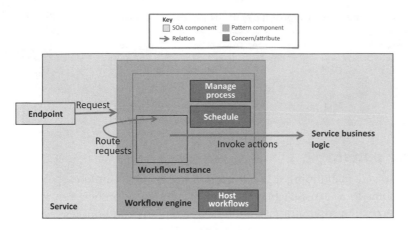

Figure 2.11   **The business process is made of the small building blocks that are relatively easy to rearrange. The workflow drives the business logic.**

The advantage of using workflows is that they give you a tool that makes you think in terms of building blocks (called *activities*) and lets you arrange and rearrange these activities into processes in a very flexible way. You model the process as a flow of activities that occur as messages arrive. Because each activity can be tested individually, reusing them requires less testing overall. By rearranging the activities, you can quickly respond to changing business needs with less risk.

How does this flexibility impact the service's contract? Usually a change in internal implementation shouldn't ripple out to affect the contract. After all, the whole point of the contract is to shield server consumers from such changes. If you apply Liskov's substitution principle to SOA (as discussed in the sidebar) there's no need to change the contract version if the overall behavior remains the same.

Liskov's substitution principle for services

Liskov's substitution principle, which is also known as *design by contract*, is an object-oriented principle that Barbara Liskov originally published as follows: "If for each object o1 of type S there is an object o2 of type T such that for *all* programs P defined in terms of T, the behavior of P is *unchanged* when o1 is substituted for o2 then S is a subtype of T."[1]

This means that a subclass can be used in place of its parent class without breaking the behavior of any users of the base class. Applied to SOA, this means that when changing the internal behavior of a service, you don't need to create a new version of the contract. The new version of the service should meet the expectations that consumers of the original service have come to expect.

---

[1]   Barbara Liskov, "Data Abstraction and Hierarchy," *ACM SIGPLAN Notices*, 23, 5 (May 1988).

Let's take another look at the mobile operator scenario and see how it looks when you apply the Workflodize pattern. To begin, you can use a workflow to route requests for new plans that don't require human intervention. You can, for example, let the customer service department register the change in the customer relationship management (CRM) system, then notify technicians to configure the network. Later, when the backend systems are ready, data can be rerouted through them. The existing, stable processing components represent reusable activities in the flow that all mobile usage plans leverage.

Adding a workflow in this scenario greatly enhances the business's ability to react and remain agile. When a competitor launches a new plan, which happens frequently in the mobile world, this mobile operator can react and launch a competing plan within a day. This is real and tangible business value.

The ability to handle long-running processes is another advantage of the Workflodize service pattern.

It can also be combined with other patterns. For example, it's easy to add job scheduling (which most workflow engines support) to implement the Active Service pattern.

A pattern closely related to Workflodize is Orchestration (discussed in chapter 7). Both patterns use the same underlying technology—a workflow engine—but there are different architectural considerations that distinguish the two. Workflodize is constrained within the boundaries of a single service, the Orchestration pattern (discussed in chapter 7) is used to coordinate multiple services.

TECHNOLOGY MAPPING

The natural technology mapping for the Workflodize pattern is the use of a workflow engine. There are many workflow engines on the market, such as Microsoft's Windows Workflow Foundation, which in .NET 4.0 finally reached a usable status. There are several other companies that provide .NET workflow solutions, such as Skelta and K2. Java has many workflow engine options, such as those from IBM, JBoss, and Flux. Oracle offers a workflow package, WF_ENGINE, along with a Java API for its database.

Many workflow engines have built-in visual designers to help you model the workflows more easily. Figure 2.12 shows a model of the Active Service pattern for report generation built with Flux's visual designer tool.

Using a visual designer such as the one in figure 2.12 is usually the preferred option for modeling flows, but you can also specify workflows by hand in XML. Several tools, such as the open source jBPM, support both a designer-based and XML-based configuration for workflows. The following listing is an example of a flow modeled in jBPM. In it, you can see a decision point where large orders will need further approval and smaller ones will go through.

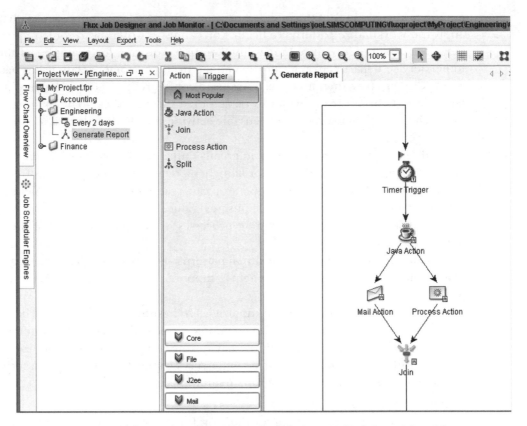

Figure 2.12   Most workflow engines come with a visual designer tool to help model workflows.

Listing 2.1   Partial XML of a credit approval workflow implemented for jBPM

```
<start-state name="start">
<transition to="credit approval"></transition>
</start-state>

...

<decision name="is user registered?">
     <handler config-type="bean"
   class="org.springmodules.workflow.jbpm31.JbpmHandlerProxy">
     <targetBean>jbpmEvaluateOrderValue</targetBean>
     <factoryKey>jbpmConfiguration</factoryKey>
     </handler>
     <transition name="large_order" to="Review And Approve"></transition>
     <transition name="normal" to="Process Paypal"></transition>
   </decision>
...
```

Some workflow engines, such as Microsoft's BizTalk, or IBM's WebSphere MQ Work-flow, are better suited to orchestrating interactions between services and not to inter-nal workflows, due to their increased complexity (and cost).

QUALITY ATTRIBUTES

The main benefit of using the Workflodize pattern is added flexibility. Programming a workflow is a visual process (at least with most workflow implementations) that is relatively easy to master. This added flexibility can result in quicker time to market for change requests, leading to greater business agility.

Table 2.4 shows two main benefits of using the Workflodize service pattern.

Table 2.4   Workflodize pattern quality attributes and scenarios

Quality attribute	Concrete attribute	Sample scenario
Flexibility	Add new business processes	Under normal conditions, adding a new prepaid plan to the system and moving it to production will take less than two days.
Reusability	Core modules	Reuse 90 percent or more of the common sales process for most new plans.

The Workflodize pattern adds a lot of flexibility to a service, enabling you to dynamically change behavior. A different aspect of flexibility can be found in the Edge Component pattern, which we'll take a look at now.

2.5   *Edge Component pattern*

The last of the foundation patterns we'll examine is the Edge Component pattern. The Edge Component pattern is classified as foundational because it's a platform used to implement other patterns. It adds a level of separation on top of business logic that enables a great deal of flexibility. Let's examine some real-world scenarios to illustrate this.

PROBLEM

Let's look at three scenarios.

Scenario 1: You have a common platform for defense solutions. This platform has base services that are reusable in many solutions. For example, one of the core services provides a unified view of military targets. The first implementation built on the platform used a messaging infrastructure based on TIBCO Rendezvous. The second implementation used a different messaging technology altogether (WSE 3.0). Both implementations are required to use the same business logic to handle and process the messages.

Scenario 2: A mobile operator needs to introduce new usage plans and offerings on a regular basis. (You'll recognize this scenario from the discussion of the Workflodize pattern.) The service interface remains stable, but the business logic keeps changing and adapting to the new plans (the opposite of scenario 1).

Scenario 3: You have a system that contains many services. Each handles a different business aspect, yet all need to perform common tasks, such as authenticate requests or log requests in an audit trail.

Within these three scenarios, you have different concerns, such as business logic, technology choices, and cross-cutting features. Each of these concerns can change independently of the others, so you need a way to enable flexibility.

> **How can you allow the service's business aspects, technological concerns, and other cross-cutting concerns to evolve at their own pace, independently of one another?**

The easiest option is to *duplicate* the service features that need to be reused in each scenario—an approach also known as "own and clone." This obviously creates a maintainability problem, as you now have multiple copies of the same business logic or cross-cutting features within several service implementations. Bug fixes and enhancements made to one need to be duplicated across all services, which is a time-consuming and error-prone process. This isn't much of a solution at all.

SOLUTION

Separation of concerns is a well-known object-oriented concept used in cases like this. The root principle is known as the Single Responsibility Principle (SRP), which states that every class should have a single responsibility, and that all its related methods should be narrowly aligned with that responsibility. Applying this to services, we get the following solution:

> ✓ **Add an edge component to the service implementation to add flexibility and separate the business logic from other concerns** (such as contacts, protocols, technology choices, and additional cross-cutting features).

The main idea behind the Edge Component pattern, as demonstrated in figure 2.13, is separation of concerns. The edge component is where you take care of all the cross-cutting features, such as auditing, specific endpoint types and contract version mediation, that aren't part the service's business logic. The business logic is then handled in a separate component that focuses solely on the business logic and remains free of other concerns. In a sense, the Edge Component pattern provides a façade, or proxy, to a service implementation.

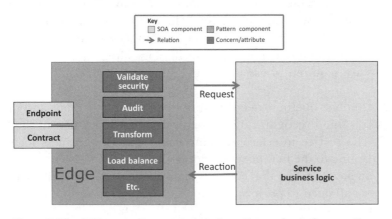

Figure 2.13   Adding an edge component allows the service to focus on the business logic and not on extraneous features.

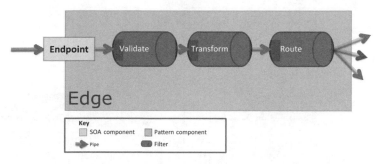

Figure 2.14   An Edge Component pattern implementation that processes incoming messages in three steps—validation, transformation, and routing— before the messages are sent to the service implementation.

You can apply a Pipes and Filters architectural style and chain several classes or components together, each dealing with a specific concern. Figure 2.14 shows an example implementation of the Edge Component pattern that starts by applying a validation filter to ensure a message is correctly formatted. Then a transformation filter translates an external contract format into an internal one. Finally, a routing filter routes the message to the correct component within the service. These subcomponents can be reused from service to service as needed, and they can change and evolve independently of specific services.

The Edge Component pattern is very useful, and *I've* introduced it in most of the SOA projects I've designed. Many of the structural patterns mentioned in this book expand and build on the Edge Component pattern.

Let's take a look at the technological aspects of this pattern.

TECHNOLOGY MAPPING
Given the wide range of uses for the Edge Component pattern, there are only a few restrictions when choosing a technology to implement the pattern, and there are plenty of examples of where you can use it.

Both JAX-WS and Windows Communication Foundation (WCF) implement the Edge Component pattern for you, but they only handle the lower-level concerns called *bindings*. These concerns are also mentioned in the various WS-* standards. With these solutions, you may still need to implement many high-level concerns, like routing, contract translations, data transformations, and so on, yourself.

An interesting technology option is a Java-based framework called Restlet. The Restlet engine, created by Restlet SAS, is a Java library for implementing RESTful services. It has built-in classes, such as filter and router, that allow you to easily build edge components. Consider the example in figure 2.15.

Here, you can see a possible edge component configuration on an Orders service whose contract has two operations: getLast (which returns the last order), and getAll (which returns all the orders for a specific customer). Before the call invokes the business logic, you have to log the request, validate its data and parameters,

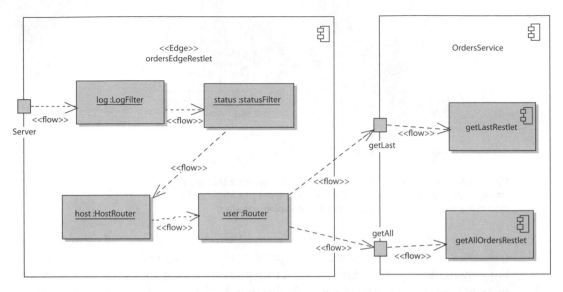

Figure 2.15   As a request is received, it goes through different steps like logging, validating parameters, and validating intent and the user before it gets to the business services on the right side of this figure—getting the last order or all the orders for a specific client.

enforce security constraints, and route the call to the appropriate business component. Adding an edge component lets you configure and reconfigure this activity without affecting the business logic components.

Another interesting example is the Turmeric SOA framework, which is an open source framework from eBay (https://www.ebayopensource.org/index.php/Turmeric /HomePage). Figure 2.16 shows the server-side architecture diagram from the Turmeric site. You can see the service implementation as a single rectangle at the far right of the diagram. Most of the diagram explains what is effectively a large edge component implementation. When a message arrives, it passes through a protocol processor and then through an incoming pipeline that handles logging, security, and globalization (G11N in the diagram).

As you've seen, the Edge Component pattern is supported by all current technologies and is even implemented internally by some of them. The further reading section at the end of the chapter contains references to other resources that expand on the technologies mentioned in this section.

QUALITY ATTRIBUTES

The Edge Component pattern can be associated with two quality attributes: flexibility and maintainability. When this pattern is implemented, it's easier to change and enhance the external properties of a service without affecting the business logic.

Table 2.5 summarizes the quality attributes for the Edge Component pattern, which is the last of the foundation structural patterns for SOA.

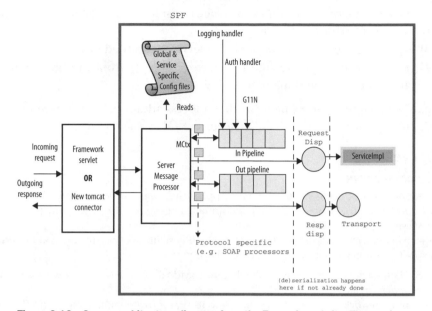

Figure 2.16   Server architecture diagram from the Turmeric website. The service implementation is the rectangle on the right of the diagram. The rest of the diagram shows some of the concerns the edge component implementation handles, such as contract endpoint (the framework servlet or tomcat connector in the diagram), logging, authorization, and globalization (G11N). (© 2011-2012 eBay Inc. All Rights Reserved. Source: https://www.ebayopensource.org/wiki/display/TURMERICDOC/ Service+Provider+Framework+%28SPF%29+Architecture)

Table 2.5   Component pattern quality attributes and scenarios

Quality attribute	Concrete attribute	Sample scenario
Maintainability	Backwards compatibility	As contracts evolve, the services should be able to support consumers using older versions of the contract.
Flexibility	Extension points	Within the next year, it is expected making the system SOX-compliant and adding auditing for all services will be required.

2.6   Summary

This chapter was the first to present SOA patterns, and it dealt with the foundation structural patterns used to build services:

- *Service Host*—A common wrapper that hosts service instances and introduces a common infrastructure that can be reused across services
- *Active Service*—Implements at least one independent thread in the service so it can safely call external services

- *Transactional Service*—Handles messages inside a transaction to gracefully recover from error conditions
- *Workflodize*—Adds a workflow *inside* the service for added flexibility
- *Edge Component*—Separates the interface (contract) from the implementation to enable flexibility and maintainability

The next two chapters discuss patterns that address additional requirements, including scalability, performance, availability, security, and management.

2.7 Further reading

SERVICE HOST PATTERN

David Chappel, "Introducing Windows Server AppFabric," *Opinari: David Chappell's Blog* (blog entry, May 24, 2010), http://davidchappellopinari.blogspot.ca/2010/05/introducing-windows-server-appfabric.html.
> This article describes Microsoft's AppFabric, which is Windows Communication Foundation's (WCF) implementation of the Service Host pattern.

Richard S. Hall, Karl Pauls, Stuart McCulloch, and David Savage, *OSGi in Action: Creating Modular Applications in Java (Manning, 2011).*
> OSGi is a framework for composable components that provide management and flexibility for hosting Java components in general. FuseESB uses an OSGi implementation (Apache Felix) and provides an implementation of the Service Host pattern.

Mark Seemann, *Dependency Injection in .NET* (Manning, 2011).
> This is a good book explaining Dependency Injection, which is one of the concepts the Service Host pattern promotes.

TRANSACTIONAL SERVICE PATTERN

Leslie Lamport, Robert Shostak and Marshall Pease, "The Byzantine Generals Problem," *ACM Transactions on Programming Languages and Systems* 4, no. 3 (July 1982), www.cs.cornell.edu/courses/cs614/2004sp/papers/lsp82.pdf.
> This seminal paper explains the basis of distributed consensus.

WORKFLODIZE PATTERN

Workflow Patterns, www.workflowpatterns.com.
> This website explains many of the patterns available for designing workflows.

EDGE COMPONENT PATTERN

Restlet engine, www.restlet.org/
> *RESTlet is a web API framework for building REST style services. RESTlet is mentioned in this book as an example of a framework supportive of the Edge Component pattern.*

Turmeric framework, https://www.ebayopensource.org/index.php/Turmeric/HomePage.
> Turmeric is an open source (Apache 2.0 license) framework for building SOAP and REST style services. Turmeric is used by eBay for many of its services, and it is mentioned in this book because it takes the Edge Component approach to handling service requests.

Patterns for performance, scalability, and availability

When you design a software architecture for a complete system, you need to make sure it will accommodate additional sets of requirements beyond the basics. You need to take care of maintainability, security, and reliability. One very important quality attribute or requirement class is *performance*. Performance involves several concerns, such as throughput and latency, which sometimes complement and sometimes contradict each other.

SOA principles and guidelines don't always help to solve performance problems. In fact, SOA is almost inherently bad for performance: by making the components distributed, it tends to increase latency and add layers of indirection. This chapter will present patterns to help mitigate these performance, scalability, and availability challenges. Availability and scalability are bundled with performance because a solution to one of these problems often helps to resolve the others.

One strategy to increasing performance is load balancing (see the Service Instance pattern in section 3.4). If implemented properly, it can also help increase service availability as each load-balanced server provides redundancy for the others.

Many people feel that performance, availability, and scalability are easily improved with more hardware. Unfortunately, this is often not the case. This is especially true where new technology or development approaches are involved. Utilizing additional hardware, implementing load balancing for services, and ensuring adequate application performance when failures do occur, are very difficult problems to solve. Fortunately, when designing SOAs, you don't need to start from scratch. Instead, you can build on the experience and solutions already in place in other environments and technologies. The challenge, and the topic of this chapter, is to bring this knowledge into the world of SOA while remaining true to the SOA architectural principles and benefits.

If you take another look at the architectural components of SOA presented in chapter 1 (as illustrated in figure 3.1) you'll see that the patterns related to performance, scalability, and availability mostly have to do with the internal structure of services. Some of these patterns are also related to more than one component of a service's interface—namely the endpoint and the contract. As mentioned in chapter 1, SOA is mainly focused on other quality attributes, such as flexibility and interoperability; it doesn't offer much guidance for performance, scalability, and availability.

We'll discuss the following patterns in this chapter:

- *Decoupled Invocation*—Handle normal request loads, peak request loads, and continuous periods of time at high load without failing
- *Parallel Pipelines*—Build services that maintain state and high throughput
- *Gridable Service*—Build services to handle computationally intense tasks in a scalable manner
- *Service Instance*—Build services that are scalable in a simple and cost-effective way

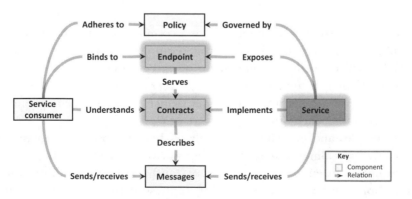

Figure 3.1   This chapter focuses on performance, availability, and scalability patterns for the service, the endpoint, and the contract components of SOA.

- *Virtual Endpoint*—Provide services with location transparency that gracefully recover from failure without affecting service consumers
- *Service Watchdog*—Increase availability and identify and resolve problems and failures that are service-specific

First we're going to look at the Decoupled Invocation pattern, which serves as a base on which other performance-related patterns can build.

3.1 Decoupled Invocation pattern

I mentioned in chapter 1 that SOA helps reduce coupling between components (services) by putting a lot of emphasis on the interface.

As you saw in the discussion of the Active Service pattern in chapter 2, SOA's reduced coupling doesn't take care of temporal coupling, though eagerly fetching and caching data can help to some degree.

Another aspect of temporal coupling is apparent in the Request/Reply pattern (discussed in chapter 5), which is what most common communications pattern SOA implementations use. With Request/Reply, you typically expect the service to return a result immediately, and this couples the consumer to the service in time, potentially resulting in a performance bottleneck. The maximum load is the maximum number of requests the service can handle concurrently.

As you'll see in this section, the Decoupled Invocation pattern solves both the temporal coupling and the potential performance problems but adds latency.

Let's look at an example.

PROBLEM

Consider an online music store. Let's say that the backend system has one backend service that deals with album orders and another that deals with single-track orders—see figure 3.2. The left side of the diagram illustrates a normal business day for this store with a mild load on both services; the purchase requests are well-distributed in time. The right side of the diagram shows what can happen on a day that some crazy hit is released. The same store suddenly has to handle a much higher number of purchase requests than normal.

Obviously, the music store needs to be able to handle all incoming requests, even under high loads, or customers will take their business elsewhere. It's important that

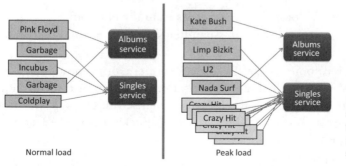

Figure 3.2 A music store's service-request loads under normal conditions versus peak loads when a popular song is released.

the service be built economically to handle normal loads but still be able to handle peak loads without failing.

How can a service handle normal request loads, peak request loads, and a continuous period of high load without failing?

One option is to estimate the peak loads and deploy enough server power to ensure you can handle them. The first problem with this approach wastes money and resources; servers may remain idle during normal operation and be used only during rare bursts of activity. The idle computers have purchase, maintenance, and operational costs. A bigger problem is that much of the service's processing may be out of your control—external credit card clearing requests, shipping requests, and others may fail under load, or slow down your internal service response times. Finally, you may need to prioritize some requests over others. You can set the overall quality of service (QOS) parameters according to the most demanding request type, but you may need more resources to be able to handle your steady ongoing load.

A good solution for this problem is to deploy to a cloud provider like Amazon, Windows Azure, or VMWare's Cloud Foundry and elastically grow the number of servers at peak load. One problem with this approach is that you need to make sure your service is cloud-ready (something you should probably take care of anyway). The more serious problem is that cloud providers will take care of scaling to peak loads, but they can't completely cover the "without failing" requirement.

What you need is something that will enable you to register requests quickly and reliably and will free up server resources to handle new requests. The solution should also let the requestors know that their request is going to be handled. This is what the Decoupled Invocation pattern is all about.

SOLUTION

When a new request enters the system, instead of immediately invoking the business logic, you can do the following:

✓ **Utilize the Decoupled Invocation pattern and separate replies from requests: acknowledge receipt at the service edge, put the request on a reliable queue, and then load-balance and prioritize the handler components that read from the queue.**

As illustrated in figure 3.3, the Decoupled Invocation pattern is composed of three basic components: a *handler*, a *queue*, and a *dispatcher* that mediates between them. Here's how the initial request processing works:

- The handler listens for incoming requests from the endpoint.
- When a new request arrives, the handler sends an acknowledgment to the sender.
- The handler is responsible for the initial treatment, or preprocessing, of incoming messages. This may include message transformation or prioritization based on knowledge it infers from the messages themselves. Overall, this processing should be kept minimal, as the goal is to quickly queue and acknowledge incoming requests.
- The message is put onto a queue.

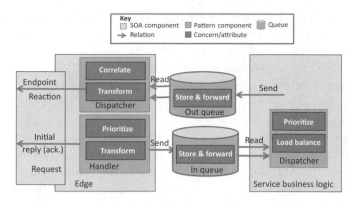

Figure 3.3 The edge component contains a handler that accepts incoming messages, acknowledges them, and queues them. The business logic then reads the queued messages at its own pace. The queue is also used for the responses.

The queue, which is the second component of the Decoupled Invocation pattern, stores incoming messages and allows the service to consume the messages at its own steady rate, thus overcoming peak loads.

You can set up the queue to be persistent so the service won't lose any requests it has already acknowledged, even if a catastrophic server failure occurs. If the queue is transactional, you can also implement the Transactional Service pattern (see chapter 2) and increase the overall robustness of the service even further.

The dispatcher is responsible for creating as many reader components as are needed for the current request load, which is measured by the number of messages waiting in the queue. The dispatcher can also prioritize incoming tasks based on internal considerations, such as resource availability. The dispatcher is a good place to introduce elasticity if the latency of handling the messages is important. (See also the further reading section for an article on the LMAX architecture, which describes a low-latency, high-performance queue between senders and receivers.)

The handler can acknowledge the request as part of the preprocessing, but it's usually best to do this inside an edge component (see the Edge Component pattern in chapter 2). This helps ensure that the service-processing load is kept to a minimum, allowing the handler to process requests as efficiently as possible.

Placing requests on the queue is a relatively low-cost operation that can be performed efficiently, making the initial request-handling less susceptible to failure during peaks (as compared to other parts of the request-handling that require more time and resources). The actual handling of the incoming requests can be performed at a reasonable pace, dictated by service resource availability and overall load. Load balancing can be achieved by running multiple readers against the queue.

When to acknowledge requests in the service

Often, request-acknowledgement processing requires some extended business logic. In this case, you need to consider whether the response is tied to the contract or if it's tied to the service's core business. If it's related to the core business, you should acknowledge the request from the service implementation; otherwise acknowledge it from the edge component.

This works well for peak loads, but if you have continuous high-request loads over an extended period of time, you may need to alter your approach or the request queue may overflow. See the Parallel Pipelines and Gridable Service patterns later in this chapter for strategies that can help with continuous loads.

Configuring the queue to be priority-based (or configuring several queues according to priority) allows you to maintain different levels of quality of service (QoS) for different message types or different contracts.

The Decoupled Invocation pattern is a good way to implement the Request/Reaction pattern discussed in chapter 5. Since the reply is delivered to the consumer as a new message, it's recommended that you correlate messages by adding an identifier that's returned to the consumer on the acknowledge message as well as the final reaction. By using a correlation ID, you can help the service consumer understand that the reaction is related to a request it sent earlier.

Let's take a look at few of the options for implementing the Decoupled Invocation pattern using currently available technologies.

TECHNOLOGY MAPPING

To implement this service, the underlying messaging technology needs to support store-and-forward queues, preferably with persistence and transactional support. Most enterprise messaging middleware packages support this, such as Microsoft Message Queue; Java Messaging Services (JMS)-compliant queues like WebSphere MQ, Progress SonicMQ, and Apache ActiveMQ; as well as Advanced Message Queuing Protocol (AMQP)-based queues like RabbitMQ and Apache Qpid. (The advantage of AMQP is that it's also a wire standard, which means you can integrate different implementations easily.)

One point to consider is whether you really need messages to be persistent; if you don't, and the service and the edge run in the same process, you can use an in-memory queue. If they're in separate processes, most message-oriented middleware supports express message delivery (without persistence) for faster performance.

You need to consider transaction support if you require a queue that supports distributed transactions. If so, you might combine the Decoupled Invocation pattern with the Transactional Service pattern described in chapter 2.

Another issue to consider is that the reply will be sent asynchronously, and you need to establish a bidirectional channel in order to do that. Messaging is a good option, and it's consistent with our approach so far. But you can also use Ajax technology, which lets you push content to the client.

In cases where acknowledgment or reply messages aren't required, you can define the contract to support one-way messages. Consider the following simple code excerpt, using Windows Communication Foundation (WCF):

```
[ServiceContract]
interface PurchaseSongs
{
    [OperationContract(IsOneWay = true)]
    void SubmitOrder()
}
```

The attribute on the `SubmitOrder` operation tells WCF to send the message without returning a reply.

You can use one-way messages if you don't care too much about the reliability of the message (for example, if it's a cyclic message, where if one is lost the next one will compensate) or if you're using a reliable transport. As usual, choosing the right technology boils down to which of the quality attributes are most important to you. In this case, it's a performance versus reliability trade-off.

QUALITY ATTRIBUTES

The Decoupled Invocation pattern helps solve the potential performance bottleneck outlined in the problem section. It does this with a queue between the caller and the message handler components. Placing a message on the queue is an efficient operation, which means the service will be free to accept new requests sooner. If you keep the handler simple, you can employ the Virtual Endpoint pattern (see section 3.5) to resolve availability problems when faults occur.

Because requests are handled asynchronously, the Decoupled Invocation pattern can help increase service flexibility, as coupling between the service and its consumers is reduced. Just as importantly, the Decoupled Invocation pattern helps with testability.

Table 3.1 lists a few quality attributes and scenarios that the Decoupled Invocation pattern can help with.

While the Decoupled Invocation pattern enables growth, scalability, and performance, the Parallel Pipelines pattern builds on it to increase overall service throughput.

Table 3.1 Decoupled Invocation pattern attributes and scenarios

Quality attribute	Concrete attribute	Sample scenario
Performance	Data loss	Under all conditions, no message acknowledged by the system will be lost.
Performance	Latency	During peak loads, the system handles incoming order requests without degrading latency (as compared to normal latency).
Testability	Isolation	Before integration tests, a service should be tested in isolation from the services it interacts with.
Flexibility	Reduced assumptions	Whenever possible, invoke services with one-way messages (fire-and-forget).

3.2 *Parallel Pipelines pattern*

The Decoupled Invocation pattern helps to handle peak loads by queuing up requests and deferring processing to off-peak hours. But this solution doesn't increase overall service scalability when increased request rates are maintained. Under a continuous high-request rate, the requests can accumulate in the queue and eventually overflow. You need another strategy to handle continuous loads.

Figure 3.4   Nominal flow for credit card processing in a credit card clearinghouse

PROBLEM

Consider a credit card clearinghouse, sometimes known as *transaction processing service.* Figure 3.4 illustrates the basic processing flow that takes place when a credit card purchase request arrives.

As illustrated, the processing for a credit card transaction begins with a check against known blacklists (bad card numbers, bad source IP addresses, and so on). Next, the service looks for fraudulent patterns in the transaction. If everything checks out to this point, it authorizes the card against the card issuer, settles the account (makes the actual payment), and produces a receipt. Naturally, if one of the checks fails, the processing enters an exception-processing path (not shown).

The primary problem is the number of steps in the process. As a secondary problem, some of the steps involve communication with external services. You may have difficulty getting a service such as this one to scale.

How can you build services that maintain state and high throughput?

One solution is to introduce concurrency (multiple threads) and have each request run in its own thread, or from a thread pool. The problem is that multithreaded programming is complex, more difficult to debug, and introduces performance and scaling issues of its own.

Here are a couple of possible solutions using other patterns:

- Introduce concurrency and use the Service Instance pattern (discussed in section 3.4), and deploy to multiple load-balanced servers. Unfortunately, the service is stateful, so this won't work unless the state is synchronized and replicated across all servers.
- Use the Gridable Service pattern (discussed in section 3.3) and introduce a computational grid. This solution is very complex and doesn't work well when external service calls are involved.

Another possibility is to use the Parallel Pipelines pattern.

SOLUTION

To maintain high throughput and be able to work with stateful components, you can use the following strategy:

✓ **Implement the Parallel Pipelines pattern, where you break the process into subtasks, add a queue between them, and make each subtask an independent component.**

The Parallel Pipelines pattern, as figure 3.5 illustrates, is an application of the Pipes and Filters architectural style (see further reading) in the context of SOA. The "pipes" represent the message transport, and the "filters" are the components that handle the subtasks.

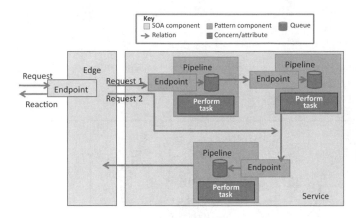

Figure 3.5   With the Parallel Pipelines pattern, the processing is broken into subtasks that are connected by queues to form a processing pipeline. Note that different requests can have different flows of tasks.

A pipeline begins with an endpoint where the messages arrive. The incoming messages are placed in a queue, and the pipeline services the queue as efficiently as possible. Each component in the pipeline works with the message and sends the results to the next component via their own outbound queue. Some components can maintain more than one outbound queue, depending upon the result of message processing. With this paradigm, you can orchestrate alternative pipeline processing paths based on request message content and variations in processing along the way.

The following are advantages of the Parallel Pipelines approach:

- The pipelines pattern is relatively simple to implement.
- Pipelines are easy to test because they operate independently (you can test them with the same technologies and principles you use to test the services that include the pipelines).
- Because the overall problem is broken into subtasks, each pipeline component tends to be simpler.
- To scale the solution, you can distribute the pipeline across as many servers as needed.
- When you need to scale the solution, the simplest option is to put each pipeline on its own server.

When deciding how to divide the process into pipelines, you can either make sure that the pipelines are independent of each other or that you pass the needed context from one pipeline to the next, so that each document gets more and more context as it passes through the steps.

The Parallel Pipelines pattern works well in combination with the other performance and scalability patterns we'll discuss in this chapter. You can use Parallel Pipelines with the Gridable Service pattern (see section 3.3) to solve a performance problem within one of the subtask components.

The challenge is to partition the process in a way that's easy to implement and deploy and that still fulfills the business goals of the parent service. It's preferable to partition according to business boundaries, so that each pipeline is a business service

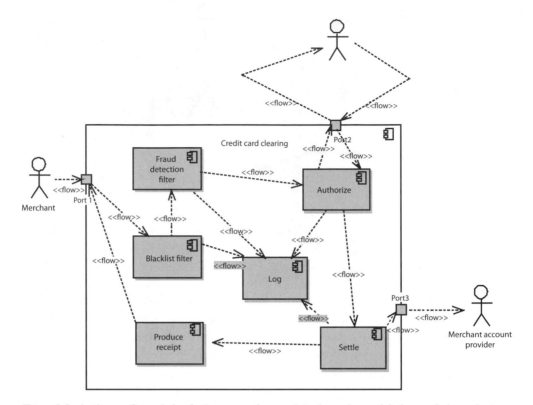

Figure 3.6   In the credit card clearinghouse service, each task can be modeled as an independent service. The Parallel Pipelines pattern has improved the overall scalability of the design.

in its own right. It's also acceptable to partition the pipelines according to a technical need; just try not to expose this partitioning to external callers. Figure 3.6 shows the credit card clearinghouse modeled with the Parallel Pipelines pattern.

As the figure illustrates, each subtask (blacklist filter, fraud detection filter, and so on) is modeled as an independent component in an overall pipeline. Each is responsible for just one task, which it can perform relatively quickly. Because there are six pipeline components, you can handle approximately six different messages in different stages of the pipeline simultaneously without the need to introduce concurrent programming within each component. Contrast this to a monolithic service, where each new request needs to wait for the previous request to be processed in its entirety before beginning on the next.

If you look at the different pipelines that make up the process in figure 3.6, you can see that most are self-contained, so they can handle the input without dependencies on other pipelines or external resources. An exception is the authorize pipeline, which needs to communicate with an external resource to complete its work. You can see here another advantage of this pattern: instead of making a lot of small requests to the external resource (each with the overhead of serialization, network, security, and so on), you can make a chunkier call for a batch of requests, which is more efficient, while other pipelines are still handling additional requests in other parts of the process.

You can orchestrate the different pipeline components with the Workflodize pattern (discussed in chapter 2), and use a workflow engine, such as JBoss jBPM, to drive the message flow through the pipeline. The easiest way to track and understand the state within the pipeline is with the Transactional Service pattern (also discussed in chapter 2). This ensures that each pipeline component performs a discrete unit of work in isolation.

TECHNOLOGY MAPPING

As mentioned previously, you can partition pipeline components based on technical considerations in addition to business needs. This sort of partitioning is acceptable as long as the overall service is exposed via an edge that implements a meaningful contract and the subcomponent breakdown isn't exposed to the caller. Also, be careful not to partition the service into too many components, or with components that are too fine-grained, as they may become difficult to manage and may make the latency unbearable.

Implementing the Parallel Pipelines pattern isn't too complicated—the design of which operations should be grouped in which subcomponents is the complicated part. You can use Akka actors—a Scala framework also usable from Java that lets you implement remote message passing between components. Akka components are called *actors*, and each actor can be a separate pipeline. Another option is to base a solution on JavaSpaces technology, which has commercial implementations like GigaSpaces (usable both from Java and .NET). The nice feature of both the Akka and JavaSpaces technologies is that, though they're different, they both allow you to make components local or remote by configuration and thus partition the logic into pipelines according to your needs and performance requirements.

As usual, we'll finish our discussion of the pattern by looking at some of the reasons you would want to use it.

QUALITY ATTRIBUTES

Remember that performance is a multidimensional trait, and one that's relative by nature. Therefore, it's sometimes hard to define clear acceptance criteria. Also, some of the subcategories of performance can contradict one another. To decrease the latency of message processing, you can choose to forgo transactions, but this increases the chances of data loss.

With the Parallel Pipelines pattern, there's a trade-off between throughput and latency. With every pipeline you add, you increase the parallelism in your application, and throughput increases as a result. This approach can also increase overall message-processing latency.

The benefits of using the Parallel Pipelines pattern typically outweigh the trade-offs. First, this pattern helps to increase service scalability tremendously. Additionally, pipelines increase testability; because the service's tasks are independent components, you can test them independently.

Table 3.2   Parallel Pipelines pattern quality attributes and scenarios

Quality attribute	Concrete attribute	Sample scenario
Performance	Message throughput	Under stress conditions, the system handles more than 10,000 requests per second.
Scalability	Increased loads	When the system needs to handle up to five times the current increased loads, you can solve the problem by adding more servers without any architecture or software changes.
Testability	Component isolation	Before integration tests, you can test each service thoroughly (coverage of 85 percent or better).

Table 3.2 outlines some of the quality attributes and benefits of the Parallel Pipelines pattern.

For the subtasks within a pipeline that are computationally intensive, you may need to apply other strategies to keep the service scalable. One such strategy is the Gridable Service pattern, which we'll explore now.

3.3   *Gridable Service pattern*

One characteristic of SOA is that it's built for highly distributed systems. Each and every service is a subsystem in itself that can run on its own machine and be located anywhere in the world. Often, services *need* to be distributed to help with computationally intensive tasks.

PROBLEM

I once managed the biometric product line of a defense systems company. One of the products we developed was a multimodal biometric platform. Such a system is used to authorize visitors as they enter a secured building or area.

This is a straightforward scenario, as you're usually dealing with a finite number of people, and each person is equipped with an appropriate identification badge. The system looks up the visitor's credentials in a database, runs some sort of biometric algorithm, and verifies the person's identity.

The same platform needs to work in other, more complex, scenarios such as a forensics system where you have a fingerprint collected at a crime scene, and you don't necessarily know who the person is ahead of time. The data must be compared against a much larger database that can contain millions of records. If you have more than one modality, such as fingerprints and DNA, the problem quickly multiplies. In the end, you need to aggregate the result sets from all the searches. The processing throughout the system can become quite intense.

Other examples of computationally intense tasks are financial calculations and simulation systems. Whatever the process entails, the same problem statement applies:

? **How can you build services to handle computationally intense tasks in a scalable manner?**

> ## Multimodal biometrics
>
> Biometrics is one solution to identification and security. It combines something you know (a password), something you possess (an identification badge card), and something that's part of you (biometrics), such as a fingerprint, face recognition, or iris recognition.
>
> Multimodal biometrics involves the combination of two or more biometric modalities. The added complexity comes from the algorithm required to aggregate the results of the different biometric engines.

One option is to scale up and get a larger, stronger server to solve the problem. This will work to an extent, but throwing hardware at the problem can also get costly fast. If you need to build redundant systems for failover and load balancing, the cost multiplies—for most organizations this isn't a feasible option. The more cost effective solution is to scale out instead.

SOLUTION

Scaling out, when it comes to computationally intensive tasks usually calls for the following solution:

✓ Introduce grid technology to the service, via the Gridable Service pattern, to handle computationally intense tasks.

Figure 3.7 illustrates the solution. The Gridable Service pattern is based on a computation grid, and possibly a data grid, as part of the internal structure of a service. When the service business logic needs to handle a task that's computationally intense, the business logic creates a job on the grid root. A job is made of one or more tasks that can be queued and executed on the grid. The scheduler distributes the tasks to one or more nodes, depending on the job type, and the grid agent then executes them.

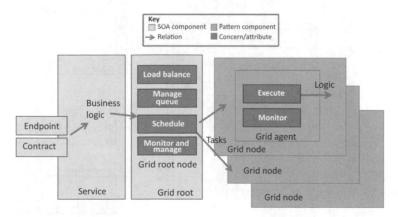

Figure 3.7   When the business logic within the service has to invoke a computationally intensive task, it creates a job on the grid root. The grid root manages all the resources within the grid or compute cluster and executes the task efficiently.

The grid infrastructure components (the agent, root node, and so on) constantly monitor resource availability. Adding hardware, configured with the grid components, enlarges the pool of available resources. The grid takes care to maximize the usage and does that based on the load of the machines. This "smart" resource allocation helps solve both scalability and load-balancing requirements. Additionally, the grid implements redundancy and failover and can pass tasks to new nodes when a node fails. The Gridable Service pattern can be combined with the Workflodize pattern (see chapter 2) by making the job's tasks into workflow instances or by having a workflow drive the jobs.

Let's return to the biometric problem presented earlier. One of the services defined in this system is a pattern-matching service, which takes a biometric pattern (sort of a hash for a biometric sample) and searches for matches in the patterns database. This is a potentially time-consuming effort, as the database may contain large numbers of records. Also, you need to use a biometric engine to compare the templates, because some information is more important than others. The distance between the eyes is more important than a beard for a face-recognition scenario, for example.

Figure 3.8 shows how the problem can be solved using the Gridable Service pattern. The edge component translates the request to an internal representation and invokes the workflow that deals with matching. Next, the workflow component works with the

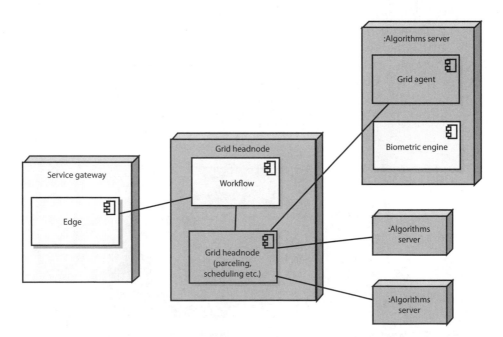

Figure 3.8   With the Gridable Service pattern applied to one of the services of a biometric platform, the different biometric engines are deployed on the grid and a workflow drives their invocation.

grid headnode to partition the matching job and schedule it. The grid infrastructure takes care of finding free algorithm servers, then invokes the appropriate biometric matching engines.

The Gridable Service pattern can help you solve your computationally intense tasks, but it sounds like a lot of work to implement this pattern. Fortunately, there are quite a few grid implementations available; all you need to do is integrate them into your SOA. Let's look at some of the available technology options.

TECHNOLOGY MAPPING

There are many grid implementations, and all of them can be applied in an SOA context to implement the Gridable Service pattern. One standard for grid computing is the Gridbus project, which defines open source specifications, an architecture, and a reference grid toolkit implementation for a service-oriented grid.

In grid scenarios, you create remote threads of execution without needing to know where the execution will take place. The grid infrastructure optimizes task execution across connected nodes, based on the available resources across them, and executes each job on the appropriate machine. Figure 3.9 shows the system console for Alchemi, which is a Microsoft .NET implementation of the Gridbus standards.

The grid software manages all member resources and can provide metrics on how the system is doing overall. The same information is used by the grid internally to distribute jobs efficiently.

Gridbus is, of course, not the only grid implementation available. Microsoft Windows HPC Server 2008 can scale your application logic out to thousands of processing cores across your existing Windows infrastructure. See www.microsoft.com/hpc/en/us/default.aspx for more information.

Pure grid computing focuses on computation. Data grid technologies are another class of grid solutions that are focused on bringing data to computation. Data grid

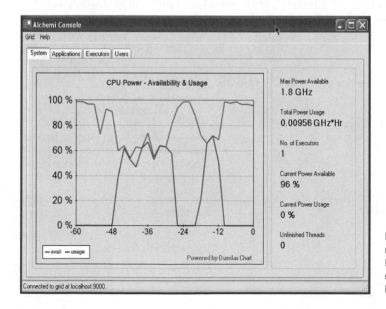

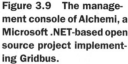

Figure 3.9 The management console of Alchemi, a Microsoft .NET-based open source project implementing Gridbus.

Table 3.3   The five protocols included in the WS-Resource Framework specification

Protocol	Description
WS-Resource	Defines the relationship of a resource on the grid to web services
WS-ResourceProperties	Defines a protocol to retrieve and set the list of features or properties of each resource
WS-ResourceLifetime	Defines the semantics to control the lifetime of a resource
WS-ServiceGroup	A standard for defining a collection of resources
WS-BaseFaults	A standard for handling problems and faults

solutions shard (partition) the data to the grid nodes and support some sort of map/reduce semantics where computation occurs locally (near the data). Only summaries are moved around the network, providing efficient computing (by minimizing I/O). There are several such options in the Java world—products such as GridGain, Hazelcast, among others.

The WS-* stack of web service protocols also addresses grid design, and there are a few protocols bundled under the name WS-Resource Framework (WSRF). Table 3.3 lists the five protocols of which WSRF is composed.

To wrap up this subject, let's review the motivations for utilizing this pattern.

QUALITY ATTRIBUTES

The Gridable Service pattern, and the grid technology it's built upon, can help with some of the common quality attributes most projects face, such as performance and availability. All of the quality attributes are met by using mechanisms that allow redistribution of computational loads based on the available resources.

Scalability is addressed by the fact that resources are pooled and constantly monitored. The grid is able to reroute work in case of failure and to redistribute the load when a new node is added.

Table 3.4 identifies a few sample scenarios and benefits of using the Gridable Service pattern.

Table 3.4   Gridable Service pattern quality attributes and scenarios

Quality attribute	Concrete attribute	Sample scenario
Performance	Latency	Under normal conditions, service requests should complete in less than a second for 99 percent of the cases and less than two seconds for 100 percent of the cases.
Availability	Hardware failure resiliency	Upon a server crash, the system will remain operational.
Scalability	Ability to scale out	It is possible to deal with increased service loads with more hardware.
Budget	Hardware costs	You can spread the load over less-expensive hardware.

One important quality attribute that's missing here is security, because it's not a core capability of the grid. But serious grid implementations should address security to some degree.

The Gridable Service pattern can help you solve some of the basic needs of distributed systems, such as performance and availability. The grid can also help achieve scalability, but grids aren't the only solution here. Let's take a look at another pattern that will also help with scalability.

3.4 Service Instance pattern

So far, we've discussed two patterns that can be used to achieve scalability: Gridable Service and Parallel Pipelines. To see why you'd need another one, let's examine a sample scenario.

PROBLEM

You might remember the blacklist service from the credit card clearinghouse example mentioned in the Parallel Pipelines discussion (see section 3.2). The blacklist service is responsible for verifying that the various attributes of an incoming request aren't in an existing list (a blacklist) of invalid items.

Let's look at the verify request operation provided by the blacklist service—see figure 3.10. Under even normal conditions, the service will experience a high number of incoming requests per second. Each needs to be validated very quickly.

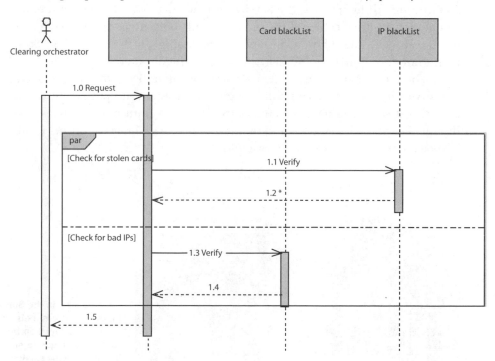

Figure 3.10   This diagram outlines the steps involved in verifying credit card purchase requests.

The blacklist service is straightforward; it communicates with a database and cache and verifies that the requester isn't in any known lists.

One very important challenge for this service is the ability to scale in cases of high request loads, such as when checking for blacklisted cards during a black Friday sales craze. Here's the problem:

How can you build services that are scalable in a simple and cost-effective way?

Two possible solutions are to use the Gridable Service pattern or the Parallel Pipelines pattern (both discussed earlier in this chapter), possibly even together.

The Gridable Service pattern, though primarily targeted at computationally intense tasks, can essentially solve most of the scalability needs. But using grid technology can be relatively complicated and expensive. You might want a more lightweight alternative to scalability.

The same is true for the Parallel Pipelines pattern. You can isolate each blacklist in its own pipeline, but this can create additional overhead for a relatively simple operation. It may even create an unacceptably large amount of latency for each request.

SOLUTION

Let's look at a simpler solution to this potentially complex problem.

Implement the Service Instance pattern by deploying multiple instances of the service business logic.

As illustrated in figure 3.11, the Service Instance pattern is built on a simple concept: you deploy multiple copies of the service. Using a dispatcher on the edge, you distribute the work to the different instances. Depending on the technology you use, you might not even have to implement anything in the dispatcher.

It's better to maintain a single endpoint and then divide the request load between the service instances. You can build on the Virtual Endpoint pattern (discussed in section 3.5) if you need multiple endpoints. The important point is that consumers of the service will be unaware of and unaffected by the scaling that occurs inside the service (see the sidebar for more information).

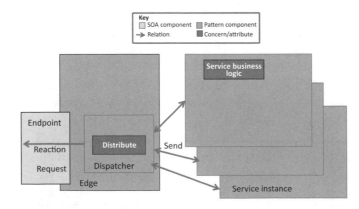

Figure 3.11 In the Service Instance pattern a dispatcher (usually deployed on the edge) routes messages to one of the instances of the service business.

> ### Scaling inside versus outside of the service
>
> When scaling is implemented outside a service, the service isn't aware that the scaling is taking place. Multiple instances of the service are deployed on the network. When scaling is implemented inside the service, the components outside of the service aren't exposed to how the scaling occurs.
>
> In most cases, it's best to scale inside the service—it hides the complexity from the consumers, which makes for easier maintenance and integration. It also lets you treat the service as an independent system and increases the overall autonomy of the service. Lastly, scaling outside the service requires that the service business logic will be stateless, which isn't always possible.

The Service Instance pattern is best suited for stateless service implementations. If you have state that needs to be shared between instances, you should probably consider using the Gridable Service pattern.

The Decoupled Invocation pattern is related to the Service Instance pattern. To combine the two, you implement the service instances as multiple readers that process the same input queue (see section 3.1 for more details).

TECHNOLOGY MAPPING

Implementing the Service Instance pattern doesn't require a particular technology. Instead, you implement a dispatcher in the language of your choice, and distribute requests to the farm of servers running your service. This is especially true if you implement this pattern on top of the Decoupled Invocation pattern.

An alternative way, and probably a more common way, to implement the Service Instance pattern is to build on the Virtual Endpoint pattern (described in section 3.5) and use one of the available load-balancing technologies. You can implement this at the application level with packages such as Apache JServ, or at the OS level with packages such as Microsoft's NLB Cluster (see figure 3.12), or one of the Linux options like HAProxy.

In figure 3.12, you can see that relying on technology (Windows NLB in this case) can simplify the scaling of the service. The edge sends the requests to the virtual IP address, and the NLB cluster takes care of routing it to the appropriate service instance. The instances themselves aren't aware that they're clustered. The obvious tradeoff here is that the granularity of control is weighted against ease of use, maintenance, and development costs.

The last issue in regard to the Service Instance pattern is shared state. As mentioned earlier, it's helpful to store shared state in a shared resource such as a database. If you still need to maintain state inside each service instance, you need to look at distributed cache solutions, such as NCache from Alachisoft or Azure Caching service on the .NET platform, or GigaSpaces and VMWare's vFabric GemFire on the JVM. Additional distributed cache options are dedicated solutions like Memcached and Redis.

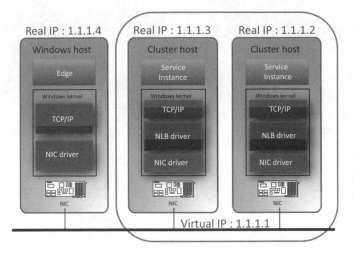

Figure 3.12   Implementing the Service Instance pattern using a Windows NLB cluster. The edge is deployed outside the cluster, and each service instance is deployed on a machine that is part of the NLB cluster.

QUALITY ATTRIBUTES

The Service Instance pattern deals with availability. Having multiple instances of the service business logic means your service is more resilient to hardware failures and you can be sure the service will stay responsive through planned downtimes (such as during upgrades). Another advantage of the Service Instance pattern is the inherent increased scalability—you can handle increased loads by adding hardware.

Table 3.5 details sample scenarios.

Table 3.5   Service Instance pattern quality attributes and scenarios

Quality attribute	Concrete attribute	Sample scenario
Availability	Hardware failure resiliency	Under normal conditions, completing service requests requires less time.
Availability	System downtime	Upon a server crash, the system will remain operational.
Scalability	Ability to scale out	It is possible to deal with increased service loads with more hardware.

The patterns so far have approached the subject of availability, but let's take a look at a pattern that addresses this head-on.

3.5   *Virtual Endpoint pattern*

At the end of the day, a service is a type of application that's hosted on a server somewhere. What happens when that server fails?

For one thing, you need to take care of restarting the failed service and resume request processing. You can look at the Service Monitor pattern (see chapter 4), Service Watchdog pattern (see section 3.6), and the Transactional Service pattern (see chapter 2) for ways to monitor services and recover from failures.

The remaining issues involve service recovery time and the failure's impact on clients.

PROBLEM

First, think about the service-level agreement (SLA) you need to support. In many cases, especially with mission-critical software, there is an agreement in place to ensure service availability and to contain outages to within a specified timeframe. You have two parameters to availability: uptime and recovery.

How can you provide services with location transparency and graceful recovery from failure without affecting consumers?

If your service is truly stateless, you can scale the service using the Service Instance pattern described earlier. But this may not provide a completely seamless solution to the service consumer. The fact that there are multiple instances of the service may be exposed to the client.

Let's explore a pattern that helps to resolve this and improves availability.

SOLUTION

The ideal solution is to run redundant instances of the service, but to have it still be accessible through one address, appearing as a single instance.

✓ **Implement the Virtual Endpoint pattern, wrapping multiple instances of the edge component to create a virtual endpoint that provides location transparency.**

The Virtual Endpoint pattern, illustrated in figure 3.13, wraps and hides the actual edge components' internal addresses. Requests are routed to one or more of the internal addresses where the edge and service exist, essentially providing location transparency for the service.

There are two variations on this pattern:

- Implement one active and one or more standby services. The standby services will be activated only in the event of a failure. The virtual endpoint will then serve as a switch between the two.
- Implement multiple active services. The virtual endpoint will route requests across all active service instances arbitrarily, or according to a load-balancing algorithm.

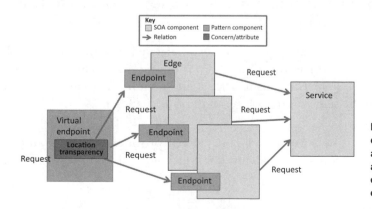

Figure 3.13   The virtual endpoint exists as a known address, but the requests are actually handled by edge components that exist on other, internal, addresses.

The first option is often simpler to implement, especially if issues exist surrounding multiple instances of a service running in parallel. This can include issues with resource sharing or locking and maintaining request message ordering. These issues can often be resolved through the use of enterprise software, such as a single shared database for resource issues and a transactional queue that maintains queued message processing order.

It's usually easier to implement the Virtual Endpoint pattern in the edge, as it's more likely to be stateless, allowing the service to maintain state independently. If you use a service registry, it can help maintain an entry for backup service addresses.

The nice thing about the Virtual Endpoint pattern is that it's very simple to implement.

TECHNOLOGY MAPPING

For services that are based on web service standards, such as REST or SOAP, the technology mapping is straightforward. You can deploy an off-the-shelf solution such as load-balancing technology. With this, you get both availability and some scalability.

If you use messaging technology rather than web technology for service interaction, you can use enterprise service bus (ESB) products like Mule or Fuse ESB (and others) to expose the virtual endpoint.

When you need smart routing to actual endpoints, such as when you have different SLAs for different tenants, you can use solutions like HAProxy (a smart load balancer) or again ESB products.

ESBs and OS-level solutions can also help introduce virtual endpoints to stateful services via clustering in active/passive setups or sharded active/active setups.

> ### Beware of the "split brain" problem
>
> When you implement a clustering solution for availability, you need to watch out for communication problems where different nodes in a pair don't see each other on the network. This "split brain" phenomenon occurs when more than one server claims to be the master. As a result, the servers and their data aren't synchronized, which can result in partial or incorrect responses.
>
> Most clustering and high-availability products address this potential problem, but you still need to be aware of this problem in case your solution doesn't protect against it.

The provider of the virtual endpoint (ESB, load balancer, or other solution) should also take care of endpoint failure and should reroute requests to an active endpoint. The provider can also help with state management by supporting session stickiness so that requests from the same source will get to the same handler.

QUALITY ATTRIBUTES

In its simplest form, the Virtual Endpoint pattern provides location transparency, which provides availability and scalability, but it can also help with maintenance and software upgrades.

Table 3.6   Virtual Endpoint pattern quality attributes and scenarios

Quality attribute	Concrete attribute	Sample scenario
Availability	Hardware failure resiliency	Upon a server crash, the system will resume operations in two minutes.
Maintenance	Upgrades	Individual service instances can be upgraded without disrupting service availability.

Table 3.6 summarizes the quality attributes.

Availability helps maintain the service when something goes wrong, but it's important to know *when* something goes wrong. The Service Monitor pattern (discussed in chapter 4) helps here, as does the Service Watchdog pattern, which we'll examine next.

3.6   *Service Watchdog pattern*

Achieving availability is a multilayered effort. You've already seen the benefits of autonomous services (see the Active Service pattern in chapter 2), and the Service Watchdog pattern will focus on another aspect of autonomy. This pattern shows how a service can proactively identify faults and try to heal itself when it finds problems.

PROBLEM

The Service Instance pattern in section 3.4 is one pattern that can cope with failure. The question is, is that enough? My opinion is that it isn't, and here's why:

- Once you deal with failure within the service, the ability to cope with additional failure is probably diminished. If the live server failed and the service transitions to a standby server, there's no additional standby if this server fails.
- The failure might be too much for the service to be able to overcome by itself. A poison message might also take the redundant or standby servers down.

To increase the service autonomy and increase overall availability, you need to identify *and* repair problems, and then notify the appropriate system operator about the service's current status.

How can you increase availability by identifying and resolving problems and failures that are service-specific?

One option is to try to infer the state of the service from the way it looks on the outside. You can periodically call the service (ping it), and if it doesn't respond within well-defined parameters (within a certain amount of time, for instance), you know the service may be down.

This approach isn't foolproof, especially if there are redundant or standby servers involved. In that case, a problem may occur and remain masked because a standby server is available to answer your pings.

Alternatively, you can install agents on each of the service's servers. This will give you a more fine-grained view of the health of each server. You may also be able to get trend information for each server, as well as warning signs about future failure potential, such as disks that are filling to capacity.

But there are problems with this solution too:

- You need to actively install software on each of the service's servers, which both decreases the service autonomy and creates a management hassle.
- You still only get an external view of the service behavior. You wouldn't be able to determine whether a service was returning stale data out of a cache because a network failure is preventing it from getting fresh data from an external source.
- Only the service really knows its wellness. Suppose the SLA of a service requires that there be at least three instances alive (for a certain load). If you have five nodes, and one is down, you still have four, so the severity of the failure isn't high. Another example is a process that's still up but is taking more time than usual. The definition of what is "usual" is something that the people who developed the service would know, and it can be part of the service's code or configuration.
- There are situations where not all of the services are under your control, and you can't access their hardware.

Yet another option is to actively contact the services and actively poll them for state. This allows you to build servers that deliberately report on potential problems and communicate trends that can lead to problems over time. They could, for example, report on growing log files, falling disk capacities, network outages or external service call failures, or low-memory situations.

This solution may not perfect because it's the observer's responsibility to request the information and act on it. If the observer doesn't sample the service frequently enough, it could miss vital information. But this approach is on the right path; all you need to do is add an element of autonomy to it, as I'll describe in the next section.

SOLUTION

A solution where the service watches over itself is often not good enough, because you normally require a human operator to be alerted to potential trouble. The solution we'll discuss here is a combination of those outlined so far.

✓ **Implement the Service Watchdog pattern, where the service actively monitors its internal state, acts on potential trouble, tries to heal itself, and continuously publishes its status.**

The Service Watchdog pattern (see figure 3.14) revolves around a single idea—you can increase the service's responsibility by combining two complementary concepts: reporting and self-healing.

The first is the *watchdog agent* concept, where the service implements the Active Service pattern (discussed in chapter 2) and contains a component in charge of monitoring the service's state. This component publishes the service's state periodically, and also when something meaningful occurs (see the Inversion of Communications pattern in chapter 5). Note that just because the service actively publishes its state

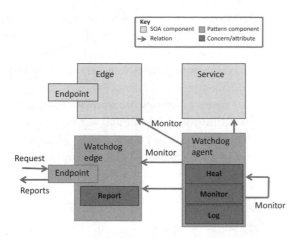

Figure 3.14   With the Service Watchdog pattern, the watchdog edge component sends health reports and listens for requests. The watchdog agent component receives these reports and tries to heal itself before the problem gets worse.

doesn't mean it can't also respond to inquiries regarding its health (akin to leaving a comment on a blog and getting a response from the author).

The second important concept in the Service Watchdog pattern is that of the *watchdog edge*. This component listens for information gathered and published by the watchdog agent component, and acts on that information in a meaningful way to increase the reliability and availability of the service.

There are many ways to implement self-healing, and many of them are application-specific. Here are a few common examples:

- Providing a fail-fast mechanism that will stop a process when the state of the component isn't certain
- Restarting failed components (as a reaction to a fail-fast)
- Implementing a circuit breaker mechanism, such as preventing a retry on a database connection when the database is down
- Clearing junk, like deleting logs, temporary files, and so on

NOTE *Watchdog* is a term borrowed from the embedded systems world. A watchdog is a hardware device that counts down to 0, at which point it takes action, such as resetting the device. To prevent this reset, the application has to "kick the dog" before the timer runs out. If the application doesn't reset the counter, it could mean that the application has stopped responding. A reset would fix that.

Let's consider the advantages of the Service Watchdog pattern over the other options presented earlier. The Service Watchdog pattern combines the benefits of an agent that actively monitors the service's health with the internal knowledge of how to maintain service continuity. For instance, a service is best equipped to know if its processing is running slower than usual. If there are many instances of the service, the service should know how many copies are really needed and how many are just for redundancy. And so on.

In one project our team inherited a situation where there were interdependencies between processes running on different servers as part of a single service. When the process was down on one server, the process on the second server didn't function properly, and vice versa. The end result was something like the situation in figure 3.15.

The watchdog agent on each server node monitors the components. The agents communicate among themselves to examine the dependencies. The watchdog edge component provides a Web Service Description Language (WSDL)-based endpoint where other services can query it for the service's health. It also publishes Simple Network Management Protocol (SNMP) traps to an external SNMP monitor (such as HP OpenView).

The simpler you keep the components, the less risk there is of failure. Let's take a more thorough look at the technology mapping options.

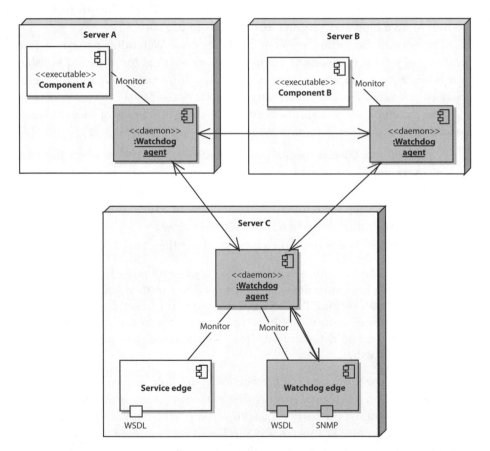

Figure 3.15   The daemon processes on the servers monitor the running components on each server. With the Service Watchdog pattern, the Watchdog edge component exposes the current state through a web-service interface, and as SNMP traps.

TECHNOLOGY MAPPING

Implementing the Service Watchdog pattern in an enterprise will usually predetermine the protocols you'll have to use. There are many third-party monitoring packages available, such as Nagios, HP OpenView, IBM Tivoli, and Microsoft Operations Manager. In these cases, you can use the SDK of the monitoring software, such as the CA Unicenter Agent SDK. There are even third-party software packages to help you build agents. OC Systems offers Universal Agent that you can use to write agents for CA Unicenter. With the emergence of SOA-specific tools, such as those from Amber-Point's SOA Management System, or WebLayers' suite of products, you can implement standard WS-* based monitoring.

At the service level, you can use standard mechanisms like performance counters on .NET and JMX MBeans in Java to emit statistics on how well the service is doing. On one system, I also configured a log listener that transmitted error and fatal log messages to the watchdog to help identify problems.

Regardless of the specific technology used, the important point is to let an agent that's controlled by the service determine when the service is healthy. The results will be manifested in an external tool, as noted earlier (and as will be discussed in the Service Monitor pattern in chapter 4).

QUALITY ATTRIBUTES

The Service Watchdog pattern helps improve the overall reliability of the service and allows it to maintain its autonomy. Monitoring and self-healing services can overcome minor problems, resulting in better overall availability.

Table 3.7 outlines some of the quality attributes that this pattern helps you achieve.

Table 3.7 Service Watchdog pattern attributes and scenarios

Quality attribute	Concrete attribute	Sample scenario
Availability	Failure detection	Upon a failure or degraded performance, the system will alert the administrator (via SMS) within a well-defined amount of time.
Reliability	Autonomy	During normal operations, the system will clear all its temporary resources continuously.

Once you begin to monitor a service and collect data, you'll begin to find new uses for that data. You can examine trends in incoming request messages to try to locate attacks on the service. Monitoring data can be used to analyze the service's behavior over time, predict failures, and help increase its maintainability.

3.7 *Summary*

Performance, scalability, and availability are related attributes of any software system. Often the best way to solve a performance problem is to scale the solution. Once you do this, you may find that the same approach can be used to increase the solution's availability. This is especially true when you combine patterns and multiply their individual quality attributes.

In this chapter, we examined structural patterns to help increase performance, scalability, and availability of services in an SOA. We covered the following patterns:

- *Decoupled Invocation*—Queues requests to deal with peak loads and increase reliability
- *Parallel Pipelines*—Breaks a process into steps to increase throughput
- *Gridable Service*—Uses grid technology for computation-intensive tasks
- *Service Instance*—Deploys multiple instances of services to help with scalability
- *Virtual Endpoint*—Provides location transparency to help with service availability
- *Service Watchdog*—Monitors and heals services

The final pattern in this chapter, Service Watchdog, serves as a good introduction to the next chapter, because it introduces the topics of maintainability and security.

3.8   *Further reading*

DECOUPLED INVOCATION

Martin Fowler, "The LMAX Architecture," http://martinfowler.com/articles/lmax.html.
    The disruptor pattern discussed in this article creates a low-latency lock-free queue between writers and readers.

PARALLEL PIPELINES

Frank Buschmann, Regine Meunier, Hans Rohnert, Peter Sommerlad, and Michael Stal, *Pattern-Oriented Software Architecture: A System of Patterns*, vol. 1 (John Wiley & Sons, 1996). The Parallel Pipelines pattern is an SOA application of the Pipes and Filters pattern described in *Pattern-Oriented Software Architecture*.

Ariel Ortiz Ramírez, "Pipes and Filters Architectural Pattern," http://webcem01.cem.itesm
    .mx:8005/apps/s200911/tc3003/notes_pipes_and_filters/.
    A short explanation of the Pipes and Filters architectural pattern.

GRIDABLE SERVICE

Robert W. Anderson and Daniel Ciruli, "Scaling SOA with Distributed Computing," *Dr. Dobb's Journal* (Oct. 5, 2006), http://www.drdobbs.com/web-development/193104809.
    This article describes the notion of adding a grid to scale SOA.

Security and
manageability patterns

4

As I mentioned in chapter 1, SOA promotes loose coupling by emphasizing interfaces, standards-based contracts, and service autonomy. SOA's loose coupling of services makes it (relatively) easy to create systems by composing services together, and it lets you update services without disrupting other services that interact with the changed service. SOA is truly an open architecture style. This openness offers a lot of benefits, like agility and easier integration, but it also opens the door to many security threats and manageability challenges. In the past, there was always a trade-off when choosing between openness and security or distribution and manageability, so you might think it would be difficult to weave security and manageability into SOA without violating SOA's principles. As you'll see in this chapter, a good balance between these somewhat contradictory quality attributes can be achieved.

Before we dive into the solutions, let's look at some of the problems they try to solve. Software systems, especially distributed and connected systems, have to deal with many threats. One example is repudiation—someone denying that they sent a message. Another example is distributed denial of service attacks, which are quite common these days.

One of the things you need to do when designing a system is threat modeling. This is a way to understand the security requirements of the system—each identified and prioritized threat needs to have some security measures to mitigate it. In *Writing Secure Code*, Michael Howard and David LeBlanc describe six threat types—spoofing, tampering, repudiation, information disclosure, denial of service, and elevation of privilege—known as STRIDE. Table 4.1 provides a short example of each threat type.

Table 4.1 **The STRIDE security threats for software systems**

Threat	Examples
Spoofing	Man in the middle replaying message; impersonating a consumer and sending a message in its name
Tampering	Changing the content of request or a reaction
Repudiation	A consumer sending a request, then denying sending it
Information disclosure	Exposing internal information in an error message
Denial of service	Flooding a service with bogus requests
Elevation of privilege	Executing a request that the consumer isn't authorized to execute

The quality attributes discussion for each pattern in this chapter will cover which of the STRIDE threats can be mitigated by using that particular security-related pattern.

One aspect of security is keeping out attackers and preventing malicious attacks. Another important aspect of security is monitoring for problems and ensuring that security guidelines are followed. The monitoring facet of security is also a part of other quality attributes—manageability and governance—which we'll also touch on in this chapter. Security, manageability, and governance are too often neglected, even though organizations pursuing SOA tend to promote governance more than before. Both security and manageability are important to ensuring that a solution will be working and running as expected—security makes sure no external and unfriendly elements interrupt the service, and management ensures that everything is well on the inside.

Figure 4.1 shows which of the SOA components mentioned in the SOA definition in chapter 1 are touched by the patterns in this chapter:

As illustrated in figure 4.1, the focus of this chapter is on the peripheral components of the service—the messages, policies, and endpoint—more than the service itself. It's better to maintain the service's focus on the business functionality than to clutter it with general concerns. Dealing with security and manageability outside of

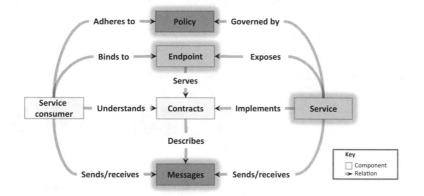

Figure 4.1   In previous chapters, our focus was mainly on the service itself. In this chapter, the focus shifts to the interface of the service—the patterns in this chapter touch the policy, endpoint, and messages components of SOA.

the service allows it to maintain that focus. You've also seen this with the introduction of the edge component (see chapter 2). This doesn't mean you shouldn't write secure code or use logs when you develop the service itself. It just means that aspects such as authentication and authorization are better handled externally.

The following patterns are discussed in this chapter:

- *Secured Message*—Secure specific messages or parts of messages that are exchanged between two or more services
- *Secured Infrastructure*—Increase the overall security of message exchange between services, with minimal impact on the services involved
- *Service Firewall*—Protect a service against malicious incoming messages and prevent information disclosure on outgoing messages
- *Identity Provider*—Implement an efficient authorization and authentication scheme in an SOA
- *Service Monitor*—Identify problems and faults in services and attend to them to ensure the overall business's availability

The first pattern we'll discuss is the Secured Message pattern.

4.1   Secured Message pattern

The first pattern in this chapter has to do with one of the most fundamental components of SOA—the message. Messages, as explained in chapter 1, are the components that transport data between services and their consumers.

SOA-based systems are, by definition, open, distributed, and, most importantly, connected, which means that you have a lot of these messages going back and forth. You can control what happens to the message inside the service, and you may have some control over the service consumers, but what about the space between the services? I remember listening to a presentation by Pat Helland on messages and data in

SOA, and he called this space "no man's land." In a sense, this space is exactly that, especially when the messages travel over a public network such as the internet.

Let's take a look at what this means.

PROBLEM

The fact that messages travel in this no-man's-land between services makes them prone to all sorts of threats. Many of the threats have to do with a class of attack known as "man in the middle." Figure 4.2 shows the basic template for a man-in-the-middle attack. Simply put, it means that when a message leaves the service or the service consumer, someone lurking on the wire can take a look at the message and tamper with it.

Figure 4.2   Man-in-the-middle attacks. An attacker listens in on messages that travel in unprotected spaces and can examine or even change the messages.

This man-in-the-middle scenario is the basis for several types of threats, and we need to find a way to protect against them. We need to find ways to:

- *Protect privacy*—Sometimes messages contain confidential information, or information that's at least private. Maybe you don't want everybody to know your company's account details when you send an order message to a supplier.
- *Protect integrity*—You don't want anyone to change the messages you send. You don't want that $100 order you've requested changed to $10,000,000.
- *Protect against impersonation*—You don't want anyone withdrawing money from your account "on your behalf" by faking the credentials you've sent in a message.

But while man-in-the-middle scenarios are important, they aren't the only threats you need to handle. You also need to protect against repudiation—you don't want your client denying sending that $10,000,000 order the minute the merchandise is received.

While these examples are for financial transactions, the same issues are relevant to other types of messages, such as transferring student grades in a university system, or sending fingerprints and personal identities in a forensic context, or any other type of data you want your services to handle.

? How can you secure specific messages or message fragments that are exchanged between two or more services?

The naïve thing to do is ... to do nothing and hope for the best. This may sound like a stupid approach, but I've seen too many systems where this was exactly the "solution" used. The obvious downsides are that the messages are prone to all the threats mentioned previously. There may be some edge cases where this sort of security doesn't matter, but as a rule, this is not a good approach to take.

One option is to use a secure channel (see the Secured Infrastructure pattern in section 4.2). This is a good option in the technical and architectural sense, as it takes the burden of security off of the service.

The main problem with this approach is that it's harder, and sometimes impossible, to make this work in an uncontrolled environment. There are situations where the infrastructure is limited and can't provide the solution you need. You may only want to encrypt part of the data—say the credit card number—but leave the other part open. Secured Infrastructure is often only suitable for point-to-point scenarios (for example, using SSL/TLS for internet security), and you may need multimessage and multiparty interactions. Furthermore, if you temporarily store the messages in a cache or other less-secure temporary storage, securing just the transport may not be enough.

SOLUTION

If you can't use the Secured Infrastructure pattern, or if the level of security it can provide isn't good enough, you'll need to take care of securing the messages yourself.

Apply the Secured Message pattern to your messages and add message-level security.

The Secured Message pattern (illustrated in figure 4.3) is composed of a single component that's responsible for enforcing the security on top of the raw messages. These are the two common security capabilities for the message:

- *Encryption or decryption of messages*—Encryption and decryption can help solve the privacy scenario because someone looking at the message will have a hard time figuring out what the message is. The strength of the encryption depends on both the strength of the algorithm used and on how protected the key is.

- *Digital signatures*—Digital signatures can help solve the integrity problem. When you digitally sign a message, you can determine whether the message was altered and doesn't match the original that was sent. Note that digital signatures tell you that something is wrong, and not what went wrong. Digital signatures can also solve the repudiation problem, because when someone digitally signs a message, they need to use their private key to sign the message, which proves that they originated the message.

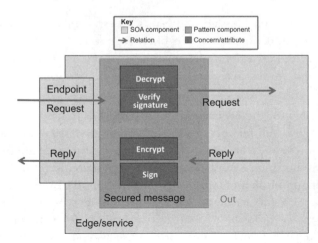

Figure 4.3 The Secured Message pattern defines a single component that handles both decryption/ encryption and digital signatures and their verification.

Idempotent messages

In addition to encryption and signing, it's also worthwhile to put time into making messages *idempotent*. Idempotence is a mathematical term that basically means that calling a function multiple times doesn't change the result $f(f(x))=f(x)$. Idempotence for messaging means that the messages should be constructed in a way that the processing service is immune to reprocessing a message. If a service receives the same message again, it should be able to handle it without changing the state of the system. In a financial scenario you wouldn't want that "withdraw $10,000,000" message to be processed more than once.

A common way to achieve idempotence in messages is to add a version number or transaction number so that you can identify the message or the origin of the message when needed. It's important to note that adding idempotence is a choice you have to make and implement on your own as part of the service implementation. Any infrastructure-level implementation won't be meaningful in the business context and will only handle network-level retries and replays.

Sometimes it's possible to make the message idempotent regardless of the receiver; for example, "set discount to $10 for order 123." Even if you handle this message several times, the discount would still be $10 (compared with a message that says "deduct $10 from order 123"). Sometimes you'll still need to make sure that the service is an idempotent receiver so that it would register which messages it has already handled and check against that list before processing incoming messages.

As mentioned previously, the Secured Message pattern isn't a replacement for the Secured Infrastructure pattern. It's best used in scenarios that aren't handled well by Secured Infrastructure, like partial encryption of data, temporary storage of data, multiparty secured sessions, and signing unencrypted data. One reason to consider partial encryption is the impact of full encryption on latency. It takes much more time to encrypt and decrypt every message than it does to encrypt several attributes or fields in a few specific messages.

Even when you use the Secured Message pattern, it doesn't mean you develop everything from scratch—if you'd do that you're likely to have insecure solutions. Instead, it's better to rely on the cryptographic capabilities of the development environment you use—I'll expand on that in the technology mapping section.

TECHNOLOGY MAPPING

The basic technology mapping for the Secured Message pattern is to use the cryptography libraries of your development technology. Both Java and .NET have the notion of a cryptographic service provider, which lets you abstract away the implementation of the cryptographic algorithms. In one application I architected, we used this feature to seamlessly replace a software implementation of an algorithm with one based on a Hardware Security Module (HSM) to accelerate encryption and decryption speeds.

When building SOAs, you're more likely than not using XML for your messages (although other options like JSON or proprietary formats are also possible). If you are using XML, two technological standards you should be aware of are XML encryption and XML signatures—both are W3C standards and both are supported by many development environments. For instance, Apache Santuario, the Apache XML security project, has implementations for Java and C++. .NET 4 has a specific namespace that deals with XML cryptography(System.Security.Cryptography.Xml).

XML encryption allows you to encrypt specific elements within an XML document; if you have the XML in listing 4.1, you might want to secure the account information, because it holds both an account ID and credit card data.

Listing 4.1 An unsecured XML message that holds sensitive data

```
<Order>
    <Account>
        <AccountID>1234-6789</AccountID>
        <Payment>
            <CardId>9999-5678-9123-4567</CardId>
            <CVV2>123</CVV2>
            <ValidBy>02/05/1999</ValidBy>
            <CardName>visa</CardName>

        </Payment>
    </Account>
    <Items>
        <Item name="Mashu">
            <ItemId>123-456-789</Id>
            <Quantity>10</Quantity>
        </Item>
    </Items>
</Order>
```

If you use one of the previously mentioned methods and encrypt it to the standard, you can get something like the XML in this listing (depending on the key and algorithm).

Listing 4.2 The XML from listing 4.1 with the account key encrypted

```
<?xml version='1.0' ?>
<Order>
    <EncryptedData Type='http://www.w3.org/2001/04/xmlenc#Element'
➥xmlns='http://www.w3.org/2001/04/xmlenc#'>
        <CipherData>
            <CipherValue>FF5BDA12C3EE3A238FCD8721AE9354</CipherValue>
        </CipherData>
    </EncryptedData>

    <<Items>
        <Item name="Mashu">
            <ItemId>123-456-789</Id>
            <Quantity>10</Quantity>
        </Item>
    </Items>

</Order>
```

Note that the XML encryption standard also defines an `EncryptedKey` tag, similar to the `EncryptedData` element in listing 4.2, to also support secure key exchanges.

Some threats, such as cross-site request forgery (CSRF, also known as XSRF) can be mitigated by using hashes and not encryption. (It's much faster to create hashes.) The Open Web Application Security Project (OWASP) suggests a "synchronizer token pattern" where for every session the server generates a unique random hash, which is hard for attackers to guess. Requests by clients should include the token so that the server knows that the requests are valid (see the further reading and the bibliography for more details).

QUALITY ATTRIBUTES

The Secured Message pattern helps deal with a few threats derived from the presence of a "man in the middle." Table 4.2 lists the threat categories and the actions that an implementation of the Secured Message pattern can take to avoid these threats.

Table 4.2   Threat categories that implementations of the Secured Message pattern can mitigate

Threat	Actions
Spoofing	Verify signature using the sender's public key to prevent impersonation
	Add time stamps, sequence numbers, or expiration times to messages, or implement idempotent messages to cope with replay attacks
Tampering	Encrypt messages so that they can't be changed without ruining the message
Repudiation	Add a time stamp and require signatures on messages to prevent senders from claiming they didn't send a message
Information Disclosure	Encrypt important information (or the whole message) to prevent someone else from reading sensitive data

In regard to general quality attributes, you can see that the Secured Message pattern is a little problematic. One problem is that it requires a lot of work on the service implementation, which means it has an impact on maintainability. Also, because it's your responsibility to implement this pattern, you need to be careful and comply with standards; otherwise, it can have a bad effect on interoperability.

Some aspects of the Secured Message pattern can be simplified by using the Secured Infrastructure pattern, which we'll discuss next.

4.2   *Secured Infrastructure pattern*

The Secured Infrastructure pattern is relatively simple from an architectural perspective, but it has a lot of details and substance in its technology mapping. The principle behind the Secured Infrastructure pattern, as its name implies, is finding a communication layer that's secured and using it for the service's communications. The complication here is deciding on the appropriate technology mapping to fit your needs and then to utilize that technology properly.

The bulk of the discussion for this pattern will be in the technology mapping section, but first let's introduce the problem and the solution.

PROBLEM

By introducing the problem, let's recap the scenarios presented in the Secured Message pattern. As messages flow in the space between services, which includes routers, networks, and sometimes even public networks (such as the internet), you need to find ways to protect the messages against prying eyes and malicious onlookers. Essentially, you need to protect privacy, protect the messages' integrity, and protect against impersonation:

- *Protect privacy*—Sometimes messages contain confidential information, or at least private information. Maybe you don't want everybody to know your company's account details when you send an order message to a supplier.
- *Protect integrity*—You don't want anyone to change the messages you send. You don't want that $100 order you've requested changed to $10,000,000.
- *Protect against impersonation*—You don't want anyone withdrawing money from your account "on your behalf" by faking the credentials you've sent in a message.

These are basically the same set of problem as for the Secured Message pattern, but with the added constraint that we want minimal work and impact on the services. Maybe there's a way to patch security on the outside without giving a lot of the work to the service and the developers who program it.

How can you increase the overall security of message exchanges between services with minimal impact on the services involved?

One option is to develop the security solution yourself. To minimize the effect on the services, you can put most of the security-related code in an edge component (see the Edge Component pattern in chapter 2). But you still have to develop the security solution, and even more importantly, test it. Also, you'd need to make sure you use security standards to enable interoperability with external parties—don't forget that openness is an important trait for an SOA.

So what's the other option?

SOLUTION

If developing a solution by yourself isn't a great option, the other option is to try to find a solution developed by someone else.

Apply the Secured Infrastructure pattern and use third-party secured solutions as the communication infrastructure for the services.

The main idea behind the Secured Infrastructure pattern, illustrated in figure 4.4, is to find an off-the-shelf solution that will solve as many of the security challenges as possible by configuration alone. This is a real boon, because you can develop your services without thinking about security, and then change a few configuration files to secure the system.

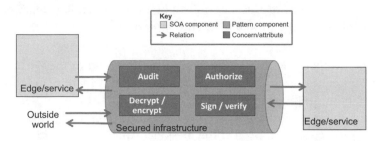

Figure 4.4   The Secured Infrastructure pattern involves buying (or building) a common secure communications infrastructure for the services that is external to the services and handles the messaging traffic for all the services.

One caveat is that when you apply the Secured Infrastructure pattern and decide to turn security "on," the granularity of the decision is usually limited. You can choose to set a secure channel, but then all the messages that go through it will be encrypted. This can have an undesired or unplanned effect on the throughput and latency of messages. Sometimes that's a necessity, because everything in every message has to be secured, but sometimes fine-grained control on security will yield both the needed level of security and better performance.

One way around this problem is to add an additional unsecured channel, then make sure you send the right messages on the right channels and that messages on the unsecure channel don't leak information that should be sent on the secure channel.

To make sure you've got the right option for the solution you're building, it's recommended that you integrate security early and conduct performance tests to assess the impact.

TECHNOLOGY MAPPING

This section usually covers both technologies where the pattern is used and ways to implement the pattern by yourself. But unless you're a technology vendor, the most likely path to take with the Secured Infrastructure pattern is to choose an off-the-shelf solution. We'll discuss the most common technological options: SSL/TLS and WS-Security, and using ESBs.

SSL/TLS

The first, and probably most approachable, option is to use SSL (Secure Socket Layer) or TLS (Transport Layer Security). These are standard internet protocols—all web browsers support them and they're in wide use today. SSL/TLS is the natural selection for securing RESTful services because REST builds on HTTP as it is.

SSL and TLS are also supported by web services based on WS-* standards, such as WCF or JAX-WS. Adding SSL support for a web service simply involves marking it in the WSDL that describes the service's contract. Suppose you have a definition such as the one in the next listing, which shows a skeleton definition of a web service exposed as a servlet endpoint.

Listing 4.3   JAX-WS definition of a web service exposed as a servlet endpoint

```
package servletws;

import javax.annotation.Resource;
import javax.jws.WebService;
import javax.xml.ws.WebServiceContext;

@WebService
public class OrderServlet {
    @Resource WebServiceContext wsContext;

    public String PlaceOrder(OrderMessage msg) {

        ...
    }
}
```

To make this web service use SSL, all you need to do is add a few tags into the WSDL, such as <transport-guarantee> CONFIDENTIAL </transport-guarantee> and <auth-method> CLIENT-CERT </auth-method>, and you're all set.

The next listing shows an except from the WSDL that configures the OrderServlet in listing 4.3 to use SSL.

Listing 4.4   WSDL excerpt for the service in listing 4.3 that configures it to use SSL

```
<security-constraint>
  <web-resource-collection>
    <web-resource-name>Secure Area</web-resource-name>
    <url-pattern>/OrderServletService/OrderServlet
    </url-pattern>
    <http-method>POST</http-method>
  </web-resource-collection>
  <auth-constraint>
    </role-name>EMPLOYEE</role-name>
  </auth-constraint>
  <user-data-constraint>
    <transport-guarantee>CONFIDENTIAL</transport-guarantee>
  </user-data-constraint>
</security-constraint>
<login-config>
  <auth-method>CLIENT-CERT</auth-method>
  <realm-name>certificate</realm-name>
</login-config>
```

> **NOTE** If you want to understand how SSL and TLS work in detail, you may want to check out Open SSL. It's an open source implementation of the two protocols.

SSL/TLS provide transport-level security and they're tied to a specific transport (HTTP), which are downsides. If you're building web services that have to use multiple transports, like Java Message Service (JMS) or Microsoft Message Queuing (MSMQ) along with HTTP, you can't do that with SSL/TLS. Another point is that messages won't be encrypted as they pass all the layers between the transport and the process on the server, and this might be a security risk in some situations. Lastly, SSL operates at the transport level, which means it's an all-or-nothing protocol—all the messages that flow on the channel will be secured, which might be overkill and create a performance bottleneck.

> **NOTE**   As an alternative, you can use IPSec, which is an even lower-level technology (compared with SSL/TLS), to implement the Secured Infrastructure pattern. IPSec sits in the network level (the IP level) and is completely external to the services. Essentially, it allows secure communications between two hardware nodes. It isn't as versatile as SSL/TLS, but it can be used to secure the communication of a closed group of services efficiently and with relatively little hassle (save for configuration and setup). IPSec suffers from the same limitations as SSL/TLS.

WS-Security

Another technology mapping for the Secured Infrastructure pattern is WS-Security. WS-Security alleviates some of the problems of SSL/TLS as it's a message-level protocol and not a transport-level one. You can choose which messages to secure and which to leave open, you don't have to encrypt a message when you just want to sign it. WS-Security is a WS-* standard that provides the means to encrypt, sign, and authenticate messages exchanged between services and their consumers.

As illustrated in figure 4.5, WS-Security adds security tokens and signatures to the message header.

The signatures are used to ensure the message hasn't changed (guaranteeing the message's integrity) and to verify the sender. As for security tokens, the OASIS standard explains that "security tokens assert claims and can be used to assert the binding between authentication secrets or keys and security identities." In plain English, a security token is the credential used for authentication, authorization, or both; a security token can be an X.509 certificate or a username that can carry with it a set of *statements* or *claims*, as the standard refers to them. Claims can be anything the sender (or

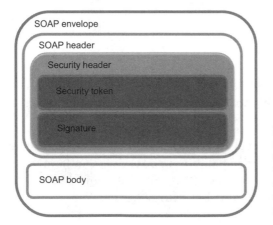

Figure 4.5   The structure of a SOAP message using the WS-Security protocol. WS-Security adds a security header to the message header where the sender can store its security token and a digital signature. Additionally, the sender can decide to encrypt the content of the message body (the SOAP body).

someone on his behalf) cares to say about the sender; a claim, for instance, can be the key that should be used to decrypt the message, the identity of the sender, and so on.

One advantage of this approach is that if you trust the security token, you can immediately process the message, whereas for SSL you need to first establish a session (exchange keys between the parties). WS-Security can use SSL if the limitations previously mentioned aren't a problem for you, and the example in code listings 4.3 and 4.4 does just that. Regarding trust, one way to gain it can be by having some trusted authority sign the security token—you can read more about this in the Identity Provider pattern in section 4.4.

One limitation of WS-Security, as compared to SSL and other options, is that it can only be used with WS-* web services (SOAP based services). This is a limitation because although SOAP-based web services are a popular option for implementing SOA, they aren't the only option. Also, if you use WS-Security for all the messages, it's likely to be slower than SSL because SSL can work at the bit level and be streamed, whereas WS-Security requires complete messages.

For REST-based systems, there is a similar approach regarding authorization called OAuth (current version is OAuth2). Like WS-Security, OAuth uses tokens in the authorization process. It can be used on top of the SSL/TLS approach mentioned in the previous section.

ESBs

The third technology option for implementing the Secured Infrastructure pattern is using an enterprise service bus (ESB). ESBs are a higher-level solution than the previous two technology options discussed here (SSL and WS-Security). In a nutshell, ESBs are integrated standards-based service communications infrastructures that provide several features, like messaging, mediation, and management. (See the Service Bus pattern in chapter 7 for a more thorough discussion.)

What's important here is that ESBs offer secured communications and they provide a means to expose services using the previously discussed technologies. You can also use ESBs to route messages, which makes it easy to introduce additional security mechanisms, such as implementations of the Service Firewall or Service Monitor patterns (both discussed later in this chapter). Essentially if you expose all your services over an ESB, you can use it as a central point to perform the three As—authentication, authorization, and auditing.

QUALITY ATTRIBUTES

The Secured Infrastructure pattern helps mitigate threats related to third-party interception or inspection of messages (man-in-the-middle threats). Table 4.3 shows the threat categories and the preventative actions that the Secured Infrastructure pattern can take.

The Secured Infrastructure pattern helps protect the channel against an external attacker when the two parties involved in the message exchange are valid. It doesn't cover malicious consumers that try to attack your service. For that, we can look at another pattern—the Service Firewall pattern.

Table 4.3   Threats categories that implementations of the Secured Infrastructure pattern can mitigate

Threat	Actions
Spoofing	Verify signature using the sender's public key to prevent impersonation
	Add timestamps to messages or implement idempotent messages to cope with replay attacks
Tampering	Encrypt messages so that they can't be changed without ruining the message
Repudiation	Add timestamps and require signatures on messages to prevent a sender from claiming it didn't send a message
Information disclosure	Encrypt important information (or the whole message) to prevent anyone from reading sensitive data

4.3   *Service Firewall pattern*

In the previous patterns, I mentioned that messages travel in "no-man's land." You can use the Secured Message or Secured Infrastructure patterns to protect the messages while they travel through that space, but what can you do if the sender is malicious? When an attacker sends you a malicious message (perhaps a virus as a SOAP attachment), the fact that the message got to you intact and without anyone else seeing it doesn't help very much.

PROBLEM

To illustrate the type of attacks a malicious sender can cause, let's look at one of them a little closer. Figure 4.6 illustrates an XML denial-of-service (XDoS) attack. In this type of attack, a malicious sender attaches a lot of digital signatures to a message. Parsers that aren't ready for this type of attack examine each of these signatures, causing the service to slow down under the load.

Another common attack scenario is XPath injection or even plain old SQL injection, where the parameters passed within a message are malicious and aim to disclose information or perform harmful operations on data within the service.

Attacks like these, using incoming messages, are one of the types of threats you need to handle. A related type of threat or problem has to do with outgoing messages. Here you need to make sure that private or classified information doesn't leak outside of the service. In this scenario, you want to find a way to make sure messages contain only information permitted to flow out of the service.

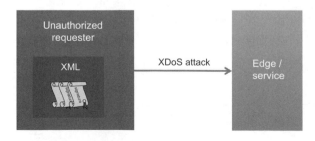

Figure 4.6   Illustration of an XDoS attack. A malicious sender prepares an XML message that looks valid but is loaded with a lot of digital signatures. An unsuspecting parser will try to verify each of these signatures, hogging CPU cycles, which can result in unavailability of the service.

? **How can you protect a service against malicious incoming messages and prevent information disclosure on outgoing messages?**

One option for dealing with malicious senders is to apply the Secured Infrastructure pattern (discussed in section 4.2) and to require certificates for authorizing clients. This means that clients who don't have a certificate won't be allowed to contact the system. One problem with this approach is that it's only good when the service is only accessible to a limited number of consumers and not to the general public. Another limitation of the certificate approach is that it doesn't handle attacks by insiders, because they're authorized to access the system.

Another option is to incorporate the security logic that screens malicious content as part of the business logic. There are several problems with this approach: One is that you get code duplication (violation of the Single Responsibility Principle), as there are many threats that are common to all services. Another problem is that the business logic gets tainted with security logic, which makes it both harder to write and harder to maintain.

The best option is to externalize the security to another component. Let's look at this option more closely.

SOLUTION

SOA messages are application-level components, but the notion of messages isn't new or unique to SOA. The computer industry already has a lot of experience with messages on a lower level of the OSI stack—the network level, specifically TCP packets and UDP datagrams. TCP and UDP have a few similarities with SOA messages, and the interesting ones, for the purposes of this pattern, are the threats they face. Since the threats are similar, maybe you can use the same solutions that work for TCP and apply them to your SOA messages.

✓ **Implement the Service Firewall pattern, intercept incoming and outgoing messages, and inspect them in a dedicated software or hardware component.**

The Service Firewall pattern is an application of the Edge Component pattern (discussed in chapter 2). Figure 4.7 illustrates how the service firewall operates.

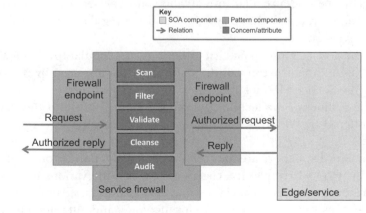

Figure 4.7 The service firewall sits between the outside world and the actual service (or edge). The service firewall scans, validates, and audits both incoming and outgoing messages. Once a message is identified as problematic, it can either be filtered out or cleansed.

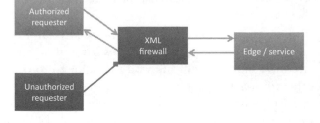

Figure 4.8   **When a request arrives at a service firewall (an XML firewall in this illustration) it's screened for validity. The firewall can check that an XML message matches the predefined XSD. Authorized requests get through and unauthorized requests are rejected.**

First, the service firewall intercepts each incoming and outgoing message and inspects it. Once intercepted, the service firewall can scan the message for malicious content such as viruses, XDoS attacks, and injection attacks as discussed previously.

Note that the firewall doesn't perform any magic that lets it deal with these threats. It's built to cope with the threats, identify the patterns that mark a message as harmful, and screen incoming and outgoing messages. Additionally, the service firewall can validate messages by making sure they conform to the contract, verifying property types, sizes, and so on. When a message is identified as problematic, the service firewall can audit and log the message and then decide whether to filter it out or cleanse the problematic content and let it through.

The service firewall acts as a first line of defense for the service. As illustrated in figure 4.8, when a request arrives at the firewall, it's scanned and verified, and requests that are authorized are then routed to the real service (or another edge component).

The idea behind a service firewall is simple. The implementation is more complicated because there is a lot of functionality that has to be implemented for each of the roles (scan, validate, filter, and so on). On top of that, you need a way to make sure the service firewall sees all the messages.

TECHNOLOGY MAPPING

The simplest way to implement the Service Firewall pattern is to create a designated edge component where you can implement the inspection and validation logic. Once the firewall logic is done, you can deploy it on the DMZ (the network subnet where public APIs and webservers are deployed and made accessible to the outside world). Deploy the real service behind a regular firewall and you're all set. The edge component will block unwanted requests that play "nice," and the regular firewall will block the other attacks.

Implementing the Service Firewall pattern without using a regular firewall is a little more problematic, as an attacker can call the endpoints that are used by the actual service and bypass the Service Firewall altogether. In these situations, you can rely on the interception capabilities of the technology you use. Figure 4.9 shows the relevant extension points offered by Windows Communications Foundation for intercepting incoming messages.

As illustrated in figure 4.9, there are four relevant extension points (out of the few dozen supported by WCF) where you use classes to perform the various roles of the Service Firewall pattern. You can have classes that verify addresses, verify contracts, inspect messages, and inspect parameters, both for incoming and outgoing messages.

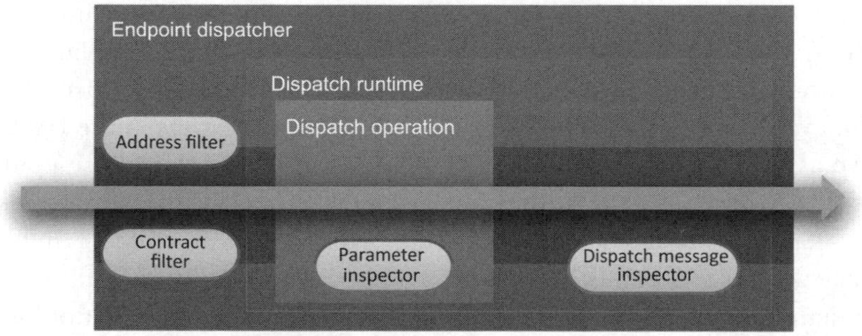

Figure 4.9 WCF supports a few dozen extension points to control the way a message is handled when it enters or leaves the service. You can use four of these extension points to implement the different roles defined in the Service Firewall pattern.

The next listing defines a new WCF web service endpoint in code and sets up a custom `ServiceAuthorizationManager` that will be the Service Firewall instance.

Listing 4.5 Getting incoming messages using WCF extension points

```
var testServer = new Tester();
var service1 = new ServiceHost(testServer,
➥new Uri(string.Format("http://localhost:{0}", TestServerPort)));

var ep = service1.AddServiceEndpoint(typeof(TestingContract), binding,
➥string.Format("http://localhost:{0}/S1", TestServerPort));
ep.Behaviors.Add(new WebHttpBehavior());

// set up an interception point for our Service Firewall
service1.Authorization.ServiceAuthorizationManager = new ServiceFirewall();

var cp = service1.AddServiceEndpoint(typeof(ImContract), binding,
➥string.Format("http://localhost:{0}/Control", TestServerPort));
cp.Behaviors.Add(new WebHttpBehavior());
```

Once you have an interception point, you can define the class that will do the actual scanning of incoming messages as shown next.

Listing 4.6 .NET skeleton code to perform validation on intercepted messages

```
public class ServiceFirewall :ServiceAuthorizationManager
 {
     public override bool CheckAccess(OperationContext operationContext,
                                 ➥ref Message message)
     {
         var isAuthorized = base.CheckAccess(operationContext, ref
                            ➥message);
         var buffer = message.CreateBufferedCopy(Int32.MaxValue);
         message = buffer.CreateMessage();
         var testMessage = buffer.CreateMessage();

         ...  // code to validate messages goes here

         return isAuthorized;
     }

 }
```

Another implementation option for the Service Firewall pattern is using hardware or embedded appliances. Companies like Layer 7, IBM (DataPower appliances), Vordel, and a few others produce XML firewall appliances. The advantage of using XML appliances is that you can deploy them along with your other firewalls in the DMZ and have them serve as the first line of defense. Another advantage is that these platforms are optimized for XML handling, so the performance impact of the appliances is lower than a self-coded solution. One disadvantage of using hardware XML firewalls is the setup costs (tens of thousands per unit); another is the increased maintenance complexity of managing an additional hardware type and performing the double management of your SOA contract (both in the service and in the appliance).

Whether you use a firewall appliance or implement the Service Firewall pattern in code, it can really boost the security of your services by helping prevent threats like denial of service attacks or even just saving validation efforts for the service itself.

QUALITY ATTRIBUTES

The Service Firewall pattern is very versatile, and it can be made to handle many types of threats. Table 4.4 lists the threat categories and the actions that an implementation of the Service Firewall pattern can take to protect against threats in these categories.

In addition to the specifics of the threats that the Service Firewall pattern helps mitigate, you can also look at it from the wider scope of quality attributes. Like most of the other patterns in this chapter, Service Firewall is a security pattern. It's interesting to note that unlike most other security patterns, it's relatively easy to add it on toward the end of a project, although this is not a completely free ride. You still have to

Table 4.4   Threat categories that implementations of the Service Firewall pattern can mitigate

Threat	Actions
Tampering	Verify signatures and make sure no one changed the content of a request or a reaction
	Validate that messages aren't malformed
Information Disclosure	Scan outgoing messages for sensitive content
	Restrict reply addresses to closed groups
	Inspect incoming messages for XPath and SQL injection attacks
Denial of Service	Prevent XDoS attacks by examining XML before validating each signature
	Block known attackers
	Restrict requestor addresses to a closed group
	Scan attachments for viruses
Elevation of Privilege	Examine an incoming message for injection attacks
	Examine an incoming message for buffer overruns by validating contracts and sizes of elements

measure its impact on system performance—it can add an overhead in regards to contract maintenance and the like.

In this chapter on security and manageability, it's about time we started talking about manageability patterns. The next pattern, Identity Provider, helps make this transition, as it has both security and manageability aspects.

4.4   Identity Provider pattern

When you move an enterprise to SOA, or even if you only build a single system based on SOA concepts, you're likely to end up with quite a few services—and quite a few more service interactions. From the security perspective, you need to make sure each of these interactions is both authenticated and authorized. This means that each of your services has to take care of this authentication and authorization.

Ay, there's the rub. This proliferation of authentication and authorization raises several challenges in regard to maintenance, management, performance, and security. Let's look at a sample scenario.

PROBLEM

Let's take another look at the journal subscription agency from chapter 2 (in our discussion of the Active Service pattern). One of the more important services for a journal subscription agency is the one that deals with the customer. Almost any other service in the system needs information from that service.

Figure 4.10 shows four simple examples— the Promotions service needs addresses, the Proposals service needs discount rates, and the Billing and Orders services both need addresses and discount rates.

So what's the problem with that? As a matter of fact, there are plenty:

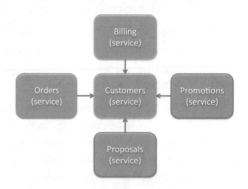

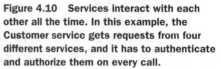

Figure 4.10   Services interact with each other all the time. In this example, the Customer service gets requests from four different services, and it has to authenticate and authorize them on every call.

- The Customer service needs to authenticate each of the services that connects to it to ensure that it's talking to an internal friendly service. But you don't want it to know about each of these services. You don't want to update the Customer service every time you add a new service. Avoiding this point-to-point integration was part of the reason of going down the SOA path.
- When you have a human in the loop, you need to make sure that person is authorized to get the customer's data. When a user works with a UI that works with the ordering service, the user might be authorized to get a customer's email address (to send an order confirmation) but not the customer's home phone number.

- You don't want each service to "know" all the users as that would cause a maintenance and management nightmare. Would you revoke the credential on all the services each time an employee leaves the company?

- If the Customer service has to authorize and authenticate every call, it will have to spend a lot of time doing so, which adds latency and increases temporal coupling.

- Management of the whole authorizations and authentications across services. For example, suppose you just added the Proposals service—how can you let the Customer service and any other service know it's OK to talk to it? How can you do that for new users?

- All the preceding problems get even worse when the service is external because the trust between organizations is naturally lower than the trust between internal components. For instance, you may have a third party that handles the promotions for you. You'll want to let them have as few details as possible about your internal structure and users, but you'd want to allow them to talk with your services and make sure that they're authenticated.

What you need is an efficient and secure way to handle authentication and authorization within a federated and distributed system.

How can you have an efficient authorization and authentication scheme in an SOA?

The first question that comes to mind is, "Wouldn't the Secured Infrastructure pattern (from section 4.2) solve this?" Well, no. The Secured Infrastructure pattern takes care of the channel, but how do you know you can talk with someone on that channel? You can communicate over a secured infrastructure to establish the identity, but you need something more.

As I mentioned earlier, the naïve option of trying to manage the security for each service on its own is a maintenance nightmare, as you'd need to do that work for each service. You also run the risk of introducing coupling and point-to-point integration for each new service consumer you introduce.

Writing this code once and reusing it (such as with the Edge Component pattern discussed in chapter 2) will only work if you or your team owns all the services. Also, you still have a management and maintenance problem, because each running instance has to be updated when a new service consumer is introduced.

Introducing an external party to handle the authorization and authentication is a step in the right direction, as you can centrally manage who is authorized to do what. But you still have to solve a few issues.

One is that most SOA implementations are sessionless, so you need to make sure that this external party won't become a performance bottleneck when each and every request has to be authenticated and authorized with it.

The second is that you don't want to couple your services to this external party, but each service does need to know somehow that it's talking to the right external party and not to some malicious impersonator.

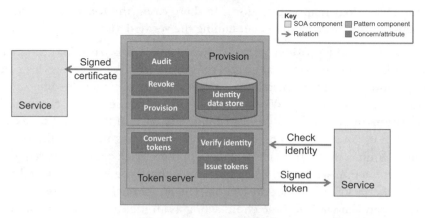

Figure 4.11 The Identity Provider pattern has two main components. One manages the identities (provisioning) and another is in charge of authentication (the token server). When a service wants to validate an identity, it passes a request to the identity provider, which returns a signed token to the service verifying the identity. If the service trusts the identity provider, it can also trust the verified identity.

SOLUTION

We need to take the "external party in charge of authentication and authorization" to the next level.

✓ Implement the Identity Provider pattern to get single sign-on for the service consumer's authorization.

The Identity Provider pattern, illustrated in figure 4.11, is an evolution of the central identity repository mentioned in the previous section. Before we look at how the pattern solves the problems left unanswered by the other options, let's explore the components of the pattern and their roles.

The Identity Provider pattern is composed of two major components, provisioning and the token server.

- *Provisioning*—This component is responsible for creating identities, privilege levels, and the like, and for storing these identities and supplying them to services. It is also responsible for revoking credentials when needed. The provisioning component can also audit and save any "identity" created, updated, or revoked.
- *Token server*—The token server is responsible for verifying claims for identities or privileges and for providing the proof that these claims are correct. It's also responsible for converting the token format. Format conversion is necessary because different services, especially if they belong to different organizations, don't necessarily understand the same tokens. Suppose the Customer service in figure 4.10 can use X.509 certificates, and the Promotions service, which may belong to an external PR agency, might use SAML assertions (more on that in

the technology mapping section). In these cases, the token server can convert between the formats while maintaining the verified identity.

How does the identity provider work? The core concept is trust, and the mechanics for using it build on previously successful infrastructures like PKI. A service consumer, which has gone through provisioning with an identity provider at some time in the past, tries to access a service. When sending a message, the service consumer makes some assertions about its identity, its capabilities, or both. If the service trusts the identity provider, it can ask the identity provider if the claims made by the service consumer are genuine, and if they are it can accept the service consumer's request.

If this interaction seems confusing, just think about the lumberjack and the choir in the "Lumberjack Song" by Monty Python. The lumberjack has two assertions: "I'm a lumberjack and I'm OK," and the choir, acting as an identity provider, confirms that, "He's a lumberjack and he's OK."

If we return to the journal subscription agency scenario presented in the problem description, the authentication and authorization can follow the steps in figure 4.12. The Proposals service gets ready to send a request to the Customer service to get a list of discounts for a customer. It will then digitally sign this request as a proof that it has credentials in the identity provider. The Customer service can then check this claim with the identity provider, which will return a token or a certificate that verifies that the Proposals service is entitled for this service. The identity provider signs this certificate with its private key. The Customer service can then verify that the identity provider signed the certificate, and because it trusts the identity provider, it can honor the certificate and return the list of discounts to the Proposals service.

The identity provider is an external party, so services, like the Customer service and others, don't have to figure out how to authenticate callers. This process also solves the coupling problem by only requiring the Customer service to know the

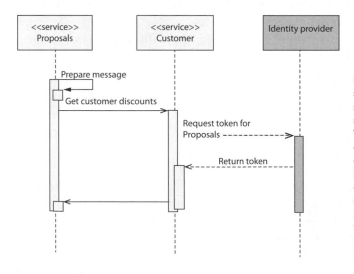

Figure 4.12 Acquiring a security token. The Proposals service sends a request and signs it with its private key. Then the Customer service checks the Proposals' credentials against the identity provider, which returns a certificate for the Proposals service signed by the identity provider. The Customer service, which trusts the identity provider, can then process the Proposals service's request.

identity provider's private key and to trust it. The Customer service isn't tied to a specific implementation of that provider.

One problem is how to prevent the identity provider from becoming a bottleneck. You could use tokens that don't expire immediately and then have the services cache them for the next calls. Another option is to preissue tokens during idle or low-traffic times and prevent the identity provider from being flooded in peak-load times. Figure 4.13 illustrates how preissued tokens would work.

Now the Proposals service requests a token from the identity provider and caches the signed token. Whenever the Proposals service wants something from other services (and as long as the token is valid) the Proposals service just sends the token along with the request. The Proposals service still has to sign the request to make sure no one else uses this token.

The identity provider can be used together with the Secured Message or Secured Infrastructure patterns (both discussed earlier this chapter) to ensure communications between the services and the identity provider are secured. Additionally, it can be beneficial to use the Active Service pattern (see chapter 2) to proactively make sure a service has a valid token—either cached or in the identity provider.

The Identify Provider pattern takes care of authentication, because the distributed nature of SOA promotes the need for federated identity. A security solution will most likely require additional components that aren't SOA-specific, like an access management component or entitlement component where you can set authorization

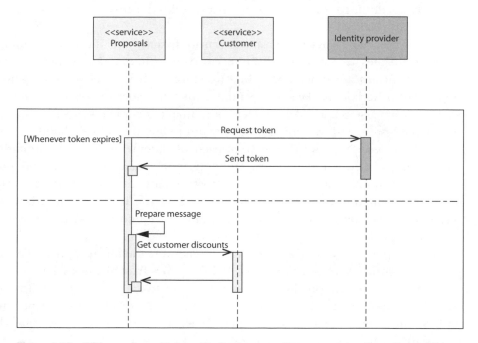

Figure 4.13   With a preissued token, the Customer service can process the call, providing the assertions made by the Proposals service were signed by a trusted identity provider.

policies, policy enforcement points to enforce these policies, and an identity reposi-tory (most likely an LDAP directory of some sort).

It's important to note that you need both a secured implementation of the Identity Provider pattern and a secured protocol and format to pass both credentials and assertions back and forth. The next section discusses these issues in more depth.

TECHNOLOGY MAPPING

As mentioned earlier, the way the Identity Provider pattern works resembles the way PKI works. This isn't a coincidence, because PKI infrastructures are both proven and successful.

As always, you can choose to implement the Identity Provider pattern by yourself, but building a scalable and secure server that will also allow cross-enterprise single sign-on scenarios isn't an easy feat. I would only recommend going down this path if you have specific needs and don't need to cater to the general cases (such as the cross-enterprise single sign-on).

There are quite a few solutions that implement this pattern for you, including Shibboleth, which is an open source implementation by Internet2, Oracle Identity Server, IBM Tivoli Access Manager, and Ping Identity's PingTrust. The identity data store can be internal to the product or it can reside on LDAP or Active Directory.

It isn't enough to have a secure sever for provisioning and token management; you also need the secure tokens themselves and a protocol for communicating the identity information. If you don't use a secure protocol, an impersonator could assume a token that is destined for an authorized party and use it to launch attacks or acquire sensitive information.

There are many ways to transport security tokens, and the most common are X.509 certificates, Kerberos ticket, and Security Assertion Markup Language (SAML). X.509 certificates are more worthwhile to keep, as they're relatively long-lived (as compared to Kerberos tickets, for example). But the more interesting technology is SAML now in version 2.0. SAML is much more than a security token—it's also a proto-col for requesting and transmitting identity information. The basic building block of SAML is the assertions, which are comprised of statements such as authentication statements and attribute statements. Authentication statements contain the informa-tion that a requestor was authenticated and which authentication methods were used to do that authentication. Attribute statements are the basis for authorization and contain information on roles, groups, and any other information that exists in the identity data store.

The last part of the puzzle is a protocol to convert the token formats. This is sup-ported by another WS-* protocol called WS-Trust. WS-Trust allows a service consumer to request an identity provider to exchange one token it already has for one in another format. As mentioned earlier, different services within an SOA may not all understand a single type of token. By using WS-Trust, a service consumer can talk to a service that requires tokens in a different format.

This listing shows a request to exchange an X.509 certificate for a SAML token.

Listing 4.7   SOAP body of a request to exchange a token from one format to another

```
<wstrust:RequestSecurityToken>
   <wstrust:TokenType>SAML</TokenType>
   <wstrust:RequestType>ReqExchange</RequestType>
    <wstrust:OnBehalfOf>
            <ws:BinarySecurityToken id="originaltoken" ValueType="X.509>
            sdfOIDFKLSoidefsdflk ...
    </ws:BinarySecurityToken>
   </wstrust:OnBehalfOf>
</wstrust:RequestSecurityToken>
```

The identity provider would authenticate that the request is genuine, and the most common way to do that is to send this request as a WS-Security signed or encrypted request (see the Secured Infrastructure pattern earlier this chapter). If the credentials are OK, it will produce a matching SAML token.

These are a lot of protocols and technologies, and utilizing them all isn't easy—the next section reminds us why it's worth going through all this trouble.

QUALITY ATTRIBUTES

The Identity Provider pattern is more important for management and maintainability than for security, or more precisely it's for management and maintenance of security-related issues. By relying on trust and certificates, the identity provider enables you to solve some of the latency issues usually related to adding a security layer.

Table 4.5 identifies a few scenarios where it's beneficial to use the Identity Provider pattern.

Table 4.5   Identity Provider pattern quality attributes and scenarios

Quality attribute	Concrete attribute	Sample scenario
Maintainability	Adding service	Configuring the security for a new service will take less than a half day's work for a single developer.
Performance	Latency	The cost of authenticating all requests won't exceed 100 msec.
Security	SSO	The system should support single sign-on for all service and human interactions.
Security	Authentication	During normal operations, a revoked right will be updated in the system within five minutes.
Security	Federated identity	Under normal operations, the system should be able to support authenticating external services (services managed by third parties).
Security	Auditing	At all times, the system should keep track of any changes to authentication or authorization rules.

As you can see in the last few quality attribute scenarios in table 4.5, the Identity Provider pattern also helps with security concerns. Table 4.6 expands on the security aspects of the pattern.

Table 4.6   Threat categories that implementations of the Identity Provider pattern can mitigate

Threat	Actions
Spoofing	Add security tokens to ensure that only authorized requests are handled by a service
Elevation of privilege	Ensure that a service consumer doesn't assert any privileges it doesn't have

The next pattern called Service Monitor. Like the Identity Provider pattern, the Service Monitor pattern is a combined manageability and security pattern, although the security aspect of the Service Monitor is secondary.

4.5   *Service Monitor pattern*

An important aspect of deploying SOA across an enterprise is governance. If you don't ensure that all the different services comply with the guidelines set out by the enterprise architect, you might not be able to capitalize on the interoperability promises of SOA, and you might encounter all sorts of performance and security problems.

On top of governance, there's the matter of the ongoing operations of the enterprise. Each service is a small independent system, and you need to find a way to manage that and make sure it all works.

The Service Monitor pattern helps solve both problems. But before we go into details of the solution, let's clarify the problem by introducing two sample scenarios.

PROBLEM

I mentioned that governance is very important for an enterprise. To demonstrate this, let me tell you about the time a very large organization invited me and a fellow architect to save their skins.

This organization, which we'll call LargeCorp (to protect the guilty), deployed a new version of a very important, mission-critical, 24 x 7 system. Shortly thereafter, the users of the system started complaining about poor performance, to the point that LargeCorp management stopped most of the development and assigned all its top developers to solve the system's problem. When we arrived, we found quite a mess, not only in regard to performance but also in issues pertaining to security and reliability, among others. We found that there were a lot of servers whose network cards were set to 10 Mbit instead of 100 Mbit. We found that sensitive information was being copied to end-users' machines and only then was the system checking whether the user was authorized to access the information. And so on. The amazing thing was that the organization already had guidelines and procedures to prevent this fiasco. It didn't have the means to make sure the procedures were followed.

In a typical SOA initiative, it's paramount that you pay attention to governance. Each service is a (relatively) independent and autonomous entity that may utilize a lot of resources, like databases and servers. If you can't achieve some control over that at the enterprise level, you may very well end up like LargeCorp.

Another even more important aspect of governance and the management of an SOA initiative is monitoring the ongoing operations. Once a system is deployed, you need a way to make sure quality of service commitments are met, to identify security problems, to verify the liveliness of services, and so on.

Figure 4.14 shows services that are likely to be found in a typical e-commerce system. The system has an Ordering service that handles the shopping cart until an order is finalized. It then interacts with an Invoicing service, which processes credit cards and other payment methods. The Ordering service also interacts with the Warehouse service to secure items or order them from suppliers and a Shipping service that monitors the activity until a package is ready. The Shipping service also interacts with the Warehouse service and with a Tracking service that verifies an order is fulfilled against multiple shipping companies.

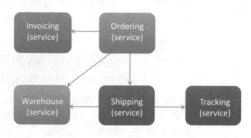

Figure 4.14   Typical services in an e-commerce system.

Looking at the relations depicted in figure 4.14, you can see that the Tracking service isn't essential in completing an ordering cycle, but if one of the other four services fails or malfunctions, you won't be able to fulfill orders in this system. If you had some way to know when a service was in trouble, you could attend to it and make sure the business gets back on track.

Remember that the scenario illustrated in figure 4.14 is a simplified version of what you'd usually find in any decently sized enterprise. In this scenario there are 5 services, and if each of them has 99.9 percent reliability, the overall reliability is 99.5 percent. Reliability decreases as the number of components grows. If you have 50 services with the same 99.9% reliability, your overall reliability will deteriorate to 95.1 percent (more than 400 hours of unavailability a year). You need a way to identify problems and fix them quickly. You need a way to take a bunch of scattered services and make sure you can maintain an operating enterprise.

How can you identify problems and faults in services, and then attend them, to ensure the overall business's availability?

One thing you can do is increase the reliability and availability of each service. This can be done by applying patterns like Service Instance or Virtual Endpoint (both discussed in chapter 3). Using these patterns will help make each service more available, but there's still a chance that something will go wrong, and then what? An even more important problem is that a service is rarely truly isolated. Services usually need to interact with other services, so the reliability of each service is also affected by the reliability of the services it has to interact with.

To try to solve this dependency problem, you can try to increase the service's autonomy—an example is the Active Service pattern in chapter 2. Nevertheless, the service needs to know if the services it depends upon are down. While an autonomous service can still operate for a while, it will eventually be updated with data from the services it depends upon.

The next level is to augment the services with internal monitoring and possibly add self-healing capabilities (see the Service Watchdog pattern in chapter 3). But this still leaves a few problems unresolved, such as making sure several services follow the same guidelines, identifying problems in the services' interconnecting infrastructure (the network that lets the services communicate), ensuring there are no system-wide security problems, and controlling and fixing problems in other services—especially those that are external to the organization.

SOLUTION

There's a limit to what can you achieve in the scope of each service, and as in other areas of enterprise management, there's no escaping centralized management.

Apply the Service Monitor pattern, and deploy a centralized management point that will monitor services' security, networks, QoS, policies, and any other governance-related issues.

As illustrated in figure 4.14, the Service Monitor pattern is composed of three main components.

The basis for everything is the collection component, whose role is to collect and store incoming statuses as well as to provide reports and summaries. The service monitor can gather many types of statuses, including performance, faults, number of calls, and data transferred.

The second component continuously monitors the data collected. It can execute different rules to validate and monitor the behavior of the services and make sure they're in order. For instance, the monitor can check performance figures against the promised quality of service. It can make sure that security policies like "channel encryption" are met.

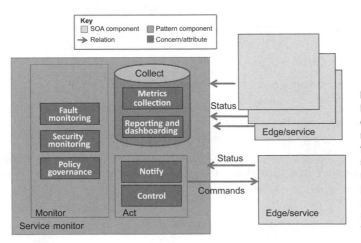

Figure 4.14 The Service Monitor pattern. A centralized component, the service monitor receives statuses from all the services in the system. The service monitor uses that information to infer policy violations, security, performance, or other failures and to allow system operators to deal with problems.

Once a problem has been identified, the third component of the service monitor goes into action and notifies the operators. It can also send commands to the monitored services, either automatically or through the actions of operators; an operator may choose to restart a faulty service, change the policy for a running service, and so on.

The Service Monitor pattern isn't a replacement for the service self-management and increased autonomy options mentioned previously. It does help solve issues these options can't by handling cross-service problems like cyclic dependencies, cross-enterprise policies, the entire service dying, and so on—problems that can only be identified by looking at the complete picture. The downside of applying the Service Monitor pattern is added complexity, but the gain in system reliability and manageability make it, in my opinion, essential for all but the simplest systems.

To help the Service Monitor pattern get an overall picture of the services in the system, consider combining it with a service registry where the service monitor will be able to find information about the services.

If you implement the Orchestration pattern (see chapter 7) and you add monitoring with the Service Monitor pattern, you may also want to enhance the Service Monitor with a business process view of the system. Then you'd be able to gain monitoring benefits such as setting and enforcing policies at the process level.

The service monitor, which is already a central hub for service interactions, can also serve as a central logger and help with auditing and debugging.

The service monitor isn't a new concept in the sense that there already are solutions based on similar concepts for non-SOA systems, with the most popular ones being CA Infrastructure Management, the IBM Tivoli suite, and open source packages like Nagios. The SOA-specific tools add a few SOA-specific features that traditional monitoring tools lack, such as the ability to handle a service's policies.

TECHNOLOGY MAPPING

Implementing the Service Monitor pattern is a relatively big task and, in my opinion, it isn't cost effective to implement it by yourself unless, maybe, you're using some nonstandard communication technology in your SOA implementation. As a result, I'll focus here on off-the-shelf technologies that already implement the patterns and on how to use them.

Many companies produce SOA monitoring and governance solutions, ranging from SOA-specific players like SOA Software to more general, larger companies like IBM and Oracle. Most of the solutions provide several layers of monitoring, starting with the basic network view, which is very similar to general-purpose monitoring solutions.

Figure 4.15 shows the Network Overview tab of Progress Actional's Looking Glass SOA-monitoring tool. This general view isn't too different from what you've likely seen in other monitoring suites. SOA monitoring tools provide additional traditional capabilities like auditing and logging. Note that even in the Network Overview, you can get some SOA-specific information, like statuses on calls and performance as well as information about dependencies and cycles.

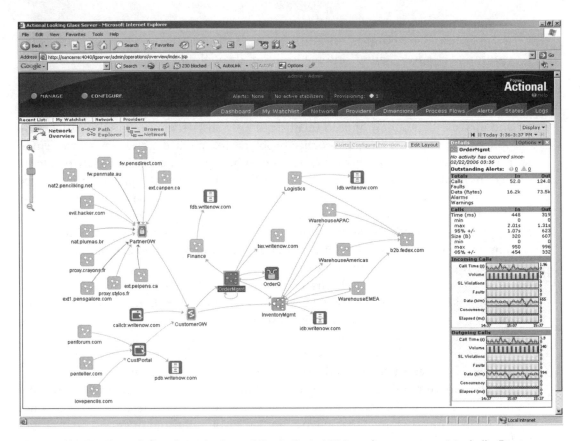

Figure 4.15   The Network Overview tab of one of the dedicated SOA service management tools (by Progress Actional). In this tab you can see an overview of the services' state and their relations, along with summary-level metrics about the services.

On top of the basic monitoring features I've mentioned, SOA monitoring tools add a few SOA-specific capabilities, like monitoring processing time, discovering services, setting and enforcing policies, and so on. Figure 4.16 shows the monitoring screenshot from Oracle's AmberPoint. You can see both the throughput and faults of the DemoManufacturerService as well as the option to examine the WSDL (contract) of the service.

You've just seen how current technologies utilize the Service Monitor pattern and let you increase the manageability of your services. I also mentioned that the Service Monitor pattern can help with security. Let's see how it all connects.

QUALITY ATTRIBUTES

The main reason to employ the Service Monitor pattern is to get central management and to help combine a bunch of services into a working enterprise, but that isn't the only reason. The Service Monitor pattern can also help you test services before you deploy them, make sure the quality of services is kept once they're deployed, ensure compatibility between services by making sure their policies match, and identify security problems like man-in-the-middle attacks.

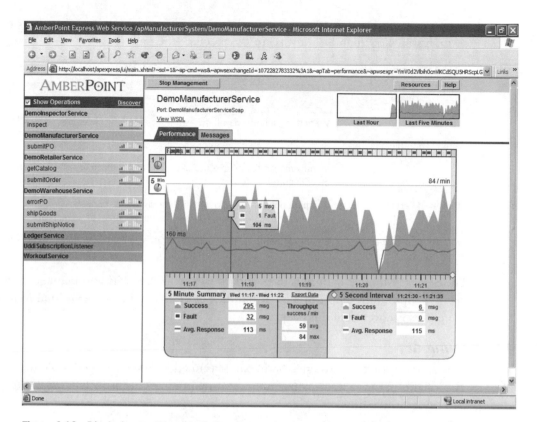

Figure 4.16 Displaying real-time statistics of a service using the Developer edition of AmberPoint. In this screenshot you can see detailed performance counters, including trends for a specific service.

Table 4.7 lists a few scenarios where it's beneficial to use the Service Monitor pattern.

Table 4.7 Service Monitor pattern quality attributes and scenarios

Quality attribute	Concrete attribute	Sample scenario
Reliability	Mean time to repair (MTTR)	Under normal operations, the time to discover a faulty service will be less than two minutes.
Manageability	Reporting	At all times, managers will be able to gain an overall view of the status and problems in handling business requests.
Testability	Performance	During stress tests, you need to be able to time the performance of each service in the system.
Security	Governance	During development and operations, the enterprise architecture team will be able to ensure that all services use secured channels.
Security	Auditing	At all times, the system should keep an audit trail for requestors and their requests.

As you can see in table 4.7, the Service Monitor pattern also helps with security concerns. Table 4.8 expands on the security aspects of the pattern.

Table 4.8   Threat categories that implementations of the Service Monitor pattern can mitigate

Threat	Actions
Tampering	Verify that all services utilize signatures for their messages
Information disclosure	Scan outgoing messages for sensitive content
	Identify man-in-the-middle attacks by watching incoming and outgoing traffic on configured routes
Denial of service	Compare both performance and the number of requests against the regular or average loads or each service to identify denial of service attacks
Elevation of privilege	Ensure different security policies for internal services and external ones

The Service Monitor pattern is the last pattern in this "Security and manageability patterns" chapter, and appropriately it handles both issues. Let's take a final look at all the patterns covered in this chapter.

4.6   *Summary*

This chapter took us through several patterns needed to secure SOA implementations. Two of the patterns also management and maintainability aspects even though they also relate to security.

- *Secured Message*—Encrypts, decrypts, and signs individual messages or message fragments to secure them when you interact with two or more parties in a conversation
- *Secured Infrastructure*—Uses or creates a secure communication infrastructure that's shared by the services in an organization
- *Service Firewall*—Inspects all incoming and outgoing messages using software or an appliance and helps protect your services from several classes of attacks
- *Identity Provider*—Uses centralized provisioning and certificate-based authentication and authorization to efficiently manage identity in a federated environment
- *Service Monitor*—Monitors and manages services from a centralized location to gain timely access to the status of your enterprise

While these patterns are, in my opinion, very useful and valuable for securing and making your SOA more maintainable, you should keep in mind that making an SOA solution (or any solution) secure and maintainable goes well beyond these patterns. The patterns listed here deal mainly with the interfaces of your SOA; you still need to make sure the business logic you write is both secure and maintainable, especially if the service is distributed internally. For instance, when you log errors or messages or persist data in the database, you should pay attention not to log sensitive information.

I highly recommended you take the time to explore the sources in the further reading section, which includes books like *SOA Security* by Ramarao Kanneganti and Prasad A. Chodavarapu (Manning, 2007) and the OWASP site, both of which cover additional aspects of security (see the next section for more info on both).

Chapters 2, 3, and 4 took a look at patterns related to building services and their interfaces. The next chapters will take a look at the interactions of services with their consumers—be they other services or humans.

4.7 Further reading

OWSAP: The Open Web Application Security Project, www.owasp.org.
   The home page of the Open Web Application Security Project has a lot of information on threats and preventive measures.

Michael Howard, David LeBlanc, and John Viega, *24 Deadly Sins of Software Security: Programming Flaws and How to Fix Them* (McGraw-Hill Osborne, 2009).
   This book discusses common security problems and their solutions. It isn't specific to SOA but it does provide general guidance.

Ramarao Kanneganti and Prasad A. Chodavarapu, *SOA Security* (Manning, 2007).
   This book discusses security in the context of SOA. Note that the book mostly talks about SOAP-based services.

SECURED MESSAGE

Bilal Siddiqui, "Exploring XML Encryption, Part 1: Demonstrating the secure exchange of structured data," *IBM developerWorks*, www-128.ibm.com/developerworks/xml/library/x-encrypt/.
   This article is a primer on XML encryption, which is one way to implement the Secured Message pattern.

Apache Santuario, http://xml.apache.org/security/.
   You can use Apache Santuario to implement the Secured Message pattern.

SECURED INFRASTRUCTURE

The OpenSSL Project, www.openssl.org/.
   The OpenSSL project, as its name implies, is an open source SSL implementation. SSL is one of the options for implementing the Secured Infrastructure pattern.

Harold Lockhart, "Demystifying SAML," *Oracle Technology Network* www.oracle.com/technetwork/articles/entarch/saml-084342.html.
   SAML is an authorization standard commonly used in SOAP-based SOA implementations.

OAuth 2.0, http://oauth.net/2/.
   OAuth is an authentication standard commonly used in REST-based systems and REST-based SOA implementations.

Message exchange patterns 5

Chapters 2 and 3 looked at patterns that can help you build services and their interfaces, like Edge Component and Service Instance. Chapter 4 covered ways of protecting and monitoring your services. Chapter 5 is the first of three that covers the different aspects of service interactions. After all, getting services to interact and enable business processes was the reason for using SOA to begin with.

As figure 5.1 illustrates, this chapter's focus is on the interaction of services with their "customers"—the service consumers. A *service consumer* is any component or piece of code that interacts with a service. The patterns in this chapter deal with the basics—the message exchange patterns. Chapter 6 looks at service consumers and chapter 7 takes a look at patterns related to service composition and integration.

The SOA definition in chapter 1 says that "each service exposes processes and behavior through contracts, which are composed of messages at discoverable addresses." This makes service interaction very simple—you just send a message in and get a message back, right? Why do we need a whole chapter, or even two, on service interactions?

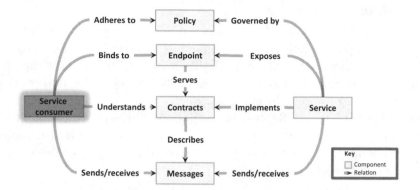

Figure 5.1   This chapter focuses on connecting services with user interfaces. It's the first chapter in this book that takes a look at the service consumers.

It's true that messages are the basic building blocks of service interactions, but there are many ways to interact using these building blocks. People similarly use sentences as the building blocks for communications and interactions. When you call a sales rep, several interactions are possible:

- You can ask a specific question and get a reply (the Request/Reply pattern in section 5.1).
- You can leave a message with a question and a telephone number, and the sales rep will get back to you later (the Request/Reaction pattern in section 5.2).
- The sales rep can call you and let you know about new products (the Inversion of Communications pattern in section 5.3).
- You can have a long correspondence with the sales rep, sending emails back and forth until your issue is resolved (the Saga pattern in section 5.4).

What's true in real life is also true for services.

Unlike most of the other patterns in this book, these core interaction patterns existed before SOA was even conceived—what this chapter will do is look at these interaction patterns from the perspective of SOA and SOA's quality attributes. We'll look at what it takes to make an interaction pattern like asynchronous communication work in a way that both complies with the SOA principles and retains the SOA benefits.

The following patterns are discussed in this chapter:

- *Request/Reply*—Enable a service consumer to interact with a service simply
- *Request/Reaction*—Temporally decouple the request from a service consumer and the reply from the service
- *Inversion of Communications*—Handle business events in an SOA
- *Saga*—Reach a distributed consensus between services without transactions

Let's start with the most basic communications form—synchronous communications. The pattern is called Request/Reply.

5.1 *Request/Reply pattern*

Request/Reply is probably the oldest, and most described, pattern in computer science. Gregor Hohpe and Bobby Woolf offer a good description of Request/Reply in *Enterprise Integration Patterns* (Addison-Wesley Professional, 2003), where they describe the pattern as answering the following question: "When an application sends a message, how can it get a response from the receiver?"

The idea behind Request/Reply in SOA is not very different. The reason to discuss the pattern in this book, however, is that there are still a few issues worth emphasizing when using Request/Reply with SOA. I'll talk about them as part of the solution discussion. First let's look at the problem.

PROBLEM

When you develop single-tier software that runs inside a single process in a single memory space, it's relatively easy to get components to interact. When a requestor component wants something from another component (a replier), it can easily gain a reference to that replier, such as by instantiating it. The requestor can then invoke a method on the replier and get the reply as a reference or an address in memory where the reply resides.

In SOA, which is an architectural style for distributed systems, the other component is generally in another memory space and more likely than not on another machine—see figure 5.2.

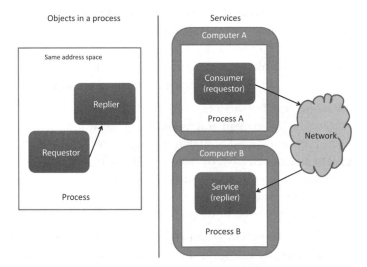

Figure 5.2   Objects instantiated within a process versus services.
With a local object, making a request from one component to another
is simple—you get a reference to the other component and you make a
request by calling it. In SOA, the requestor and consumer aren't in a
single address space. They're also likely not to be on the same
computer, and maybe not even on the same LAN. Making a request
under these conditions is a lot more complicated.

NOTE Remote calls have been technologically solved before SOA—but for other architectural styles. Most of these technologies can also be used for SOA—the difference is how you use them. I'll discuss this later in this pattern.

The first thing you want to do is find a way for services to interact with their consumers.

? **How can you enable a service consumer to interact with a service simply?**

There are several alternatives for service interactions detailed in this chapter: asynchronous Request/Reply (Request/Reaction pattern), long-running interactions (Saga pattern), or events (Inversion of Communications pattern). They're all more powerful than the Request/Reply pattern, but that extra power comes with a price—they're all more complex than Request/Reply both to implement and to support.

SOLUTION

There's a place for sophistication, but sometimes you want to have a simple synchronous interaction between two remote components.

✓ **Send a request message from the consumer, handle the request synchronously, and send a reply message from the service. Both the request and the reply belong to the receiving service.**

The Request/Reply pattern, illustrated in figure 5.3, is the most basic interaction pattern, so there aren't any special components needed to make it happen. What you do need is a piece of logic that accepts a request, processes it synchronously, and returns a reply or a result. One thing to pay attention to is that both the request and reply messages belong to the contract of the service and not the service consumer (which is a common error for SOA novices).

The Request/Reply pattern only covers the message exchange; a complete interaction also needs communications infrastructure. You could utilize the Service Bus pattern (discussed in chapter 7), which handles exposing services on reachable (or even discoverable) endpoints as well as routing replies.

The roles of the request and reply are rather obvious. The request holds the intention or the task that the service is expected to perform, along with the input needed to perform it. The reply holds the results of performing the task.

The main problem with the Request/Reply interaction style is that it's suspiciously reminiscent of remote procedure calls (RPCs)—that DCOM/CORBA, distributed-

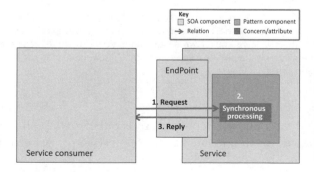

Figure 5.3   The Request/Reply pattern defines request and reply messages in the service's contract. When the service gets a request in the appropriate format, it processes it synchronously and returns the reply message to the service consumer.

object stuff. You should be wary of modeling the services' contracts on the RPC mind-set—this can have several unfortunate effects on your SOA, ranging from poor perfor-mance to completely nullifying SOA. Instead of using the RPC approach, you should try to model your contracts on a document-centric approach. What in the world is a "document-centric approach"? Good question.

In a nutshell, *document-centric* means that the message contains enough information to represent a complete unit of work and doesn't instruct the service on how to handle the message. In contrast, RPC calls tend to be command-oriented and geared toward sending just the parameters needed to perform the action; they have some stateful expectations from the service side as well as implicit expectations about what's going to happen on the consumer side. Document-centric messages don't make these assump-tions; having a complete unit of work means that the service has enough information or context in the message to understand all the state it needs. This also means that doc-ument-centric messages are usually more coarse-grained than their RPC counterparts.

NOTE   There's a third message type called *event messages*. We'll discuss it in the Inversion of Communications pattern in section 5.3.

The following table outlines three ways document-centric messages can contain more context.

Two things to note are that the message can combine more than one type of con-text, and the same document can be exchanged back and forth between a service and its consumers, possibly adding detail as it moves, to allow complete business processes.

Table 5.1   Options for providing context within a document-centric message

Context	Explanation
History	The message can contain the interactions up to this point, sort of like bread-crumbs in the Hansel and Gretel tale. In an ordering scenario, if the first step was to get customer data and the current step is to set the order (each step being performed by another service), the message would contain the customer information when it goes to the ordering service.
Future	The message can include the options the consumer can take to complete the interaction. If you think about an ordering scenario, if the previous step was to reserve the order (see the Reservation pattern in chapter 6), the return mes-sage could include the information needed to confirm the reservation.
Complete future	Another way to provide context is for the message format to contain the com-plete details needed for the interaction. For the ordering example, this would mean that the message would have a skeleton to support all the order and related details, and the parties involved would fill in the blanks as the interac-tion progresses.

TECHNOLOGY MAPPING

The technology mapping for the Request/Reply pattern is rather trivial. All the tech-nologies I can think of enable you to implement the Request/Reply pattern in one form or another.

Most technologies make it extremely easy to expose objects remotely, which encourages RPC style-interactions; they make it hard to get to document-centric interaction. The code in listing 5.1 is an excerpt from the New Project wizard for the WCF service library in Microsoft's Visual Studio 2010. The sample code shows a developer how to take a simple class and expose its methods as web services.

Listing 5.1   Code from the New Project wizard for creating a WCF service

```
namespace WCFServiceLibrary1
{
    [ServiceContract()]
    public interface IService1
    {                                                     Exposes method
                                                          as web service
        [OperationContract]
        string MyOperation1(string myValue);
        [OperationContract]
        string MyOperation2(DataContract1 dataContractValue);
    }

    public class service1 : IService1
    {
        public string MyOperation1(string myValue)
        {
            return "Hello: " + myValue;
        }                                                 Accepts document
        public string MyOperation2                        (data contract) as
    (DataContract1 dataContractValue)                     parameter
        {
            return "Hello: "
    + dataContractValue.FirstName;                        Handles document in
        }                                                 an RPC way (doesn't
    }                                                     return document)

    [DataContract]                                        Defines basic
    public class DataContract1                            document (missing
    {                                                     links to related data)
        string firstName;
        string lastName;

        [DataMember]
        public string FirstName
        {
            get { return firstName; }
            set { firstName = value; }
        }
        [DataMember]
        public string LastName
        {
            get { return lastName; }
            set { lastName = value; }
        }
    }
}
```

On the surface, this code may seem like a good example for the Request/Reply pattern (except maybe for the naming). A service consumer can send the `MyOperation1` message with a string in it and get the "Hello" concatenated to the string as a reply. But the `MyOperation1` implementation is a classic RPC interaction.

The situation is a little better for the second method (`MyOperation2`). Here a simple document is passed to the method. But the sample code handles that document in an RPC way too, and doesn't return a document as a reply.

This approach isn't unique to .NET—as another example you can consider the REST style. Whereas the REST principles promote the document-centric approach, the basic HTTP verbs are PUT, GET, POST, and DELETE, which again make novices think about CRUD interfaces.

A document-oriented approach results in richer messages that contain some context if not the whole of it. Consider the XML excerpt in listing 5.2.

Listing 5.2   A sample document-centric reply

```
<feed xmlns='http://www.w3.org/2005/Atom'
    xmlns:gd='http://schemas.google.com/g/2005'>
<id>http://www.google.com/calendar/feeds/johndoe@gmail.com
➥/private-0c1e3facdd1a4252aad07effeb7d68cc9/full</id>
  <updated>2007-06-29T19:22:12.000Z</updated>
  <title type='text'>John Doe</title>
  <link rel='http://schemas.google.com/g/2005#feed'
➥ type='application/atom+xml'
    href='http://www.google.com/calendar/feeds/johndoe@gmail.com
➥/private-0c1e3facdd1a4252aad07effeb7d68cc9/full'></link>
  <link rel='self' type='application/atom+xml'
    href='http://www.google.com/calendar/feeds/johndoe@gmail.com/
➥private-0c1e3facdd1a4252aad07effeb7d68cc9/full'></link>
  <author>
    <name>John doe</name>
    <email>johndoe@gmail.com</email>
  </author>
  <generator version='1.0' uri='http://www.google.com/calendar/'>
  CL2
</generator>
  <gd:where valueString='Neverneverland'></gd:where>
  <entry>
    <id>http://www.google.com/calendar/feeds/johndow@gmail.com
➥/private-0c1e3facdd1a4252aad07effeb7d68cc9/full/
➥aaBxcnNqbW9tcTJnaTT5cnMybmEwaW04bXMgbWFyY2guam9AZ21haWwuY29t</id>
    <published>2007-06-30T22:00:00.000Z</published>
    <updated>2007-06-28T015:33:31.000Z</updated>
    <category scheme='http://schemas.google.com/g/2005#kind'
      term='http://schemas.google.com/g/2007#event'></category>
    <title type='text'>Writing SOA Patterns</title>
    <content type='text'>shhh…</content>
    <link rel='alternate' type='text/html'
      href='http://www.google.com/calendar/event?eid=
➥aaBxcnNqbW9tcTJnaTT5cnMybmEwaW04bXMgbWFyY2guam9AZ21haWwuY29t'
      title='alternate'></link>
    <link rel='self' type='application/atom+xml'
      href='http://www.google.com/calendar/feeds/johndoe@gmail.com/
➥private-0c1e3facdd1a4252aad07effeb7d68cc9/full/
```

```
➥aaBxcnNqbW9tcTJnaTT5cnMybmEwaW04bXMgbWFyY29guam9AZ21haWwuY29t'>
➥</link>
   <author>
     <name>John Doe</name>
     <email>johndoe@gmail.com</email>
   </author>
   <gd:transparency
     value='http://schemas.google.com/g/2005#event.opaque'>
   </gd:transparency>
   <gd:eventStatus
     value='http://schemas.google.com/g/2005#event.confirmed'></
    gd:eventStatus>
   <gd:comments>
     <gd:feedLink
        href='http://www.google.com/calendar/feeds/johndoe@gmail.com/
➥private-0c1e3facdd1a4252aad07effeb7d68cc9/full/
➥aaBxcnNqbW9tcTJnaTT5cnMybmEwaW04bXMgbWFyY29guam9AZ21haWwuY29t
➥/comments/'>
     </gd:feedLink>
   </gd:comments>
   <gd:when startTime='2006-08-14T20:30:00.000Z'
     endTime='2012-03-28T22:30:00.000Z'></gd:when>
   <gd:where></gd:where>
  </entry>
</feed>
```

This listing shows the result of requesting a full calendar from Google Calendar. In addition to the calendar details (title, update date, owner name, title, and so on) you get all the listings with their full details as well as a pointer to get each calendar entry directly. The result uses Google's GData protocol, which in turn builds on the Atom Publishing Protocol (APP). Note that the contract for accepting this XML is also simpler than that in listing 5.1, because you just need to handle a single XML parameter. The consumers aren't bound to specific operations that can change over time.

To sum up this section, the Request/Reply pattern is supported by all the technologies that allow remote communications. The choice between RPC and document-centric approach is a design decision that isn't enforced by the technologies. That has to be done by the developers or architects of the solution.

QUALITY ATTRIBUTES

The Request/Reply pattern is a simple pattern that connects a service consumer with the service that it wants to interact with. As a basic pattern, it doesn't solve a lot of quality attribute concerns, except for providing the functionality needed (getting the consumer and the service to interact).

One quality attribute that can be important is simplicity. Because Request/Reply is a simple pattern, it's easy to implement and support and thus helps reduce the complexity of the solution.

Table 5.2 lists sample scenarios in which you might consider using Request/Reply.

Table 5.2   Request/Reply pattern quality attributes and scenarios

Quality attribute	Concrete attribute	Sample scenario
Time to market	Development ease	During development, exposing a new capability (already developed) in a service should take less than half a day to implement and test.
Testability	Coverage	During development, each capability of a service should have 100 percent test coverage.

I mentioned earlier that Request/Reply is the basic synchronous communications pattern. The next interaction pattern takes a look at implementing asynchronous communications under the SOA constraints and principles.

5.2   *Request/Reaction pattern*

Synchronous communication, as described in the Request/Reply pattern (in the previous section), is very important, but it isn't enough. The synchronous nature of Request/Reply means that the service consumer needs to sit and wait for the service to finish processing the request before the consumer can continue with whatever it was doing. There are situations where the service consumer doesn't want or can't afford to wait but is still interested in getting a reply when it's available.

Clear as mud? Let's take a look at a concrete example so I can better explain.

PROBLEM

In contemporary border-control systems, when travelers get to the immigration officer, the officer searches for the traveler's details in the system (swipes the passport, types in the password number, and so on) and then looks at the passport and tries to match the face to the passport holder. In the last few years, countries around the world have begun the move to e-passport systems. E-passports contain several elements, including an RFID chip, machine-readable code, and a couple of biometric samples (usually a photo of the face and fingerprints).

Figure 5.4 shows a high-level view of the flow for issuing an e-passport.

As you can see, one of the steps in the flow is to enroll the person in the biometric database (which is part of the Biometric service). While it isn't apparent from just looking at the interaction, the enrollment task can take quite some time to complete because internally the Biometric service also checks for duplicates, which is essential in ensuring the integrity of the database and preventing mistakes as well as intentional impersonations. This step involves comparing each sample (each face, for example) against every other sample already in the database, which could contain hundreds of millions of records (the population of the country).

Making this type of request using the Request/Reply interaction pattern is problematic because the wait time between the request and the reply is too long. It may be even worse if you decide to do the duplicate checks in a nightly batch.

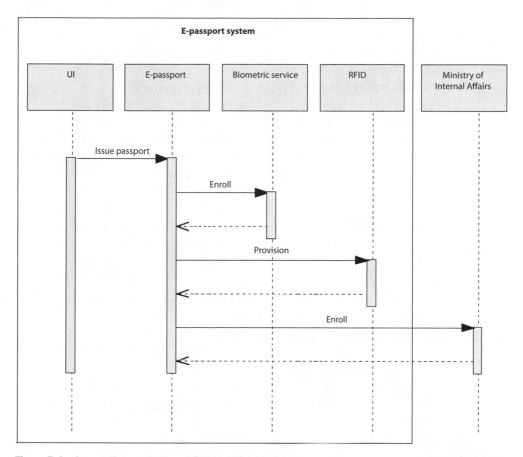

Figure 5.4   An enrollment process. When the UI asks the e-passport service to issue a passport, the service has to interact with several other services to fulfill the request.

This situation isn't unique to e-passport systems. Similar situations occur in other systems. When you buy shares in a trust fund, for example, the transaction doesn't happen immediately, but you probably want to know when it's been completed. Another example is requesting a travel-planning system to locate the best deal for your next vacation. Here's the problem:

How can you temporally decouple the request from a service consumer and the reply from the service?

One option is to solve the temporal coupling on the client side. To do this, you spawn a new thread before you send a request to the service; you then let that thread wait for the reply while the rest of the UI stays responsive. .NET has a component called BackgroundWorker that performs this separation and allows the UI to dispatch long-running work without blocking the UI thread.

This solution has its drawbacks. For one, the "waiting" isn't resilient—if the service consumer happens to crash, the reply would be lost when the consumer wakes up again. Plus, the thread takes up resources on the consumer—what would happen if the request takes hours or days? Additionally, it's a matter of responsibility. The service is the one that has a task that's time-consuming—it should be the service's responsibility to solve the matter and not throw it at the consumers.

Another approach to solving the temporal decoupling is to circumvent it and break the interaction. When you order an item online, for example, you don't sit and wait until the system ships the item to you. Instead, the system lets you know that the item was ordered. Registering the order takes much less time than fulfilling the order.

The downside here is that you don't know if the item has shipped unless you check the order status from time to time. Again, as in the previous approach, it's your responsibility as the service consumer to solve the shortcomings of the service.

There are interaction solutions that support complex interactions, like the Saga pattern (which we'll discuss in section 5.4). Implementing the Saga pattern will solve this issue, but it's like killing a fly with a cannon. It's overkill when all you really need is a delayed replay.

SOLUTION

When Saga is overkill, breaking the integration works, but it hurts the service consumers, and you want to avoid client-side integration because of its bad implications. What you really want to do is somehow implement asynchronous communications over SOA, and do that in the simplest manner possible. This is what you need to do:

✓ **Introduce the Request/Reaction pattern and implement asynchronous communication between service consumers and the service. Implement the message exchange as two one-way messages—a request from the consumer and a reply from the service side.**

The idea behind the Request/Reaction pattern, illustrated in figure 5.5, is to have two distinct interactions between the service consumer and the service. The first interaction sends the request to the server, which may return an acknowledgment, a ticket, or an estimate for finishing a job to the consumer. Once the processing is complete, the service has to initiate an interaction with the service consumer and send it the reply or reaction.

NOTE   The service has to manage the knowledge about where to return the reply—we'll discuss that later.

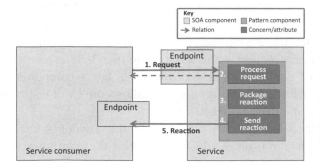

Figure 5.5   The Request/Reaction pattern defines both request and reply messages in the service's contract. When the service gets a request, it processes it and prepares a reaction. When the reaction is ready, the service sends the request back to the consumer.

The Request/Reaction pattern is more aligned with the basic premise of messaging because it lifts the time coupling. In contrast, Request/Reply is more aligned with RPC.

Figure 5.6 shows the use of the Request/Reaction pattern with the biometric service. Now when the biometric service receives an enrollment message, it reacts with an "enrolling" message notifying the client that the request has been received. Once the service finishes the enrollment either successfully or with an error, it will prepare an enrollment reply with the enrollment records and send it to the client.

NOTE In the scenario illustrated in figure 5.6, it makes sense to use the Saga pattern (discussed in section 5.4) to roll back the other services if the duplication check in the biometric service finds a duplicate identity.

The Request/Reaction pattern is used in the Decoupled Invocation pattern (discussed in chapter 2). The difference between the two patterns is that Request/Reaction decouples the response from the request; the Decoupled Invocation pattern also decouples the processing of the message.

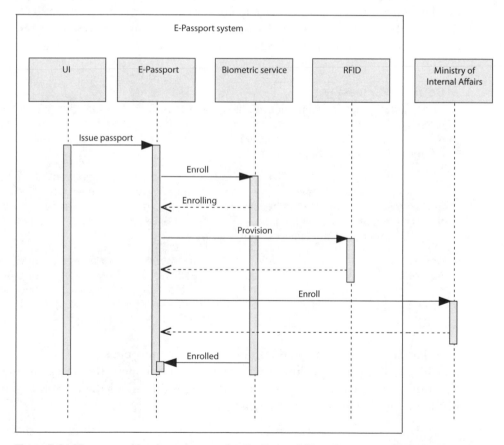

Figure 5.6 The passport-issuing process using the Request/Reaction pattern. Now the biometric service returns two messages. First it returns an acknowledgment that it is processing the message; then, when the process is finalized, it returns a status.

The interaction semantics of the Request/Reaction pattern are limited. If the e-passport scenario included the possibility of canceling the enrollment (if, for example, the RFID provisioning failed), it would be problematic coordinating this with a bunch of requests and reactions. In these long-running interactions, you may want to consider more advanced patterns, such as the Saga pattern described in section 5.4.

The Request/Reaction pattern offers more flexibility than the Request/Reply pattern, but this flexibility comes with a price. The Request/Reaction pattern is more complicated than Request/Reply, and it requires more work on the service (or edge) side.

Let's look at some of the implementation details that you'll need to take care of.

TECHNOLOGY MAPPING

The basic way of implementing the Request/Reaction interaction pattern is to use two one-way messages. If you're using web services, it would mean two HTTP channels. If you're using messages, you'd need a queue (endpoint) for each of the involved parties.

The first hurdle is the temporal decoupling. Because the request and the reaction (reply) are separated in time, other messages can get in between. This means that you need to provide a way for the service to know where to send the reaction. It also means that both the service and the service consumer need a way to correlate the request and reaction messages—see the "correlated messages" sidebar for more details.

> **Correlated messages**
>
> One challenge of asynchronous messaging comes from the fact that the reaction message and the request aren't directly related. The reaction can arrive quite some time after the original request was sent. What you need in this case is a way to identify that the two messages are related.
>
> The mechanism that solves this problem is known as a correlation identifier, and as the name implies, it involves adding a token to messages that the service consumers and services can use to identify related messages. This isn't very far from the idea of session cookies in a web application. The correlation identifier can include a message ID, a token for the conversation, and so on.
>
> Correlation is supported by a wide variety of the WS-* standards. For instance, WS-Addressing has a relationship message ID header that can be used for correlation. Another example is WS-BPEL, which has even better support for correlation by letting developers define multiple correlation sets and the content of those sets.

Both Java and .NET offer solutions to deal with one-way messages. The Apache Axis2 Java library even provides the infrastructure to implement the complete Request/Reaction pattern out of the box. The following listing shows the consumer-side code needed to send an asynchronous message.

Listing 5.3 Client code sending a message using the Request/Reaction pattern

```
boolean useTwoChannels = true;

...

OMElement messageBody = helper.FormatmMessage(data,type);
Call msgSender = new Call();
msgSender.setTo(
        new EndpointReference(AddressingConstants.WSA_TO,
                "HTTP://www.example.org/ServiceName"));
msgSender.setTransportInfo(Constants.TRANSPORT_HTTP,
    Constants.TRANSPORT_HTTP, useTwoChannels);
Callback callback = new Callback() {
        public void onComplete(AsyncResult result) {
          //code to handle the Reaction goes here
        }

        public void reportError(Exception e) {
          //code to handle errors..
        }
};
msgSender.engageModule(new Qname("addressing"));
msgSender.invokeNonBlocking("MessageName", messageBody, callback);
```

From the architectural point of view, the reaction is a message that's sent by the service. From the implementation point of view, though, it can also be implemented by pulling from the service consumer.

Implementing Request/Reaction on top of Request/Reply isn't too complicated. Figure 5.7 illustrates the steps. When the service consumer sends a request, it will get as a reply the address of the reaction (the URI in this case). The consumer will also get a time token designating when the answer will be expected. Once that time has elapsed, the consumer will make a second request to the service, this time asking for the reply (for example, using the GET command).

> **NOTE** You can use the Active Service pattern, discussed in chapter 2, in the consumer to keep track of time.

The time to go down this path (of using *pull* instead of *push*) is when you can't create an active independent endpoint on the consumer side. Again, the preferred approach is to get the Request/Reaction pattern right. If you can't do that, you can implement the *pull* approach and still conform to the general idea behind the pattern, which is to offer flexibility and temporal decoupling.

QUALITY ATTRIBUTES

I've mentioned that temporal decoupling and the flexibility it brings are the main quality attributes that drive using the Request/Reaction pattern. The pattern can also help with the performance quality attribute. When sending a message to the service doesn't block the consumer, it allows the consumer to allot CPU cycles to other

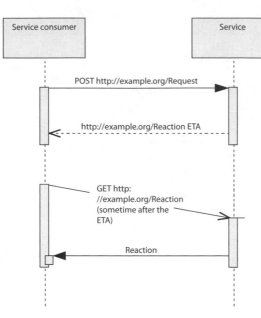

Figure 5.7   Implementing Request/Reaction on top of Request/Reply. The request's return message explains where to find the reaction the estimated time or arrival (ETA). Sometime after the ETA, when the Service Consumer isn't busy, it can go to the Reaction address on the Service and obtain the reaction itself.

problems (such as handling requests from other services). Compare that with the blocking Request/Reply pattern, which holds resources on the consumer side while it waits for the reply.

Table 5.3 presents a couple of sample scenarios where Request/Reaction is more applicable than other patterns.

The Request/Reply pattern demonstrates synchronous communications between service consumers and services. The Request/Reaction demonstrates asynchronous communication. What we need to do now is check whether we can communicate using an event-driven architecture without violating any SOA constraints and assumptions.

Table 5.3   Request/Reaction pattern quality attributes and scenarios

Quality attribute	Concrete attribute	Sample scenario
Flexibility	Temporal coupling	Under normal conditions, the system should notify the ordering party about order shipment within two hours of shipping the package.
Performance	Responsiveness	Under normal conditions, the UI won't hang while long operations are performed (such as searches and course recalculations).

5.3   *Inversion of Communications pattern*

The Request/Reply and Request/Reaction patterns are geared toward interactions where the consumer wants to get information or an action from a service. In order to get the action or information, the service consumer is willing to pay the coupling

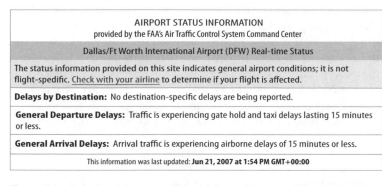

AIRPORT STATUS INFORMATION provided by the FAA's Air Traffic Control System Command Center
Dallas/Ft Worth International Airport (DFW) Real-time Status
The status information provided on this site indicates general airport conditions; it is not flight-spedific. <u>Check with your airline</u> to determine if your flight is affected.
Delays by Destination: No destination-specific delays are being reported.
General Departure Delays: Traffic is experiencing gate hold and taxi delays lasting 15 minutes or less.
General Arrival Delays: Arrival traffic is experiencing airborne delays of 15 minutes or less.
This information was last updated: **Jun 21, 2007 at 1:54 PM GMT+00:00**

Figure 5.8   Arrival and departure delays information as provided by the FAA (http://www.fly.faa.gov/flyfaa/usmap.jsp). This can be a source of information for an airline traffic control system.

price associated with knowing about the other service, its service capabilities, and the protocol (contract) it uses to expose these capabilities.

But what happens when the potential consumers don't know that they need to go and ask a service for new information? Will the service let them know? Will the service be willing to pay the coupling price?

This situation may at first sound unlikely to happen, but let's look at a few examples. You'll see that it's a common enough business situation, and may be the norm.

PROBLEM

Suppose you wanted to create a service for an airline that will proactively take care of delayed flights. When a flight is expected to arrive late, you'd want to find new flights for passengers who won't make their connections, free up their places in their current connecting flights, and adjust the rates for these flights.

To do that, you'd have to interact with several services—some of them would be part of your system (such as a service that tracks all the active flights), and some would be external to your system (such as services that provide weather reports and airport statuses). Figure 5.8 shows delay information that you can get from the FAA in the United States.

Figure 5.9 shows a Delays service and a few of the services it can consume to work its magic.

Figure 5.9   Some of the services that a Delays service would need to interact with. The Delays service drives some of the services directly (such as Reservations and Schedules) but it's driven by data coming from the other services (Weather, Operational Picture, and Airports).

NOTE If you do an internet search for business events, you'll notice that airline examples are quite popular but there are many other more down-to-earth (pardon the pun), run-of-the-mill IT examples. Just think about someone wanting to know when stock prices reach a certain level, or someone who needs to know every time an order larger than a certain value is placed. Similarly, an inventory system will need to know to order new parts when the supply gets below a certain threshold, and dashboarding and business activity monitor (BAM) solutions need to know about problems they should be reporting on.

While SOA seems to be rooted in Request/Reply, you'll also need to find a way to support business events within the SOA constraints and tenets. In other words,

How can you handle business events in an SOA?

One option is to stick with the base SOA approach and have the service that generates the event actively send a message to all interested services. Note that the source service has to know about all the interested services, which would include understanding their contracts, to support this scenario. This is problematic because it introduces needless coupling between the event source and other services. In the previous example, the Weather service would have to know about the Delays and Operational Picture services. Similarly, if the Airport service wants to know about the weather so that it can update the airport status, you'd have to change the Weather service to notify that service as well. You need to keep in mind that unlike a classical Request/Reply scenario, the source service here doesn't care about the target services.

Another option is to allow the interested services to poll for updates. Every event basically has a time to live when it's still available in the current state of the providing service. An interested service can poll the event-generating service and find out about the interesting events. The advantage of this approach over the previous option is that now the dependency direction is correct. The services that do the polling are the ones interested in the information. The problem with polling is that if the polling interval is too long, you'll miss important events, and if it's too short, you'll cause unnecessary network loads. (You can overcome this problem—I'll talk about this as a variation on the solution.)

You can alleviate the service's coupling problem in the polling option by externalizing the relationship from the services. One way to do this is by using the Orchestration pattern (discussed in chapter 7), which involves an external workflow engine. The event source can then have a single dependency on an endpoint of the workflow engine. The workflow engine knows about all the interested parties and forwards the messages to them.

This is a step in the right direction because the services aren't coupled and it's easy to make changes to the workflow and add additional services. The downside is that it federates the logic between the services and the workflow.

We've considered three different solutions, and each has some advantages, but maybe we can do better? I think we can.

SOLUTION

The solution to handling business events has been there in the background all the time. If you want to add events, why not adopt an architectural style that's built around events and incorporate that into SOA? As it happens, we don't have to reinvent the wheel—there is already such an architectural style, and it's called event-driven architecture (EDA).

An *event* is any significant change that happens within the event generator or within a component that's observed by the event generator. Event specifications in EDA are structured entities akin to SOA contracts and messages. An event specification consists of a header and a body, where the header contains the metadata and the body contains the actual information about the event. Unlike traditional messages, events don't have a specific destination.

EDA is similar to publish/subscribe, but it also has several differences such as the historical perspective that's gained by treating events as streams instead of isolated occurrences.

To accommodate an event-like message exchange pattern within SOA, you can do the following:

✓ **Implement the Inversion of Communications pattern by supplementing SOA with EDA—you can allow services to publish streams of events that occur in them instead of calling other services explicitly.**

The Inversion of Communications pattern, illustrated in figure 5.10, basically reverses the direction of the information flow. Instead of the service consumers calling on the service to get information, the service reaches out to the consumers with updates. This change in roles requires two components within the service, or rather within the edge (because they aren't really business-oriented).

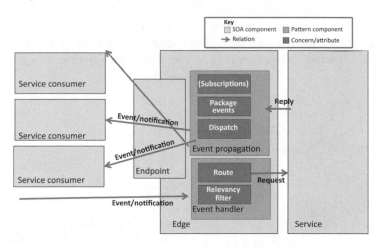

Figure 5.10   In the Inversion of Communications pattern, the service's edge accepts and filters incoming events in addition to "standard" requests. When the service has some reply or reaction to an event ready, the edge also packages and dispatches it as an event to service consumers.

The first component is for event propagation. Events should be packaged in the format agreed upon for the SOA initiative (or, if there is no common contract, according to the service's contract) and distributed (the following technology mapping section discusses this).

The second component, the event handler, enables the service to act as a service consumer for events sent by other services. The first task for the event handler is to filter incoming events for relevancy. This is important, because many of the events received might not be relevant, especially if the infrastructure between services isn't smart enough to route or manage subscriptions. The second role of the event handler is to route the relevant events to the components of the service that can react to the events—the components that in a Request/Reply model would get the new information as requests.

One thing you've probably noticed is that even though the Inversion of Communications pattern talks about events, it doesn't include a subscription-management component on the edge. That's because subscriptions management requires too much effort that isn't really related to the services, like routing and persistent subscriptions. An alternative to subscriptions on the service is to move the responsibility to the consumer or infrastructure (or both). To do that, you can provide known names (URIs, queues, and the like) where events can be found, and then have any interested services listen to them.

Let's look at the Delays service mentioned in the problem description. Figure 5.11 shows that now the Airports, Weather, and Operational Picture services push their changes to the Delays service instead of the other way around. This has a positive effect on network traffic, because the Delays service no longer has to worry about missing an important change in the three services it monitors. Also note that applying the Inversion of Communications pattern does not mean you have to move all your interactions to events. In this example, the Delays service still has Request/Reply interactions with the Schedules and Reservations services. If the Delays service identifies a delay, it can try to reserve places on later flights for people who would miss their connections.

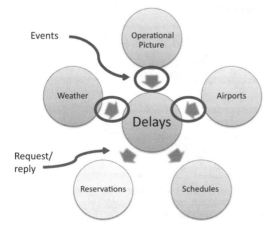

Figure 5.11 The relations between the services shown in figure 5.9 when using the Inversion of Communications pattern. Now the Weather, Airports, and Operational Picture services push their changes to the Delays service.

One thing to note when you combine the Inversion of Communications pattern with the Request/Reaction or Request/Reply patterns is that in addition to replying to the service consumer (or as an alternative to doing this), the service should also raise an event informing listeners of the effects of handling the request, so that other subscribed services can handle the effects of the change.

Inversion of Communications is about implementing EDA on top of SOA. Up to now, we've looked at the simple side of that, which involves handling sporadic or isolated events. But a very strong concept that EDA defines is *event streams*. This means you don't look at each event on its own, but rather at a chain of related events over time. Event streams can give you both trends and a historical perspective. Used well, this can give you real-time business intelligence and business-activity monitoring. The Aggregated Reporting pattern discussed in chapter 7 shows an application of this capability.

Another pattern you can combine with Inversion of Communications is the Parallel Pipelines pattern (discussed in chapter 3). This combination can be used to provide an SOA implementation of a staged event-driven architecture (SEDA). In a nutshell, SEDA can provide a way to increase the concurrency and throughput of a solution in a relatively simple way.

The downside of using Inversion of Communications is the added complexity of designing the whole system using events. The way to deal with this problem has already been mentioned—don't use Inversion of Communications exclusively; rather, combine it with the other message-exchange patterns mentioned in this chapter.

One other thing to watch out for and avoid when using the Inversion of Communications pattern is a vicious event circle, where an event triggers a chain of events that gets back to the original event source and causes it to refire the same or a similar event. I haven't yet seen it happen in real business scenarios, but the possibility exists. The way to handle this problem is logging and monitoring, such as by using the Service Watchdog pattern discussed in chapter 3.

Moving to Inversion of Communications also makes it more complicated to debug processes. When something goes amiss, you need to trace the problem back to the butterfly whose wings initiated the chain reaction that led to the problem. The way to counter this is via centralized logging throughout the development process (and possibly in production) that enable you to replay the system. This is more complicated than following a direct call stack.

Another challenge of moving to Inversion of Communications is adding it in the middle of an SOA initiative, when you already have services deployed that utilize simpler message-exchange patterns. I can't provide general guidance on the interaction remodeling because it's very situation-specific, but as with the SOA initiative itself, the secret here is to perform the transition gradually.

The other set of challenges related to the Inversion of Communications pattern has to do with the implementation details. After all, many SOA infrastructures (most obviously HTTP) don't support events or multicasts. Let's see if we can clear up these obstacles.

TECHNOLOGY MAPPING

There are several technology mapping options for implementing the Inversion of Communications pattern.

The first option, which is also the most natural fit, is to use an ESB. Most ESB implementations can accommodate all of the common message-exchange patterns, including publish/subscribe. The next listing shows how you could configure a subscription on Apache ServiceMix (an open source ESB). To configure the subscription, add a subscriptions section (`sm:subscription`) in the configuration section of a component (`sm:activationSpec`).

Listing 5.4   Configuration excerpt including subscription for a "picture" component

```
<sm:activationSpecs>
    <sm:activationSpec componentName="sub" service="foo:Subscriber">
...
        <sm:subscriptions>
            <sm:subscriptionSpec service="cop::picture"/>
        </sm:subscriptions>
    </sm:activationSpec>
</sm:activationSpecs>
```

When you want to implement the Inversion of Communications pattern with an ESB, you delegate the responsibility of passing the events and of managing subscriptions to the infrastructure, and you can concentrate on planning the events and the other business activities.

You can get even looser coupling by using a messaging infrastructure (or ESB) that supports topics, even though this isn't a common service infrastructure for SOA. Topics are more loosely coupled because the subscribers don't know who the publisher is—they just know about the topic that they find interesting. The problem with that approach is that the subscribers don't know who the publisher is, so the infrastructure needs to make sure only authenticated and authorized services can post events.

Now let's consider the more problematic infrastructures, like HTTP (RESTful services) and plain TCP. There are two options here.

The first option is to write the necessary infrastructure as part of the edge component of each service. In other words, develop your own logic to persist subscriptions and actively send each generated event to all the interested subscribers. Although it's technically feasible, I don't recommend going down this path unless you're a middleware vendor. It's better to focus on your core business and business value for your solution and not try to develop a delicate piece of infrastructure you aren't likely to get right on the first try.

The second option, which I find more interesting, has to do with a push (well, actually *pull*) application that you probably use daily—blogs and blog newsreaders. When I publish a new event (post) in my blog, it isn't immediately sent to my blog subscribers. In fact, it's never actively sent. Instead, the new event is added to an events stream (RSS or Atom feed) that contains the most recent events. The subscribers, who manage the subscription on their side without any regard to me (loose coupling), decide how often they need to poll my event steam so that they don't miss important events. That decision is based on how many items I keep in my feed, the frequency of new events, and the latency they can afford in handling the events. Note that consumers who need low latency from event occurrence to notification will probably need the online event notification and won't be able to use this method.

As you've seen in the Request/Reply pattern (section 5.1) the Atom Publishing Protocol is a popular choice for formalizing collection in RESTful web services, as are the JSON versions, like OData and GData.

An event's time to live

Whether you use feeds or a queue-based approach for publishing events, you need to consider the event's time to live (TTL). By TTL, I mean the time during which the event should be available to consumers before it becomes irrelevant.

When you use events in a programming language, the TTL is inherent ("You snooze, you lose"). If a consumer isn't there when the event is raised, that's the consumer's problem. In SOA, it's wiser to allow temporal decoupling between the time the event was raised and the time it's consumed. This temporal decoupling allows increased autonomy and loose coupling for both the event generator and the event consumer. The flip side is that you now have to consider the TTL of events to prevent the processing of obsolete information, too much latency, and performance problems.

The TTL changes depending on the business meaning of the event, so there aren't any firm rules. Two rules of thumb I can give are that the TTL for cyclic events, like stock price updates, is usually the cycle frequency, and the TTL for one-time events, like a new order, tends to be much longer.

One point mentioned briefly in the previous section was that the EDA part of the Inversion of Communications pattern allows you to treat events as a stream rather than as isolated instances. Event streams can enhance your solutions even more if you add additional architectural concept known as complex event processing (CEP). As its name implies, CEP involves taking a look at event streams and examining them for complex patterns. This is probably best explained through an example.

Listing 5.5 shows a sample query in an embeddable CEP engine I wrote a few years ago (it was based on C# LINQ). The query examines a stream of login events and raises an alert whenever there are three failed logins in a row from the same user.

Listing 5.5 A continuous query to raise an event on three consecutive failed logins

```
var loginRecords = engine.GetEventSource<Login>();

engine.AddQuery(() => from names in loginRecords.Stream
                      group names by names.Name
                      into logins
                      from login in logins
                      let next = logins.FirstOrDefault(
```

```
➡t => t.LoginTime > login.LoginTime)
                         let nextNext = null == next ? null
➡ : logins.FirstOrDefault(t => t.LoginTime
➡> next.LoginTime)
                     where
                       !login.Successful &&
➡(null != next && !next.Successful) &&
➡(null != nextNext && !nextNext.Successful)
                   select login, HanleAlert);
```

There are many commercial CEP engines from companies like SAP, TIBCO, and IBM, as well as few open source options like Esper from EsperTech.

The Inversion of Communications pattern presents a good opportunity to introduce CEP to a project, but that isn't the main reason to use the pattern. As usual, we'll finish our discussion of the pattern by exploring some of the motivations for using it.

QUALITY ATTRIBUTES

Inversion of Communications is a powerful pattern. Events-based interaction greatly helps increase the autonomy and composability of a system, and the reuse within a system. This is great news for SOA, so much that Gartner called EDA and SOA "Advanced SOA." While it's important to remember the challenges involved in the implementation of Inversion of Communications, like complicated debugging and the added work of designing events, it's an important pattern to have in your toolkit because all of its benefits.

Table 5.4 identifies some scenarios that might make you think about using the Inversion of Communications pattern.

Table 5.4   Inversion of Communications pattern quality attributes and scenarios

Quality attribute	Concrete attribute	Sample scenario
Flexibility	Decoupling	Services should know as little as possible about each other.
Reuse	Interfaces	All services should support some common service APIs in addition to any specific requests they may serve.
Changeability	Add feature	Assuming the development for a new capability is done, you should be able to integrate it into the system in three weeks or less.

The Inversion of Communications pattern wraps up the basic message-exchange patterns by showing how you can do eventing or publish/subscribe within SOA. The last message exchange pattern we'll cover in this chapter is the Saga pattern, which enables you to get transaction-like behavior between services.

5.4 Saga pattern

In chapter 2, we talked about the Transactional Service pattern as a way to make a service handle requests in a reliable manner. But using the Transactional Service pattern only solves one part of puzzle. Let's take another look at the scenario that we looked at in chapter 2 and see what we still need to do.

Figure 5.12 shows an Ordering service that processes an order. The interesting issue here is in steps 2.3 and 2.4. Within the internal transaction of handling the request, the Ordering service has to interact with two other services: it requests a bill from an internal Billing service, and it orders something (parts or materials) from an external Supplier system.

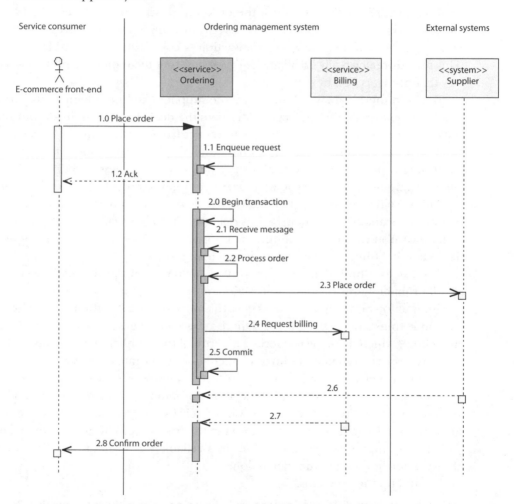

Figure 5.12 Sample message flow in an e-commerce scenario (talking to an Ordering service). The front end sends an order to an ordering service, which then orders the parts from a Supplier service and asks a Billing service to bill the customer. Note that all the handling of the Place Order message (step 1.0) is done within a single local transaction (steps 2.0 to 2.5).

There are two major problems lurking here. Consider what will happen if instead of committing the internal transaction at step 2.5, the Ordering service decides to abort its (internal) transaction. Also, consider how the ordering service would go about getting some commitment from the other services so that it could continue its work based on that commitment. You may want to get a confirmation from the supplier that the ordered items have been secured before you confirm the order to the customer.

PROBLEM

The obvious solution to the two problems mentioned in the previous section is to extend (or flow) the Ordering service's internal transaction into the other services. This extended transaction is known as a *distributed transaction*.

Using distributed transactions, the ordering service would have to call both the Billing service and the Supplier system as part of a single transaction, and if all the services agree to commit, the whole transaction is committed and completed together. This sounds really, really great, and we even have the technology to do that—technology that predates SOA by many years.

But, and there's always a but, what if the supplier can only complete its part of the transaction after a senior manager authorizes the deal? Can you hold all your internal locks while you wait for that manager to return from vacation in the Bahamas sometime next week? Probably not. And what if the supplier also happens to be a competitor. It might prolong the transactions to disrupt your business—you're holding locks on internal resources while you wait for the supplier to complete the transaction.

This specific scenario might be too far-fetched, but the point is that you can't make assumptions about how other services operate. This is especially true for services you don't own. You can read about other reasons to avoid cross-service transactions in the Transactional Integration antipattern (in chapter 8).

Even if you think that cross-service transactions aren't problematic as a concept, you'll probably agree that long transactions aren't very good. The more conversational the interaction between the services gets, the more you need to think about alternatives to atomic transactions. In figure 5.12 there are two messages going out from the Ordering service, which might be borderline in terms of the number of interactions. But business processes can sometimes involve much more elaborate conversations.

A lot of messages flowing back and forth between services isn't recommended, because it increases latency and the chances of failure. Nevertheless, few and sparse interactions aren't realistic either. Services rarely live in complete isolation; interoperability is one of the reasons for using SOA in the first place. This means you need a way to handle complex service interactions in a reliable way without bundling the whole thing in one lengthy atomic transaction.

To sum up the problems,

How can you reach distributed consensus between services without transactions?

I think by now it's clear that using a single transaction isn't an option. If all the services involved are under your control, you might want to break the long process into multiple steps and run each step in its own transaction. Smaller distributed transactions are definitely a step in the right direction, but you're still bound by cross-service transactions, and because everything isn't bounded by one single transaction, you have problems like canceling the effect of a first step if something fails in the third or fourth step.

Another option is to model the contract so that you'll never need this kind of complex interaction. You can minimize interactions between services if you increase the granularity of the services. But there's also a limit to how large you want your services to be—you don't want to end up with a single monolithic service that does everything. And just like objects, services need to be cohesive and adhere to the Single Responsibility Principle. When you do that, you can contain some interactions within the service boundary, but you still need to handle cross-service interactions to implement business processes.

The option you're left with is to break the service interaction—the business process—into a set of smaller steps, and model that into a long-running conversation between the services.

SOLUTION

The Saga interaction pattern is about providing the semantics and components to support the long-running conversation mentioned at the end of the previous section.

✓ **Implement the Saga pattern and break the service interaction (the business process) into multiple smaller business actions and counteractions. Coordinate the conversation and manage it based on messages and timeouts.**

Hector Garcia-Molina and Kenneth Salem defined the term "saga" in 1987 as a way to solve the problem of long-lived database transactions. Hector and Kenneth described a saga as a sequence of related small transactions.[1] In a saga, the coordinator (a database in their case) makes sure that all of the involved transactions are successfully completed. Otherwise, if the transactions fail, the coordinator runs compensating transactions to amend the partial execution.

What made sense for databases makes even more sense for service interactions in SOA. Figure 5.13 illustrates how you can apply the saga notion to SOA. You can break a long service interaction into individual actions or activities and compensations (in case there are faults or errors).

The first component to notice in figure 5.13 is the initiator. The initiator triggers the Saga pattern by creating the context, which is the reason for the interaction. It then asks one or more other services (participators) to perform some business activities. The participators can register for coordination (depending on how formal the Saga implementation is). The participants and initiator exchange messages and requests until they reach some agreement or they're ready to complete the interaction.

---

[1] Hector Garcia-Molina and Kenneth Salem, "Sagas," in *SIGMOD '87: Proceedings of the 1987 ACM SIGMOD International Conference on Management of Data* (1987), 249–59.

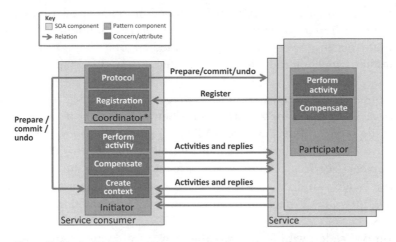

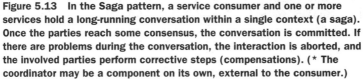

Figure 5.13 In the Saga pattern, a service consumer and one or more services hold a long-running conversation within a single context (a saga). Once the parties reach some consensus, the conversation is committed. If there are problems during the conversation, the interaction is aborted, and the involved parties perform corrective steps (compensations). (* The coordinator may be a component on its own, external to the consumer.)

This is when the coordinator requests all the participants (including the initiator) to finalize the agreement (prepare to commit) and commit.

If there was a problem during either the interaction or the final phase, the activities that occurred have to be undone. In regular ACID transactions you can roll back, but in a saga you have to perform a counteraction, called *compensation*, which may not be the exact opposite of the activity that must be undone. If the result of the original activity caused the service to cross some threshold, it may not wish to undo the action it took. Or it may be impossible to undo the effect, such as if canceling the action requires something from the service that requested the action in the first place (maybe a cancellation fee) or if too much time has passed which makes it impossible to undo the effect. As another example, if the result of a saga was to launch a missile, the compensation would be to abort the mission and blow up the missile in midair—you can't just pull the missile back into the pod.

The Saga pattern is sometimes also referred to by the name "Long-Running Transaction." It's true that you can conceptually think of a saga as a single logical unit of work and that it does make use of transaction semantics. But a saga doesn't really adhere to the transaction tenets like atomicity or isolation, mostly because the interaction is distributed both in time and space. For instance, when you call a compensation, it might be too late to undo the original action, so that there might be consequences like cancellation fees or partial deliveries. The "Saga" term better reflects the fact that the interaction is lengthy and that the messages are related.

Let's take a look at what the ordering scenario in figure 5.12 might look like when you utilize the Saga interaction pattern. Figure 5.14 demonstrates a scenario where the supplier is out of stock of the ordered items. In this case, both the ordering and billing need to be canceled. You also need to notify the front end that there was a problem and let the supplier know that you closed the interaction.

In this Saga pattern version of the ordering scenario, all the services involved (Ordering, Billing, and the Supplier system) send notifications about their ability to complete the saga or not. For instance, the Supplier system emits a fault message to let the Ordering service know that it had a problem processing the "place order" request. When the coordinator component inside the Ordering service gets the fault message, it requests that the other parties (the Ordering service itself, and the Billing service) compensate, and once that's done it notifies the Supplier that the interaction has completed handling the fault.

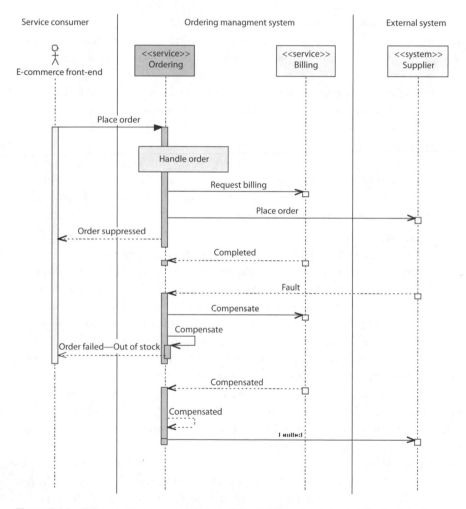

Figure 5.14 The e-commerce scenario from figure 5.12 remodeled using the Saga pattern. The interaction with the Billing service and the Supplier system is now coordinated in a saga. The Ordering service can handle problems in a more robust way by canceling the order and notifying the front end instead of hoping for the best.

The front end is notified about the failure during the compensation of the Ordering service. It isn't a task of the coordinator.

The interaction in figure 5.14 has the service consumer and services controlling the interaction internally. One good way to do this is to use the Workflodize pattern (discussed in chapter 2) so that each service has an internal workflow that follows the sequence and different paths of the interaction. Another pattern related to the Saga pattern is the Reservation pattern (see chapter 6).

Another approach you can take to implement the Saga pattern is to use an external coordinator for the conversation—see the Orchestration pattern in chapter 7 for more details. The semantic difference between an internally coordinated Saga implementation and an externally coordinated Saga implementation is that with external coordination the coordinator holds the "big picture" of what the saga is trying to achieve, whereas with internal coordination you can get coordination without any one service having the complete picture. Internal coordination is more flexible, but it's harder to manage.

The main effort involved in implementing the Saga pattern is deciding on the business activities and compensations. You can use techniques such as business process modeling to determine what these activities might be (Business Process Modeling and Notation, BPMN, is discussed in the section on the Orchestration pattern in chapter 7).

Even though the main effort in implementing the Saga pattern is on the business side, modeling business processes and activities that will support long-running conversations, there are also a few technological aspects that have to do with the messages and protocols—let's take a look at them.

TECHNOLOGY MAPPING

At a minimum, the Saga pattern requires you to add compensation messages to any state-altering message that can participate in a saga. Again, it's important to emphasize that the compensation may not be able to undo the original activity, but it does have to try to minimize the effects of the activity.

The internal processing of the compensation messages varies depending on what needs to be done to cancel the effect of the original message. It's usually better to set statuses to canceled rather than to delete records, especially at the database level, because the original action might have triggered other business processes and actions that rely on those records. For instance, if as a result of a message you added an order, another service might have produced a bill. Chances are that the billing also occurred within the same saga, but you might not know or control that within the Ordering service. Making a change that leaves traces behind it (like setting a status to canceled) is better than deleting a record because it allows you to resolve problems manually if the need arises. Note that in some industries, like banking, you're required by law to register cancellations as new changes rather than to delete or amend the original records. (See Pat Helland's "Accountants Don't Use Erasers" article in the further reading section for more about not deleting records.)

Another message type that's important for the Saga pattern is the failure message. When you have a simple point-to-point interaction between services, the reply or reaction that a called service sends is enough to convey the notion of a problem. The calling service consumer, which understands the service's contract, can understand that something is amiss and act accordingly. When you implement the Saga pattern, however, you may have more than two parties involved, and you also have a coordinator. The coordinator isn't as business-aware as the service's business logic, but it does define control messages in order to understand the status of the interactions.

As you probably know (or have noticed by now) web services are considered the primary technology for implementing SOA, and the Saga pattern isn't any different. The WS-* stack of protocols has produced the WS-BusinessActivity protocol as part of WS-Coordination.

WS-BusinessActivity has two variants:

- *Business Agreement with Coordinator Completion*—The coordinator decides and notifies the participants when to complete their roles within the activity. This approach is a little more ordered.
- *Business Agreement with Participant Completion*—The participants decide when to complete their roles within the activity. This approach is a little more loosely coupled, with the cost being increased chances for compensation.

WS-BusinessActivity defines an orderly protocol and states for both the participating services and the coordinator. WS-BusinessActivity also defines two coordination types:

- `AtomicOutcome`—All the participants have to close (commit) or compensate.
- `MixedOutcome`—The coordinator treats each participant separately.

Figure 5.15 shows the state transitions for a participating service using WS-Business-Activity with participant completion.

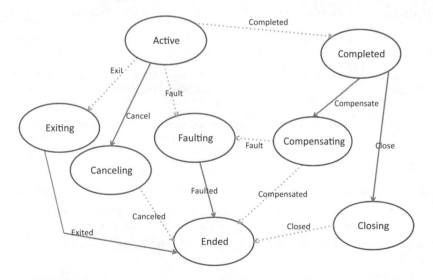

Figure 5.15 State diagram from the point of view of a participating service using the completion-by-participants variant of the WS-BusinessActivity protocol. The state transitions can be either the result of decisions by the service (the dotted lines) or by messages from the coordinator (the solid lines).

Another important technology option for implementing the Saga pattern is to use BPEL (Business Process Execution Language) or its WS-* implementation known as WS-BPEL (or BPEL4WS in previous versions). Additionally, you can also use a non-BPEL-compliant orchestration engine. These technology mappings all fall under the external coordinator mentioned previously and are covered in more depth as part of the Orchestration pattern in chapter 7.

QUALITY ATTRIBUTES

The main reason to employ the Saga pattern is to increase the integrity of the system. As I've mentioned in the previous sections, transactions are problematic when it comes to distributed environments in general, and they're even more so when using SOA. Nevertheless, you'll still want to be able to coordinate the behavior of services and have meaningful interactions. By coordinating the behavior and failure handling, you can introduce reliable, predictable, long-running conversations.

In a distributed environment, it's relatively hard to know what the outcome of a complex interaction will be, and this is especially true if you use other patterns, like Inversion of Communications (discussed in section 5.3). The Saga pattern introduces some control into the interactions and verifies that the outcome of a complex interaction will be along known paths (either completed or compensated).

The outcome of increased predictability is also increased correctness. When you know how the system is going to behave, it's easier to construct system tests to verify that the desired outcome indeed happens.

Table 5.5 presents sample scenarios for the preceding quality attributes.

Table 5.5 Saga pattern quality attributes and scenarios

Quality attribute	Concrete attribute	Sample scenario
Integrity	Correctness	Under all conditions, an order processed by the system will be billed.
Integrity	Predictability	Under normal conditions, the chances of a customer getting billed for a canceled order shall be less than 5 percent.
Reliability	Handling failure	When resuming from a communications disconnection, all the processes that were interrupted shall remain consistent.

Writing compensation logic is relatively complicated. As the timeline advances, the number of changes in the service can get rather large, which makes it harder to achieve predictability when you try to undo an early change. One way to try to cope with that is to implement the Reservation pattern, which you'll read about in the next chapter.

5.5   Summary

One distinct characteristic of all the patterns in this chapter is that none of them are new. All the interaction patterns predate SOA by many years. Nevertheless, I've spent more than 30 pages discussing them with you, instead of just pointing you to Hohpe and Woolf's excellent *Enterprise Integration Patterns* book, which covers these patterns as well. The reason for this is that although these patterns seem relatively simple and well known, each has some aspects that makes them a little complicated when you try to implement them and adhere to SOA principles:

- *Request/Reply*—This pattern talks about synchronous communications, but in SOA it's better to use document-based interactions. That's in contrast to RPC-based interactions, which are the norm in traditional distributed architectures for synchronous communications.
- *Request/Reaction*—This pattern implements asynchronous communications. Again, it's a simple pattern, but it can be tricky to implement when you use consumers that don't support callbacks.
- *Inversion of Communications*—This pattern implements eventing, but with a few twists such as implementation on transports that don't support eventing. Another interesting aspect is providing event streams.
- *Saga*—Sagas are a way for services to reach distributed consensus without relying on distributed transactions.

The next two chapters will look at less basic interaction patterns. Some of them are complementary to the patterns discussed here, such as the Reservation pattern in chapter 6, which complements the Saga pattern, or the Aggregated Reporting pattern in chapter 7 that uses the Inversion of Communications pattern. The other patterns we'll look at have to do with aspects of interactions and aggregations beyond the underlying message exchange patterns, such as the Composite Front End pattern in chapter 6.

5.6   Further reading

Gregor Hohpe and Bobby Woolf, *Enterprise Integration Patterns: Designing, Building, and Deploying Messaging Solutions* (Addison-Wesley Professional, 2003).
This book discusses fundamental integration patterns in a general context, and many of them are applicable to SOA as well.

Google Data APIs, http://code.google.com/apis/gdata/overview.html.
Google's Google Data Protocol (GData) is an example of a document-centric protocol for interacting with services.

INVERSION OF COMMUNICATIONS

Arnon Rotem-Gal-Oz, "Bridging the Gap Between BI & SOA," www.infoq.com/articles/BI-and-SOA.
This article shows an application of the Inversion of Communications pattern (as well as Aggregated Reporting).

INVERSION OF COMMUNICATIONS

Matt Welsh, "SEDA: An Architecture for Highly Concurrent Server Applications,"
www.eecs.harvard.edu/~mdw/proj/seda/.
Combining the Inversion of Communications pattern with the Parallel Pipelines pattern
gives an SOA implementation of SEDA.

SAGA

Pat Helland, "Accountants Don't Use Erasers," *PatHelland's WebLog*, http://blogs.msdn.com/b/
pathelland/archive/2007/06/14/accountants-don-t-use-erasers.aspx.
Pat Helland explains the merits of retaining prior states.

Service consumer patterns

The previous chapter focused on the basics of service interactions—the message exchange patterns. This chapter also focuses on the interactions of services with their consumers but it covers a wider range, looking at patterns that support these interactions. Like chapter 5, this chapter's focus is on the service consumer in the SOA components model (see figure 6.1).

Service consumers aren't necessarily other services (though that's common as well). One important type of nonservices that are service consumers are UIs. It's important to talk about connecting UIs to services, because SOA, in itself, doesn't really pay attention to the needs of UIs. SOA separates business concepts into different services, whereas users working with a UI want a unified view.

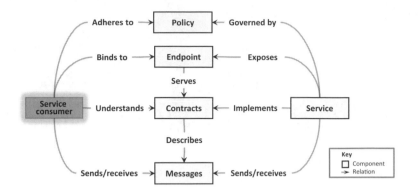

Figure 6.1   This chapter's focus is about connecting services with service consumers in the levels and layers beyond the basic message exchange patterns.

The following patterns are discussed in this chapter:

- *Reservation*—Efficiently provide a level of guarantee in a loosely coupled manner while maintaining services' autonomy and consistency
- *Composite Front End*—Interact with multiple services, get an integrated, cohesive UI, and still preserve SOA principles and modularity benefits
- *Client/Server/Service*—Connect an SOA to UIs where integration is problematic (such as when the client side isn't SOA-aware or it uses incompatible technologies)

The first we'll look at is the Reservation pattern, which is closely related to the Saga pattern discussed in the previous chapter. The Reservation pattern also exists in its own right to allow a service to give partial commitments to service consumers.

6.1   *Reservation pattern*

The Reservation pattern is an SOA-friendly way for services to provide partial commitments and guarantees. To better understand why that's needed, let's look at transactions and distributed systems.

When you use transactions in "traditional" *n*-tier systems, life is relatively simple. When you run a transaction and an error or fault occurs, you abort the transaction and roll back any changes, getting back your system-wide consistency and peace of mind. This is possible because a transaction isolates changes made within it from the rest of the world. One of the base assumptions behind transactions is that the time that elapses from the beginning of the transaction until the end is short. Under that assumption, you can afford the luxury of letting the transaction hold locks on your resources (such as databases) and prevent changes by others while the transaction is in progress. Transactions provide four basic guarantees—atomicity, consistency, isolation, and durability—usually remembered by the acronym, ACID.

Unfortunately, in a distributed world (SOA or otherwise), it's rarely a good idea to use atomic short-lived transactions (see the discussion of the Transactional Integration antipattern in chapter 8 for more details). The fact that cross-service transactions are discouraged is one of the main reasons for using the Saga pattern in the first place.

One of the obvious shortcomings of sagas is that you can't perform rollbacks. The two conditions mentioned earlier, locking and isolation, don't hold in sagas, so you can't provide the needed guarantees. Still, because interactions, and especially long-running interactions, can fail or be canceled, sagas offer the notion of compensations. Compensations are cool; you can't have rollbacks, so instead you reverse the interaction's operations and have a pseudorollback. If you added 100 (dollars or units or whatnot) during the original activity, you can just subtract the same 100 in the compensation. Easy, right? Wrong. As you probably know, it isn't easy.

PROBLEM

There are a number of problems with compensations, arising from the fact that, unlike ACID transactions, the changes made by the Saga activities aren't isolated. This lack of isolation means that other interactions with the service may operate on the data that was modified by the saga, rendering the compensation impossible. To give an extreme example, if a request to one service changes the readiness status of a missile to "all-set," and another service caused the missile to launch based on that status, it would be a little late for the first service to try to reverse the "all-set" status now that the bird has flown the coop. A more down-to-earth (pardon the pun) business scenario is any interaction where you work with limited resources, such as ordering from a limited stock.

Look at the scenario in figure 6.2. A customer orders an item, and the Ordering service requests the item from the warehouse, as it wants to ship the item to the customer (probably by notifying another service). Meanwhile, on the Warehouse service, the item order causes a restocking threshold to be hit that triggers a restocking order from a supplier.

Then the customer decides to cancel the order—now what? Should the restocking order be canceled too? Can it be canceled under the ordering terms of the supplier?

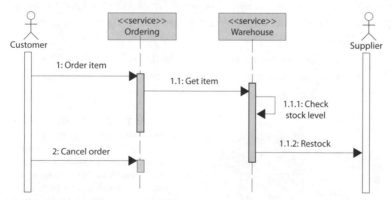

Figure 6.2   A simple ordering scenario where the customer changes their mind and cancels the order after the order has already created additional actions on the ordering system

And what about customers who request the item between the ordering and cancellation—they might get an out-of-stock notice that would send them off to the competition. This can be especially problematic for orders that are prone to cancellations, like hotel bookings, vacations, and so on.

Another limitation of compensations and the Saga pattern itself is that a coordinator is required. Involving a coordinator means services are trusting an external entity (one outside most of the services involved in the saga) to set things straight. This is a challenge for some of the SOA goals because it compromises autonomy and introduces unwanted coupling to the external coordinator.

This, then, is the problem:

? **How can you efficiently provide a level of guarantee in a loosely coupled manner while maintaining the autonomy and consistency of the services?**

I've mentioned a couple of challenges of compensations. Another risk of using compensations is that the external coordinator may fail or the compensation request might get lost, which might result in the service getting to an inconsistent state.

I've also mentioned that distributed transactions aren't the answer because they lock internal resources for too long (a saga might go on for days) and they put excess trust in services that may be external to the organization. So what's the solution?

SOLUTION

This seems like a quagmire of sorts, but fortunately real life has already found a way to deal with a similar need for fuzzy, half guarantees—reservations! (See figure 6.3.)

✓ **Implement the Reservation pattern and have the services provide a level of guarantee on internal resources for a limited time.**

The Reservation pattern has an internal component in the service that will handle the reservations. It has three responsibilities:

- *Reservation*—Making the reservation when a message that's deemed "reserving" arrives. When an order arrives, in addition to updating durable storage (such as a database), the component needs to set a timer or an expiration time for the order confirmation. Alternatively it can set some marker to indicate that the order isn't final.

- *Validation*—Making sure that a reservation is still valid before finalizing the process. In the ordering scenario, this step would involve making sure that the items designated for the order have not been given to someone else.

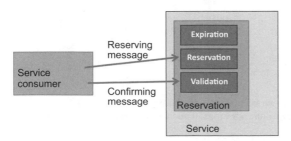

Figure 6.3 A service that implements the Reservation pattern considers some messages as "reserving" messages, and it tries to secure an internal resource and sends a confirmation if it succeeds. When a message considered to be "confirming" is received, the service ensures that the reservation still holds. In between, the service can choose to expire the reservation based on internal criteria.

- *Expiration*—Marking invalid reservations when the conditions change. If a VIP customer wants a reserved item, the system can assign it to the VIP and invalidate an existing reservation, so that when the non-VIP client tries to claim it, the system will know it's gone. Expirations can also be timed, as in, "we're keeping the book for you until noon tomorrow."

Reservations can be explicit (the scenario in figure 6.2 would also have a Reserve item action) or implicit. In the case of an implicit order, the service decides internally what will be considered a "reserving" message and what will be considered a "confirming" message. An action like placing an order might trigger the internal reservation and an action like making a payment could serve as the confirming message. When the reservation is implicit, the service consumer implementation will probably be simpler because the consumer designers are likely to treat reservation expirations as simple failures, whereas when the reservation is explicit, the service consumer is expected to have specific behavior to handle the reservation state (reserved, expired, overbooked, and so on).

Reservations happen in business transactions every day. The most obvious example is booking a hotel. You send in a request for a room (initiating a saga) saying you'll arrive on a certain date and check out on another date (performing an action within the saga). The hotel says "OK, we have a room for you (a reservation), provided you confirm your arrival by a set date (a limited time). Even if everything goes well, you may still arrive at the hotel and find out that your room has been given to another person (a limited guarantee).

The idea of the Reservation pattern is to copy this behavior to the interaction of services so that services that support reservations offer a sort of "limited lock" for a limited time and with a limited level of guarantee. A *limited level of guarantee* means that, like in real life, services can overbook and then resolve the overbooking by various strategies such as first come, first served; serving VIPs first; and so on.

It's easy to understand the Reservation pattern being applied to services that handle real-life reservations as part of their business logic, such as ordering services for hotels or airlines. But reservations are also suitable for a lot of other scenarios where services are asked to provide guarantees on internal resources. In one system I worked on (discussed at length in chapter 9), we used reservations as part of the saga initiation process. The system used the Service Instance pattern (discussed in chapter 3) where some services needed to be stateful. Naturally, services have limited capacity to handle consumers—an instance can handle a limited number of concurrent sagas or events. Because of the statefulness of instances, the services needed to know which service instances were allocated to a saga. As long as a single service instance initiates sagas, everything is fine. But when two or more services (or instances) initiate sagas concurrently, they may both try to allocate the same service instance to their particular sagas (and given enough load and time, they will).

In figure 6.4 you can see that both Initiator A and Initiator B want to use Participant A and Participant B. Participant A has a capacity of 2, so everything is fine for

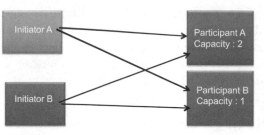

Figure 6.4 **A situation that can benefit from the Reservation pattern**

both initiators. Service B, however, has limited capacity, so at least one of the sagas will have to fail the allocation and not start.

The Reservation pattern enabled us to manage this resource allocation process in an orderly manner by implementing a two-pass protocol (somewhat similar to a two-phase commit). The initiator asks each potential participant to reserve itself for the saga. Each participant tries to reserve itself and notify back whether it's successful, so in the scenario in figure 6.4, Participant A would say yes to both requests and Participant B would say yes to one of them. If the initiator gets an OK from all the involved services (within the timeout) it tells all the participants the specific instances within the saga (initiating the saga). The participants only reserve themselves for a short period of time. Once an internally set timeout elapses, the participants remove the commitment independently.

> **NOTE** The initiator and other saga members can't assume that a participant will be there just because it's officially part of the saga. The system still needs to handle the various failure scenarios. In the preceding example, the Reservation pattern is used only to prevent overallocation; it doesn't provide any transactional guarantees.

A reservation is somewhat like a lock, so it introduces some of the risks distributed locks present. These risks aren't inherent in the Reservation pattern but can easily surface if you don't pay attention during implementation (such as if you use database locks to implement reservations). Let's look at the risks:

- *Deadlock*—Whenever you start reserving anything, especially in a distributed environment, you introduce the potential for deadlocks. If both participants in figure 6.4 had a capacity for single saga, and Initiator A first contacted Participant A and then Participant B, and Initiator B used the reverse order at the same time, you'd have had a potential deadlock.

  There are several mechanisms that can prevent this sort of deadlock. The first is inherent in the Reservation pattern—allowing the participants to release the lock themselves. But if there is a retry mechanism to reinitiate the sagas when they fail after the timeout, the same resources would be reallocated over and over, and there might be a deadlock after all.

- *Denial of service*—DoS, whether caused maliciously or as a byproduct of misuse, can result from similar reasons as a deadlock; if you incur a deadlock you also have a DoS. Another way for DoS to occur is by exploiting the reservations by constantly re-reserving. Depending on the reservation timeout, regular firewalls might fail to detect the DoS, so you may want to consider using the Service Firewall pattern (discussed in chapter 4) to help mitigate this threat.

- *Additional network calls*—When you introduce the Reservation pattern, you're likely to add additional network calls. You might, for example, introduce another call to tell saga members which instances are involved in the saga.

In addition to the Service Firewall pattern, mentioned in the discussion of DoS, another pattern related to Reservation can be the Active Service pattern (see chapter 2). The Active Service pattern can be used to handle reservation expiration when it's implemented with timeouts.

NOTE   Sometimes it's better, resource-wise, to handle expiration passively and not actively. See the discussion of implementation options in the next section.

TECHNOLOGY MAPPING

Unlike a lot of the patterns in this book, the Reservation pattern is more a business pattern than a technological one. This means there isn't a straight one-to-one technology mapping you can use. On the other hand, code-wise, the pattern is relatively easy to implement.

One thing you have to do is to keep a live thread in the service to make sure that when the lease or reservation expires, something will be there to clean up. One way to ensure this is to use the Active Service pattern and to use technologies that support timed events that provide the wakeup service. If you're running in an EJB 3.0 server, you can use single action timers (timers that only raise their event once) to accomplish this. The following listing shows a simple code excerpt that sets a timer to go off based on the time received in the message. When the timer expires, the reservation can be validated again, and if it's still valid, perform the action in the message. Other technologies provide similar mechanisms to accomplish the same effect.

Listing 6.1   Setting a timer-based Reservation (using JBoss)

```
public class TimerMessage implements MessageListener {

  @Resource
  private MessageDrivenContext mdc;

   ...

  public void onMessage(Message message) {
    ObjectMessage msg = null;                              Retrieve entity
    try {                                                  from message
      if (message instanceof ObjectMessage) {
        msg = (ObjectMessage) message;
        TimerDetailsEntity e = (TimerDetailsEntity) msg.getObject();
        TimerService timerService = messageDrivenCtx.getTimerService();
        // Timer createTimer(Date expiration, Serializable info)
```

```
        Timer timer = timerService.createTimer(e.Date, e);      ⊲┐ Push entity
    }                                                              │ into timer
} catch (JMSException e) {
    e.printStackTrace();
    mdc.setRollbackOnly();
} catch (Throwable te) {
    te.printStackTrace();
}
    }
...
```

Timer-based cancellations might be overkill if the reservation implementation is simple. The Reservation pattern implemented in C# in the following listing, is used by the participants, as was discussed in the Saga and Reservation example in the previous section.

Listing 6.2   Simple, in-memory, nonpersistent reservation

```
public Guid Reserve(Guid sagaId)
    {
        try
        {
            Rwl.TryWLock();
            var isReserved =
➡Allocator.TryPinResource(localUri, sagaId);       Manage capacity
            if (!isReserved)                            ⊲┘ of service
                return Guid.Empty;
                                                        Add code to manage
            //Missing expiration logic              ⊲┘ expiration here
            return sagaId;                          ⊲┐ Return saga ID on
        }                                              successful reservation
        finally
        {
            Rwl.ExitWLock();
        }

    }
```

Because the Reservation implementation in listing 6.2 doesn't involve heavy service resources (such as a database), you can implement passive handling of reservation expirations, which will be more efficient than timer-based expirations. The following listing shows a revised Reservation implementation, which removes timeout reservation before it commits.

> **NOTE**   When using this code, an expired reservation can still be used if no other reservation has since occurred or if the capacity of the service isn't exceeded.

Listing 6.3   Passive reservation expiration handling added to listing 6.2

```
private readonly TimeSpan MAX_RESERVATION = new TimeSpan(0, 0, 0, 1, 0);
...
public Guid Reserve(Guid sagaId)
        {
            try
            {
                Rwl.TryWLock();
                RemoveExpiredReservations();          Add method to
                var isReserved =                      clean up expired
 ➥Allocator.TryPinResource(localUri, sagaId);        reservations
                if (!isReserved)
                    return Guid.Empty;
                                                      Record when
                OpenReservations[sagaId] =            reservation
 ➥DateTimeOffset.Now + MAX_RESERVATION;              will expire
                return sagaId;

            }
            finally
            {
                Rwl.ExitWLock();
            }

        }

private void RemoveExpiredReservations()
        {
            var reftime = DateTimeOffset.Now;
            var ids = from item in OpenReservations
 ➥ where item.Value < reftime select item.Key;
            if (ids.Count() == 0) return;
            var keys=ids.ToArray();
            foreach (var id in keys)
            {
                OpenReservations.Remove(id);
                Allocator.FreePinnedResources(id);
            }

        }
```

The preceding code listings show that implementing the Reservation pattern can be simple, but implementations can be more complex, such as if you need to persist the reservation or distribute a reservation between multiple service instances. At its core, implementing the Reservation pattern shouldn't be a heavy or complex process.

Another implementation consideration is whether reservations should be explicit or implicit. Explicit reservations employ a distinct "Reserve" message. This usually means there will also be a "Commit" type message and that the service or workflow engine that requests the reservation might find itself implementing a two-phase commit protocol, which isn't very pleasant.

The other alternative is implicit reservations, where the service decides internally when to reserve and under what conditions to commit the reservation or reject it. As usual, the tradeoff is between a simple implementation in the service or a simple implementation for the service consumer.

QUALITY ATTRIBUTES

Because it's a complementary pattern to Saga, the Reservation pattern also has similar quality attributes.

The main driver for using the Reservation pattern is the need for commitment from resources. The Reservation pattern helps provide partial guarantees in long-running interactions, so the quality attribute that points you toward it is integrity. Table 6.1 provides a couple of quality attribute scenarios relevant to the Reservation pattern.

Table 6.1   Reservation pattern quality attributes and scenarios

Quality attribute	Concrete attribute	Sample scenario
Integrity	Correctness	Under all conditions, failure to receive payment within five business days will cancel the order and shipping.
Integrity	Predictability	Under normal conditions, the chances of a customer getting billed for a canceled order shall be less than 5 percent.

The Reservation pattern is a protocol-level pattern that involves the exchange of messages between service consumers and services. The next couple of patterns take a look at a component that may need to use reservations when it talks to services—we're going to look at the UI and how to tie it to services running at the back end.

6.2   *Composite Front End (Portal) pattern*

When you think about service consumers, the obvious candidates are other services. But there are other software components that interact with services, such as legacy systems, non-SOA external systems, and reporting databases. The Composite Front End pattern deals with yet another type of service consumer—the UI.

First, let's clarify that UIs aren't services. One reason is that they enable several business areas to converge. For example, a UI might let you enter an order, look up information about the customer, browse the product catalog, and view open invoices.

In addition to convergence, UIs are data producers instead of data processors.

> **NOTE**   There's one exception to this, where the UI is the front of a "human service." See the Orchestration pattern in chapter 7 for more details.

The main challenge caused by UIs comes from their main difference from services: UIs try to aggregate or converge data from several services into a cohesive and useful whole; services want to keep their data isolated from that of other services.

PROBLEM

To better understand the challenges involved in having UIs work with multiple services, let's consider an example with just a single point of friction.

In a project I worked on, we designed a C4ISR (Command, Control, Communications, Computers, Intelligence, Surveillance, and Reconnaissance) system for an Unmanned Naval Patrol Vehicle (UNPV). One of the services in the system was dubbed "Common Operational Picture" (COP). The COP's responsibility was to handle anything that's detected by sensors: ships, planes, radar stations, and so on. One of the main UI representations of the COP was a map that showed all the detections (see figure 6.5). Clicking on a map icon presents some related information the COP has about it, such as ID, nationality, and course.

The system had a few other services in addition to the COP, including the UNPV service. The UNPV service was responsible for anything related to the UNPV itself, such as setting its course and turning it around. The UNPV service had several UI screens that allowed the user to manage and monitor these functions. Another responsibility of the UNPV service was to send the UNPV's location to the COP (locations are the COP's responsibility, remember?), so in the COP UI, one of the icons on the map is the UNPV.

When a user clicks on the UNPV icon on the map, the desired outcome is to display a pop-up menu with options related to controlling the UNPV. In an object-oriented model of the COP, everything that is detected by a sensor (ships, submarines, radar stations, and so on) might be considered a "detection." Under this model, the UNPV might be a subclass of a detection, so it would accept the same events as any other detection but respond in a more specialized way, as appropriate to its particular subclass. Here, however, the COP and the UNPV are completely different services, developed by two different groups and maybe even two different companies.

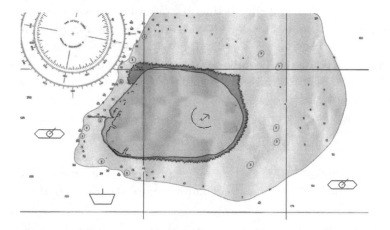

Figure 6.5   **A simplified illustration of a front end for a COP service for a naval command and control system. You can see a shoreline and some icons using NATO symbology: a radar, two submarines, and a ship (the UNPV).**

You may be able to dismiss this specific example and solve it with a specific solution: add an `if` statement somewhere to call up the correct commands and to interact with the correct services. The problem is that this example is just the tip of the iceberg. How do you handle security? Do you need to log in for each service separately? How do you handle things that all the services need? SOA's premise is that you'll have a sort of LEGO-like enterprise where you can compose different business processes easily. Is there any way you can get that in the UI?

?

How can you interact with multiple services, get an integrated, cohesive UI, and still preserve SOA principles and modularity benefits?

One option is to write client-specific code, as mentioned previously. Using this approach, an *application* is any specific composition of services. For the preceding example, the application would include the two services (COP and UNPV) and a UI that ties them together. The upside of this approach is that each application delivers a consistent experience for the user. After all, a specific or tailored application can be made to be very cohesive. Additionally there are many tried and tested ways to build flexible UIs with a proper separation of concerns, such as using model-view-controller (MVC) and its variations in a multitude of rich client and web technologies. You could probably reuse some of the UI-side logic from application to application.

Nevertheless, you do lose flexibility. Any service change that has UI aspects needs to be modified for each of its UI instances (applications). Similarly, because the UI ties multiple services together, changes in one service may cause another to malfunction within the unified UI. You also lose on composability—the ability to replace services and to create new business flows (relatively) easily. Overall, writing client-specific code is a bad option in the long term, but it can be made to work as a short-term solution.

A related option is to tie several services together, but instead of integrating the services together on the client side you can integrate them on the server side. This approach has the same pros and cons as the previous solution. Nevertheless, there are specific circumstances where it does make sense to follow this approach, and you can read about them in the next section on the Client/Server/Service pattern.

You can have independent UI components for each service. This will overcome the limitations I've mentioned because each service's UI can evolve independently, and you can cram as many of them together as you like to create an application. Unfortunately, this approach won't solve problems like the one in the example. It won't produce a cohesive UI that works across services.

SOLUTION

What you need, essentially, is to provide mechanisms to glue services together as a cohesive whole while still keeping them autonomous. That's what the Composite Front End pattern is about:

✓ **Apply the Composite Front End pattern to aggregate services while still providing them with unified client-side services like layout and theming, as well as coordination services for client-side service integration.**

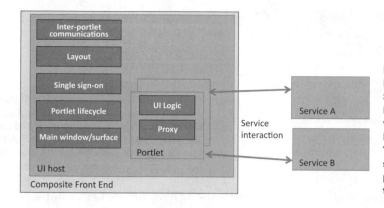

Figure 6.6　The Composite Front End pattern. Each Service has a Portlet which is a Service Agent combined with a UI logic (most likely Model in a MVC UI pattern). The UI host provides services for the different portlets to weave them together into a coherent UI.

The Composite Front End pattern, illustrated in figure 6.6, is about taking the ideas (and sometimes the technologies) behind web portals and applying them to SOA services. Web portals provide unified access points that aggregate multiple web pages. They also provide single sign-on and personalization. SOA interfaces need that and more.

The Composite Front End pattern is composed of two main components: the portlet and the host.

Portlet

The portlets are the building blocks, the *composites*, that are fused together to form the UI. The portlets are made of at least two components: the UI logic (views and controllers in MVC lingo) and the service proxy (or agent).

The service proxy is the more interesting component from an SOA perspective—it's a client-side representation of a service. The proxy serves as the model for the UI components. It's usually recommended that you have a single proxy for each service, just as it's recommended that each service maintain its own data store. From a product management perspective, the service proxy can be seen as part of the service itself.

Host

The host is the value-added part of the Composite Front End pattern. The host provides the glue that ties the different portlets into a cohesive whole. As such, the host performs several roles:

- Provides the canvas or surface on which the portlets are displayed
- Controls the lifecycle of the portlets
- Provides capabilities like interportlet communications and single sign-on

Let's revisit the problem discussed in the previous section. A right-click on a UI component (the map) should produce a context menu with options from two services (COP and UNPV). How would that work in the context of the Composite Front End pattern?

One option is that a click would be first intercepted by the host, which would then dispatch it to any registered portlet. Another option, illustrated in figure 6.7, is for the

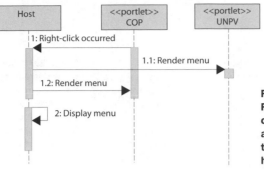

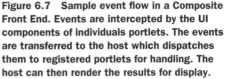

Figure 6.7   Sample event flow in a Composite Front End. Events are intercepted by the UI components of individuals portlets. The events are transferred to the host which dispatches them to registered portlets for handling. The host can then render the results for display.

click to be intercepted by the first portlet (the COP in the earlier example), the COP would then notify the host, and the host would ask all the portlets involved to render the right-click menu. The COP portlet should pass enough information as part of the event for the other portlets to do something meaningful with it. Both options are valid; the second is usually simpler to implement because you don't have to interfere with the UI framework to ensure the host gets the events.

The Composite Front End pattern is a service consumer pattern, so the proxy will utilize the various service interaction patterns, like Saga, Request/Reply, and so on (see chapter 5). It can also benefit from the service composition patterns, such as Orchestration and Service Bus (see chapter 7).

You've probably noticed that I've been using the term *portlet* to describe the service agents, and you might be wondering why the pattern is named Composite Front End rather than Portal. The main reason is that the pattern can also be used with rich-client implementations and not just web implementations. We'll explore that further in the technology mapping section.

TECHNOLOGY MAPPING

Normally, you won't be developing your own Composite Front End container. Instead you'll use existing products that provide the framework and usually also the tooling to help build the portlets.

The obvious examples are web portal frameworks. Modern enterprise web portals usually support anything from JSR 168/286 (Java Portlet Specification) to WSRP (Web Services for Remote Portlets) to open web standards like RSS, plain REST services, or OpenSocial. There are a lot of products in this area, both commercial like IBM's WebSphere Portal Server and Microsoft SharePoint and open source like JBoss's GateIn and Liferay Portal. Figure 6.8 shows the layout of the UI host as it's implemented in GateIn.

Web portals aren't the only option for implementing the Composite Front End pattern. You can also implement the concept for desktop (rich client) applications. An example is the Prism framework from Microsoft's Pattern and Practices group. Prism implements the Composite Front End pattern for both Silverlight and WPF applications. It provides all the functionality of a UI host and lets you write portlets that consume these capabilities.

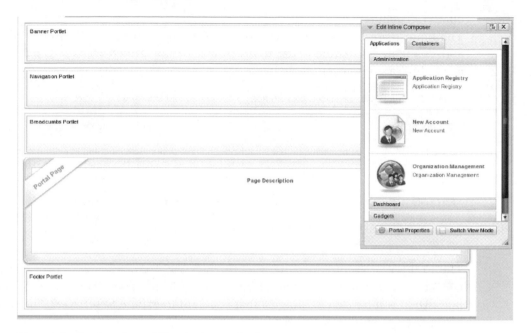

Figure 6.8   The layout capability of a Composite Front End UI host as it's implemented in JBoss's GateIn Portal.

The following listing demonstrates how you could use an EventAggregator facility that allows interportlet communications (needed for the previous map component example):

Listing 6.4   Sample use of Prism's EventAggregator

```
[Export(typeof(SampleView))]
  public partial class SampleView : UserControl
  {
      [ImportingConstructor]
      public SampleView([Import] IEventAggregator eventAggregator)
      {
          InitializeComponent();

          eventAggregator.
             GetEvent<CompositePresentationEvent<ItemSelectedEvent>>().
                 Subscribe(OnItemSelectedReceived);          Subscribe
      }                                                       to event

      public void ItemSelectedReceived(ItemSelectedEvent item)
      {
          //do something with item...
      }
  }
```

In addition to using web portal frameworks and desktop frameworks, you can roll your own implementation of Composite Front End. But it's usually better to choose one of the available options, because it's quite an investment to get it right.

QUALITY ATTRIBUTES

The main reasons to use the Composite Front End pattern are flexibility in adding and changing services and the desire for a well-integrated UI. Table 6.2 provides examples for both quality attributes.

Table 6.2 Composite Front End pattern quality attributes and scenarios

Quality attribute	Concrete attribute	Sample scenario
Usability	Operability	Under normal system use, the end user wants to achieve business tasks fluently. The system should reuse entered data (like personal details) between different tasks.
Flexibility	Changeability	Under normal conditions, changing the billing process to support a new credit card clearance provider should take less than one week.

The Composite Front End pattern is generally the preferred way to provide an SOA UI. But there's still the problem of integrating UIs that aren't SOA-aware. What happens when you have an existing UI that you want to expose to services? The next pattern will try to answer that question.

6.3   *Client/Server/Service pattern*

It's always nice to work on "green-field" projects because they have fewer constraints. There are no existing systems that you need to work with or around. Most projects aren't like that. You have systems in place and existing assets you need to integrate and work with. This is especially true for SOA projects, which are usually large transition projects that happen gradually over time—no one will stop the enterprise while you get the system ready to ship.

In the discussion of the Composite Front End pattern in the previous section, we looked at building a UI for SOA in a manner that's akin to a green-field project, creating a new UI, from scratch to consume newly developed services. In contrast, the Client/Server/Service pattern helps solve the problem of UI and SOA integration when you already have a working system in place and you want to evolve it to SOA.

As usual, let's start with a scenario to get a better grasp on the problem.

PROBLEM

I worked on a project where the company had just finished converting its UI to a three-tier solution, based on Microsoft Silverlight connected to an application back end. Our team was tasked with building new services as well as replacing existing business capabilities with new services that added additional functionality. To help complicate things, the technology chosen for the new system was Java and related technologies. Figure 6.9 shows a simplified illustration of the problem.

On the left side of figure 6.9, you can see the current system, which has components for single sign-on (SSO) and some business logic to handle customers, orders, and invoices. On the right side are the services that are going to be developed, with

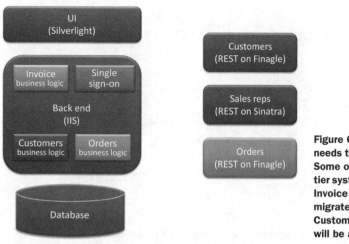

Figure 6.9 A three-tier system that needs to integrate with new services. Some of the capabilities of the three-tier system will remain intact (such as Invoice Business Logic), some will be migrated and expanded (such as Customers BL), and some new ones will be added (such as Sales Reps).

Orders and Customers destined to subsume and expand the current implementations and a new Sales Reps service that introduces new business capabilities.

Our "dream" solution might be to use the Composite Front End pattern (described in the previous section), where you have a portal-like UI that directly integrates all the new services. This is possible if the current architecture and technologies of the current UI are compatible. In the project I've descried here, if the UI was based on Prism and the back end services were based on ASP.NET, it would have been possible to stitch the new services into the existing system. But most of the time that's not the case, and you're left with this question:

 How can you connect an SOA to UIs where integration is problematic (for example, the client side isn't SOA-aware or it uses incompatible technologies)?

We've discussed the possibility of not compromising on the UI for the services and of building the optimal service UI. Unfortunately this would require a major rewrite, and there would be a long wait before the business users could use the new capabilities (a long time to market). Not to mention that even in the simplistic example illustrated in figure 6.9, it's likely that not all the existing functionality is planned to move to SOA in the near future, which can be another barrier for this kind of move.

Another option is to integrate the services within the existing UI. The main problem with that approach is that it's hard to maintain a cohesive and unified user experience when you're integrating two UI concepts together. The secondary problem with this approach is the difficulty of integrating technologies due to the different tools or skillsets of the services and UI developers.

SOLUTION

We need to find a way to integrate the new functionality, begin the SOA transition, and get a reasonable time to market. This is the answer in most cases:

Apply the Client/Server/Service pattern and use an intermediate server between the UI and the services.

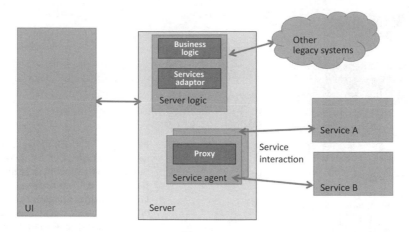

Figure 6.10   The Client/Server/Service pattern integrates new services on the server side to minimize the impact on existing UIs and functionality.

The Client/Server/Service pattern, illustrated in figure 6.10, is a simple one. It suggests integrating existing UIs with new services on the server-side or back end of that UI. Essentially, on the server you'd have a service agent that represents the service. The service agent includes a proxy that's used for communicating with the services.

The existing service logic on the server must then be changed to integrate with the new service. The recommended way to do that is to change all the writers to write both to the existing implementation and to the new one, then get all the readers to read from the new implementation, and finally retire the old readers. This way, you can keep the application running and operational while you're making changes.

"Wait a minute," you might say. "How is that different or better than integration on the UI side?" The main reason integrating the new services on the server side is better is that the communications mechanism from client to server needs increased security as compared to server-to-server integration (inside the firewall). Switching security contexts and maintaining single sign-on can be tricky across technologies. Additionally, there is a wider selection of integration technologies for server integration than for client-to-server integration. Finally, when it comes to smart clients, there are even more reasons for server-side integration, such as the increased complexity of maintaining a uniform look and feel when integrating different architectures.

The Client/Server/Service pattern works well with the various service integration patterns (discussed in chapter 7) and it utilizes the message exchange patterns (see chapter 5). It can also make use of the Identity Provider pattern (see chapter 4) for passing the security context between the existing system and the new services.

Let's take a look at how Client/Server/Service can be used to implement our example scenario.

TECHNOLOGY MAPPING

Implementing the Client/Server/Service pattern doesn't require any specific technology, although employing integration patterns can help. In particular, tools like ESBs (see the Service Bus pattern in chapter 7) can help weave disparate technologies and architectures together. Alternatively, you can integrate services and existing systems by building on simpler concepts like REST.

Let's recap the example scenario. As illustrated in figure 6.9, there's a Silverlight service in a classic three-tier setup, and you need to integrate it with a few new services. This scenario identifies three new services: Customers, Orders, and Sales Reps. Let's look at a few code excerpts and see how you could introduce the Sales Reps service into the existing system.

The first thing you need to change is the UI itself. Listing 6.5 shows a short excerpt from the ViewModel of the sales rep page in an MVVM Silverlight UI implementation.

NOTE In case you're not familiar with Silverlight, Silverlight applications generally use a pattern called Model, View, ViewModel (MVVM). Listing 6.5 is an excerpt from the ViewModel component. See the further reading section for more information about MVVM.

Listing 6.5   Code excerpt with C# UI code calling to the server (via web service)

```
public class SalesRepPageViewModel : INotifyPropertyChanged
{
    private ISalesReps salesRepService;

    private ObservableCollection<Employee> salesReps;
    public ObservableCollection<Employee> salesReps
    {
        get{return salesReps;}
        set
        {
            if (value != salesReps)
            {
                salesReps = value;
                RaisePropertyChanged("salesReps");
            }
        }
    }
    [Inject]
    public PageViewModel(ISalesReps proxy)                    ❶ WCF proxy
    {                                                            to SalesRep
        salesRepService = proxy;                                 web service
        salesReps = salesRepService.GetCurrentShift();   ←❷ Web service call
    }
}
```

You can see that the UI has a WCF proxy that exposes web services for the remote business logic ❶. You can see the call to retrieve the sales reps on the current shift ❷.

The Sales Rep service, in contrast, uses a mix of a RESTful interface for setting and getting state along with AMQP queues to push events out to subscribers, such as the current shift is an event that's pushed whenever a new shift starts. The following listing shows an excerpt of the Ruby code that handles subscription registration and allocates (binds) queues.

Listing 6.6   Code excerpt with a Ruby back end that handles the Sales Reps service

```ruby
class Sub < Sinatra::Base
    def self.init
      @@registered_queues={}
      @@rabbit_wrapper=Bunny.new
      @@rabbit_wrapper.init
      …
    end
    put '/salesrep/subscribers/:name' do |n|
      if  not @@registered_queues.key?(n)
        @@registered_queues[n]=@@rabbit_wrapper.allocate_queue n
      end
      status 200
        # return hyperlinks to subscriptions and subscribers...
    end

    get '/salesrep/subscribers' do
      puts "Subscribers list"
      if not @@registered_queues.empty?
         @@registered_queues.each { |queue| puts queue }
      end
    end

    post '/salesrep/subscriptions/:name'  do |n|

      request.body.rewind
       values=request.body.read.split(",").each do |agent_id|
       @@rabbit_wrapper.subscribe_topic n, Topic+sales_rep_id+".#"
      end
      status 201
      #return ref to the subscription
    end
  end
```

To tie the Silverlight (C#) code with the AMQP messages received, you can use a proxy on the business logic server that looks like a regular WCF service from one side, so that the Silverlight client can interact with it, and that also uses REST and AMQP to communicate with the service. The following listing shows an excerpt from the mediation code, written in C#, that creates subscriptions for changes in sales reps.

Listing 6.7   Excerpt from the Sales Reps service proxy on the back end service

```csharp
public static void Subscribe(string subscriberName, string s)
        {
            var addr = new Uri(HOST_URI, SUBSCRIPTIONS + subscriberName);

            var req = CreateHttpRequest
```

```
➡(addr, new TimeSpan(0, 0, 0, 30), WebRequestMethods.Http.Post);
        AddBody(req,s);
        var response = CallApi(req);

    }
public static void AddSubscriber(String subscriberName)
    {
        var addr = new Uri(HOST_URI, SUBSCRIBER+ subscriberName);

        var req = CreateHttpRequest
➡(addr, new TimeSpan(0, 0, 0, 30), WebRequestMethods.Http.Put);
        var response = CallApi(req);
    }
```

Naturally, there's a whole lot more code involved to provide the actual interface, mediate between the service and the UI, and provide the business value. But the idea is that by utilizing the Client/Server/Service pattern, you can deliver the quality attributes you need and get a working system.

QUALITY ATTRIBUTES

The main drivers for using the Client/Server/Service pattern aren't technical. A pattern like Composite Front End is a technically superior way to provide services with a UI. Nevertheless, when you want to migrate an existing system to SOA and you want to get a faster time to market, or when you don't want to make minimal changes to an existing UI while introducing SOA, the Client/Server/Service pattern provides a good solution.

Table 6.3 provides two quality attribute scenarios for these two motivations.

Table 6.3   Client/Server/Service pattern quality attributes and scenarios

Quality attribute	Concrete attribute	Sample scenario
Usability	Efficiency	When the user needs to learn to use new features, the experience should be streamlined to ensure a minimal learning curve.
Business drivers	Time to market	The time to market of new changes should be less than six months.

An additional reason for utilizing the Client/Server/Service pattern that isn't directly related to quality attributes is the specialization of your development teams. If you have teams that are adept in different technologies, you may want to minimize the interfaces between the teams. Providing a centralized access point by using the Client/Server/Service pattern can help achieve that.

> **NOTE** It's important to remember that the Client/Server/Service pattern is usually a transient pattern. In these cases, it's a stepping-stone that's used while making the move to SOA from an existing system.

6.4   *Summary*

This chapter covered three patterns related to how service consumers can better integrate with services:

- *Reservation*—Deals with providing time-bound guarantees that allow consumers to work and coordinate with several services (while avoiding distributed transactions)
- *Composite Front End*—Describes a pattern for integrating UIs with services in a way that keeps the SOA premise for agile integration and adaptability
- *Client/Server/Service*—Shows a way to deal with the transition period of moving from an *n*-tier architecture to SOA while avoiding large rewrites

Naturally, a lot of other patterns are relevant to service consumers. UIs have patterns like Model-View-Controller (and related ones, like MVVM, MVP, and so on), but most of these patterns aren't directly related to SOA. One notable pattern (or concept) that I recommend exploring is Command Query Responsibility Segregation (see the further reading section).

In chapter 5, we looked at several patterns related to how services and service consumers communicate. In this chapter, we looked at how consumers integrate with services. The next chapter talks about service integration patterns to complete the picture of how you can tie services together to deliver complete solutions.

6.5   *Further reading*

Martin Fowler, "CQRS" (Command Query Responsibility Segregation), http://martinfowler
.com/bliki/CQRS.html.
  CQRS is an interesting pattern that focuses on information flow from the UI to services
  and back to the UI. It can be used as a complementary approach for client-service
  communications.

COMPOSITE FRONT END

OpenSocial, http://docs.opensocial.org/display/OS/Home.
  OpenSocial is an open standard pioneered by Google that can be used to implement the
  Composite Front End pattern with web technologies.

"Prism," *Microsoft Patterns & Practices*, http://compositewpf.codeplex.com/.
  Prism is a desktop implementation of the Composite Front End pattern developed as a reference model by Microsoft.

"Project Silk," *Microsoft Patterns & Practices*, http://silk.codeplex.com/.
  Project Silk is a Microsoft project that implements the Composite Front End pattern for
  (Microsoft-related) web technologies.

CLIENT/SERVER/SERVICE

"Model View ViewModel," *Wikipedia*, http://en.wikipedia.org/wiki/Model_View_ViewModel.
  This is an explanation of the MVVM pattern mentioned in the technology mapping section
  of the Client/Server/Service pattern. MVVM is a common UI pattern for WPF/Silverlight
  applications, as well as for the upcoming WinRT (Windows 8) applications.

Service integration patterns

7

The previous chapter looked at how service consumers integrate with services to achieve their goals. This chapter takes a look at the higher-level integration of services to achieve goals that are beyond those of a single service, such as several services collaborating to create a complete business process or a report based on information from multiple services. As illustrated in figure 7.1, integration patterns involve all of SOA's components.

The following patterns are discussed in this chapter:

- *Service Bus*—Make services interact in a decoupled manner over different protocols, dynamic configurations, and routing
- *Orchestration*—Make business processes agile and adaptable while using services based on the Request/Reply or Request/reaction interaction patterns
- *Aggregated Reporting*—Get efficient business intelligence and summary reports spanning the business when the data is scattered and isolated in autonomous services

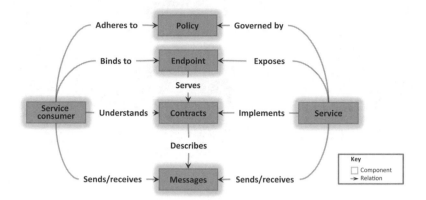

Figure 7.1   This chapter's focus is on service integration—connecting and making services work together to achieve business goals.

The first pattern we'll look at is the Service Bus pattern, which is a communication building block that helps services integrate and collaborate with each other.

7.1   *Service Bus pattern*

Congratulations, you're starting a new enterprise and you think that it would be a good idea to model it using SOA. Since there aren't any legacy systems around, you choose to use your favorite technology, a messaging technology to match (perhaps JMS, REST, or WS) and you are all set. You've got a heterogeneous environment. Each of the services you develop can easily talk to the other services because they're all built using the same technology stack.

Homogeneity may seem a reasonable assumption when you develop everything. But as Peter Deutsch and a few others noticed early in the 1990s, assuming that the "network is homogenous" is one of the fallacies of distributed computing.[1] The eight fallacies are assumptions that newcomers to distributed computing tend to make, which prove wrong in the long run. One of these fallacies is that the "network is homogenous."

The Service Bus pattern can help you mitigate the problem of heterogeneity, but first let's explore the problem.

PROBLEM

You can build your homogenous system, and it will hold for a while, but sooner or later you'll have to integrate with a third-party vendor, or maybe your company will merge with another, or you'll have to integrate a legacy system, or maybe the technology you're using will be updated. In other words, regardless of your starting point, you're likely to find yourself in a situation similar to the one illustrated in figure 7.2.

---

[1]   Peter Deutsch, "The Eight Fallacies of Distributed Computing," https://blogs.oracle.com/jag/resource/ Fallacies.html.

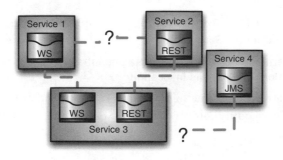

Figure 7.2 In this Tower of Babel, services using different protocols—WS-* web services, REST, and messaging (JMS)—need to be integrated. Some services may have more than one endpoint, like Service 3, but most won't. Even if you choose to have two endpoints for each service, what will you do when a third technology or protocol appears?

You'll have a bunch of services using different technologies, not all of them under your control, and you'll have to integrate them all.

Your initial thought when this happens might be to add another endpoint. Service 3 does just that—it has both a WS-* endpoint and a RESTful one—so both Services 1 and 2 can interact with it. But this doesn't solve Service 3's own problem of consuming Services 1 and 2 because it still needs to support the two protocols. Not to mention the problem of integrating Services 1 and 2.

Different communication protocols, as depicted in figure 7.2, are just one problem you may encounter when trying to integrate services. Other examples include bridging different security protocols, transforming messages (like XML to JSON), or handling big decimals on various platforms and technologies.

Another related problem has to do with message routing, especially if you use the Inversion of Communications pattern (discussed in chapter 5). If you use subscriptions and messages, having each and every service manage these subscriptions involves overhead not unlike supporting multiple protocols in each service.

To solve all these types of problems, you need to find a way to get different services interacting, regardless of protocols, languages, and other differences.

How can you make services interact in a decoupled manner over different protocols, dynamic configurations, and routing?

Having multiple interfaces or endpoints for each service, as mentioned previously, can be a good option if you want to make sure your service is usable from other services, but it isn't a good path to choose for integration. You can't control all the services; if you could, you'd be unlikely to have a problem getting them all to speak the same protocol. In the best case scenario, multiple interfaces will only solve half of the problem—other services could communicate with your services, but you'd still need to figure out and write integration code for services you'd want to consume, and you'd have to do that for each service. That's precisely the point-to-point integration problem SOA is supposed to avoid.

The better solution is to use a central piece of software to perform the integration. One such option is extract, transform, load (ETL) tools, but they're batch-oriented, and SOA messaging needs to be in real time or near real time.

SOLUTION

You need the same concept that ETL provides (externalizing integration logic), but you need it applied to SOA—you need a Service Bus:

✓ Implement the Service Bus pattern and use a unified messaging infrastructure for message transformation, mediation, routing, and invocation.

The crux of the Service Bus pattern is abstracting away the communications between services. To achieve that, the Service Bus pattern combines several enterprise integration design patterns, including:

- *Message bus*—Connects the different services
- *Message router*—Determines what message to send where
- *Channel adaptor*—Converts formats and protocols

As illustrated in figure 7.3, the Service Bus pattern is composed of three main roles:

- *Service registration*—The bus needs to know where to find services so that it can invoke them. It also needs to provide a facility to allow services to configure and expose additional endpoints that other services can consume.
- *Message handling*—The service bus provides capabilities to invoke registered services using the endpoint they've defined on the bus. The bus also routes messages to the registered service. The service bus also transforms protocols or messages to make sure that the targeted service can handle the messages.
- *Publish/subscribe*—The bus provides subscription services (which can be thought of as a type of registration). Then, when services publish messages, the service bus can use routing, transformations, and invocation to call the subscribed services.

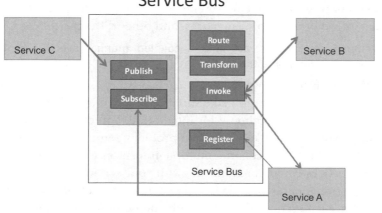

Figure 7.3 In the Service Bus pattern, services can interact with each other using the bus as an intermediary. For instance, Service A registers its endpoint with the service bus and subscribes to messages such as ones published by Service C. Both new messages from Service C and requests from Service B can find their way to Service A, either directly or by being routed and transformed before the actual invocation of Service A.

An architectural diagram of a solution that uses the Service Bus pattern will usually look something like figure 7.4—a few services with a central entity connecting them all.

In reality, there are three deployment options for the Service Bus pattern, as illustrated in figure 7.5: hub and spoke, bus (peer-to-peer), and federated (a mix of the other two).

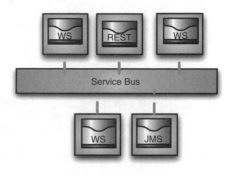

Figure 7.4 Typical representation of a service bus—a single entity with all the services connecting to it

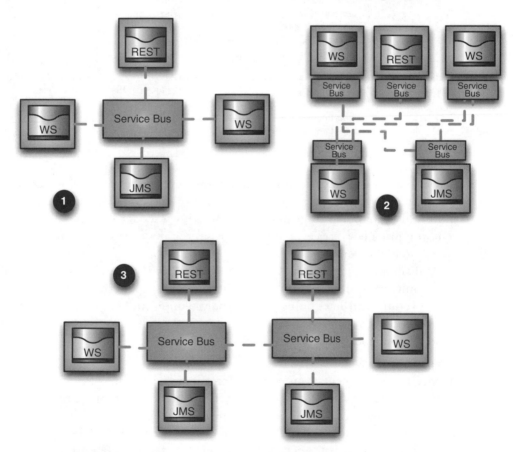

Figure 7.5   Three possible deployment topologies for the Service Bus pattern. First, a hub-and-spoke setup with a central service ❶. Second, a bus where each service has a service bus (agent) nearby, and the service buses themselves connect in a peer-to-peer manner ❷. Third, a federated setup, where each service bus is a central service for a few services, but the buses also coordinate so that services can communicate with services connected to remote buses ❸.

The most common setup is hub and spoke, because it's easier to deploy and maintain. But the other two options do have some merits that you should consider. Naturally, each option also has drawbacks. Table 7.1 contrasts the three deployment options.

Table 7.1   A comparison of service bus deployment architectures

Deployment	Description	Pros	Cons
Hub and spoke (option ❶ in figure 7.5)	There is one centralized server (or two servers for availability) that all the services connect to.	– Easy management – Easy to debug	The server is a bottleneck (all traffic goes through it) Limited scalability (only scale up)
Bus (option ❷ in figure 7.5)	Each service has a bus or a bus agent instance. Services communicate with their local service bus, and the service buses connect with each other so they seem like a single network.	– Scalable – Flexible – High-availability (with store and forward)	Complex topology Relatively hard to configure and debug
Federated (option ❸ in figure 7.5)	Multiple small hubs are interconnected. You can have hub-and-spoke service buses at the departmental level, and connect them together in a federated solution across the enterprise.	– Scalable – Simpler than the bus option	More complex than hub and spoke

The Service Bus pattern adds a level of indirection, so it has an effect on the overall latency of operations. On the other hand, it provides a lot of benefits in terms of flexibility and decoupling. You can choose not to use a service bus if you have a small system with just a few services, but in most cases you'd want a service bus of some sort in your SOA implementation.

Unlike most of the patterns in this book (but like most of the patterns in this chapter), you're most likely to implement the Service Bus pattern by choosing an off-the-shelf product and integrating it into your solution, rather than implementing one yourself (though that sometimes happens, as in the case study in chapter 9). Let's take a look at some of the options available today.

TECHNOLOGY MAPPING

Service Bus implementations come in three main flavors: message buses, pure service buses, and ESBs. Table 7.2 provides a brief explanation of these types.

Looking back at SOA projects I've reviewed or participated in, I'd say the most common implementations of the Service Bus pattern use ESBs. The most likely reason for that is that most vendors have ESBs and ESBs offer more features.

The most common deployment model I've seen for the Service Bus pattern is hub and spoke. That's likely because this is the most common deployment model for ESBs and it's the most cost-effective in terms of licensing prices. (ESBs are usually priced per server, so if you have a lot of them it can get costly.)

Table 7.2 Service Bus implementation types

Implementation type	Details	Sample products
Message bus	Message-oriented middleware or solutions built atop message-oriented middleware can be used as service buses when your services use messaging (see the Inversion of Communications pattern in chapter 5).	– Java–Apache ActiveMQ, MQSeries – .NET–MassTransit – Other—RabbitMQ, OMQ
Service bus	In contrast to message buses, service buses support SOA concepts like contracts. While they can support publish/subscribe, they also support the Request/Reaction and Request/Reply patterns.	– Java—Apache CXF, Apache Camel – .NET—NServiceBus, Windows Azure service bus
ESB	ESBs are service buses that also support additional patterns or capabilities and are packaged as single products.	– Java—Mule ESB, Fuse ESB, WebSphere ESB – .NET—Neuron ESB

Nevertheless, when you evaluate Service Bus implementations, I recommend not dismissing the bus implementation (option 2 in figure 7.5). Having Service Bus instances running on each server goes a long way toward availability and flexibility.

> **DEFINITION** Enterprise Service Buses (ESBs) are products that cover a lot of service infrastructure aspects in addition to implementing the Service Bus pattern. In addition to service mediation and routing, ESBs will usually add capabilities like orchestration (see the Orchestration pattern in section 7.2), provide management capabilities (see the Service Monitor pattern in chapter 4), help deliver some reliability features (such as the Virtual Endpoint pattern in chapter 3), and so on. Additionally, ESBs usually come with a lot of connectors for easy integration with third-party systems and protocols.

As mentioned previously, you're more likely to buy a service bus than to implement one, but you still need to configure it. Sometimes that will be done using visual designers, sometimes with XML, and sometimes in code.

The following listing shows Apache Camel's Scala DSL (domain-specific language) being used to configure a simple route for routing messages according to the tenant ID. (This assumes an earlier route authenticated the request so that the tenant ID is correct.)

Listing 7.1 Routing with Apache Camel

```
package com.rgoarchitects.camelDemo.routes
import org.apache.camel.scala.dsl.builder.RouteBuilder

class SlaRoute extends RouteBuilder {
  when (req=>RouteValidator.checkSlaLevel(req.in("TenantId"))==High)
    --> "http://betterServiceUri"
  otherwise -->   "http://waitInLineUri"
}
```

Another example is shown in the next listing—it shows the XML configuration for declaring a Jersey (REST -JAX-RS JSR-311 implementation) endpoint in Mule ESB. This sample configuration file uses Mule's Jersey connector (www.mulesoft.org/jersey).

Listing 7.2   Declaring a REST endpoint in Mule ESB

```
<?xml version="1.0" encoding="UTF-8"?>
  <mule xmlns="http://www.mulesource.org/schema/mule/core/2.2"
        xmlns:xsi="http://www.w3.org/2001/XMLSchema-instance">
        xmlns:jersey="http://www.mulesource.org/schema/mule/jersey/2.2"
        xmlns:vm="http://www.mulesource.org/schema/mule/vm/2.2"
        xsi:schemaLocation="http://www.springframework.org/schema/bean
        http://www.springframework.org/schema/beans/spring-beans-2.5.xsd
        http://www.mulesource.org/schema/mule/core/2.2
        http://www.mulesource.org/schema/mule/core/2.2/mule.xsd
        http://www.mulesource.org/schema/mule/jersey/2.2
        http://www.mulesource.org/schema/mule/jersey/2.2/mule-jersey.xsd
        http://www.mulesource.org/schema/mule/vm/2.2
        http://www.mulesource.org/schema/mule/vm/2.2/mule-vm.xsd">

     <model name="CategoriesResource">
          <service name="categoriesResource">
          <inbound>
               <inbound-endpoint address=
➥"jersey:http://localhost:8991/" synchronous="true"/>
          </inbound>
    <component class="com.rgoarchitects.sample.Categories"/>
               </service>
      </model>
   </mule>
```

The interesting lines in this listing start with the `service` tag, where you configure an inbound endpoint and tell Mule to call the class (`com.rgoarchitects.sample` `.Categories`). The result of this configuration is that the URL http://localhost:8991/ will go to a categories REST API defined in the class. Note that once you have the endpoint set up, you'd probably wrap that with a route that will perform authentication and authorization and expose it to the outside world.

Figure 7.6 shows a screenshot of NServiceBus (a .NET service bus implementation) modeling tools for Visual Studio that can be used to design publishers, subscribers, and messages for service-to-service interactions.

To summarize, there are many Service Bus pattern implementations out there, and they come in all shapes and sizes. Depending on your technology stack and needs, you can likely find a solution that will work for you.

QUALITY ATTRIBUTES

The main reason to use the Service Bus pattern is the need for loose coupling of service interactions. The Service Bus pattern provides flexibility, openness, and contributes toward the adaptability of SOA implementations.

Table 7.3 presents a few quality attribute scenarios.

Another integration pattern that's geared toward flexibility is the Orchestration pattern. Let's explore that next.

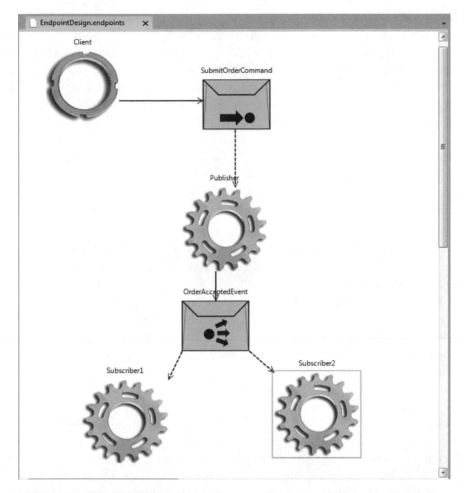

Figure 7.6 Designing message flows, subscribers, and publishers with NServiceBus tools for Visual Studio. The designer shows two messages—a submit order command and an order accepted event as well as a publisher service with two subscribing services.

Table 7.3 Service Bus pattern quality attributes and scenarios

Quality attribute	Concrete attribute	Sample scenario
Availability	Effort to change—deployment	Under normal conditions, adding a server for scaling purposes should take no longer than four hours (including installation, and configuration).
Changeability	Replace component (vendors)	During development, replacing a credit card processing gateway should take one week or less.
Flexibility	Interfaces	During development, adding a REST API to the system should be supported.
Interoperability	Integration	During operations, integrating a new subsystem should take less than two calendar months.

7.2   *Orchestration pattern*

Service Bus, the pattern presented in the previous section, enables services to communicate in a decoupled manner. That's a good start—it lowers the technical barriers to getting services to talk to each other. The next challenge is the business processes.

What's a business process? As you know, services partition enterprise capabilities into functional areas, but for the business to accomplish anything meaningful, services need to work together. Even a simple shopping cart scenario needs information from the customer, orders, invoices, inventory, and so on. The sequence of related messages between services required to achieve a business goal is a business process.

The Orchestration pattern provides a way to build business processes in a flexible way, but first things first. Let's take a look at the problem that would make us want something like this.

PROBLEM

One project I worked on was an e-commerce site for produce (fresh vegetables, fruit, and dairy products). Once the produce was ordered, it was picked up from participating farmers and grocers.

Figure 7.7 shows the basic business flow once a shopping cart is submitted. The user fills a cart from multiple shops and submits the cart, which creates an order. The order is then billed, and a delivery person goes from grocer to grocer to pick up the goods and fulfill the order (reporting back to the system about the items that were delivered).

This looks simple and clean, so let's say you develop that. You now have a Cart service that calls the Orders service, which does its thing and then calls Billing.

If you do that in real life, you'll soon discover that the process is wrong. True, when you order a carton of milk, the preceding process works. But you're dealing with produce here, so when you order a kilo of tomatoes, you might actually get 0.96 kilos or 1.051 kilos. Also, you're dealing with small businesses here, so they might be out of a certain product at the time of pickup. That means you need a new process: after registering the order you secure the order amount with the credit card company, and during fulfillment you update the order and set the final billing. This means you'd need to change your process so that orders can be updated from Fulfillment and not just from the Cart. You'd also need Billing to be called twice (once to secure payment and once to process the billing).

Now let's consider what will happen when you enter another market and find out that the fulfillment works in some other way. Not to mention, sales processes where you want to add promotions, coupons, and other options.

Business processes are bound to change, either because you gain a better understanding of the business or because business requirements change (perhaps a new

Figure 7.7   A basic e-commerce flow—the user fills a shopping cart and places the order. The user is then billed and the order is sent to fulfillment.

competitor enters the market). You can't go on hand-wiring services to other services every time that happens—you need a way to make the business processes more flexible.

How can you make business processes agile and adaptable while using services based on the Request/Reply or Request/Reaction interaction patterns?

Obviously, hardcoding the interaction pathways as described previously won't get you very far. We looked at just one business process, and a solution would usually have quite a few of those, and they'd be changing. Hardcoding would involve too much work for several reasons:

- You'd have to create new versions of a service just to change the flow.
- The business process would be scattered about and hard to isolate.
- The services would be hard to change when the need arises.

Section 7.1 introduced the Service Bus pattern, which, among other things, provides message routing, and you might be thinking you could use the flexibility it introduces to help solve this problem. Routing at the Service Bus level will help with most of this problem, particularly externalizing the routing logic and making it easy to change. In reality, Service Bus implementations lack the sophistication needed to implement complex business processes. They're more suited to mediating between services than controlling their interactions. Not to mention situations where the complete process includes human workflow (steps that require human interactions).

In many cases, especially when the business processes are simple, the Inversion of Communications pattern (chapter 5) can be enough. The problem with events is that they limit the visibility of the complete business process, making it hard to understand what's happening and why. (See the sidebar on orchestration vs. choreography in the next section for some further discussion.)

To get all the properties we want, you need something different—you need Orchestration.

SOLUTION

Implement the Orchestration pattern to externalize business processes from the services and allow these processes to be governed, controlled, and changed dynamically.

The Orchestration pattern, illustrated in figure 7.8, is relatively simple—in essence, it's about adding a workflow engine that's external to the services. You model the different business processes as flows of service interactions, and let the engine execute, monitor, and manage them to carry out the process.

The main component is the workflow engine. It manages workflows, providing users with the means (usually visual) to define, edit, and delete workflows. The workflow engine also hosts workflow instances and monitors their progress.

Each process is instantiated as a workflow instance that can schedule and manage the process itself. The workflow instance is capable of forking (sending requests in parallel), joining (waiting for replies or reactions from multiple services), and handling failures. A workflow can be a short-lived process, but in most cases it will be a longer running process.

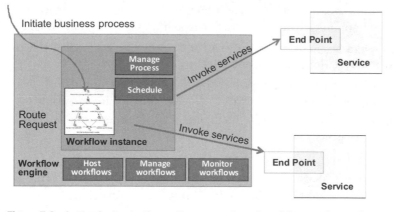

Figure 7.8   In the Orchestration pattern, an external workflow engine activates a sequence (simple or compound) of services to provide a complete business service.

We've already covered a pattern for long-running processes—the Saga pattern (chapter 5). In a sense, the Orchestration pattern is a particular implementation of the Saga pattern where the coordinator is external to all the participants. The Saga pattern is more generic, as it can also be implemented without a central component that knows what steps need be done and when to complete the business process. This has the advantage of keeping services more autonomous, with emergent and flexible processes, but the cost is a lack of clarity as to what constitutes a business process and resulting difficulties in monitoring and understanding the current state of those business processes.

Note that most workflow engine implementations don't hold the workflow instance live as it's running but rather save its state between calls and retrieve it when a new message arrives (a process called *dehydration* and *hydration*).

Orchestration vs. choreography

The problem statement for the Orchestration pattern specifically mentions using the Request/Reply and Request/Reaction communication patterns, which begs the question, "Why not use publish/subscribe or event-based communications (such as the Inversion of Communications pattern in chapter 5) with the Orchestration pattern? It turns out that Orchestration isn't a good fit in this situation.

Orchestration is a metaphor for a conductor telling each service what to do. Events lend themselves to another arts-related metaphor—choreography: each service plays its part, independently publishing events that occur within it and subscribing to events it needs to perform its role. The resulting "dances" are the different business processes of the organization.

Choreography isn't described as a pattern in this book because it's more an emergent property of using events than a deliberate pattern. Choreography provides even greater flexibility than the Orchestration pattern does, and it allows for emergent business processes and behaviors not planned in advance.

> On the downside, choreography lacks the explicitness of business processes that the Orchestration pattern provides. To compensate for that and ensure that the system will be correct, services should be developed to be as autonomous as possible (see the Active Service pattern in chapter 2) to keep the problem each solves as localized as possible. Also, it's recommended that you externalize the events into an event catalog to allow for both reuse and system-wide governance (see the further reading section for an article I wrote on event ownership).
>
> Notations like BPMN 2.0 (Business Process Model and Notation) support the design of choreographies in addition to workflows.

Figure 7.9 shows the revised flow of order handling in the produce e-commerce solution described in the problem description. As mentioned previously, the process needs more coordination between the different services than the original flow in figure 7.7 showed.

You can study the figure for the details of the flow, but the more important point here is that it's modeled as a workflow with several decision points that can alter the process. You can abort the whole ordering process depending on your ability to secure the funds for the order ❶. Changing the workflow will change the business process

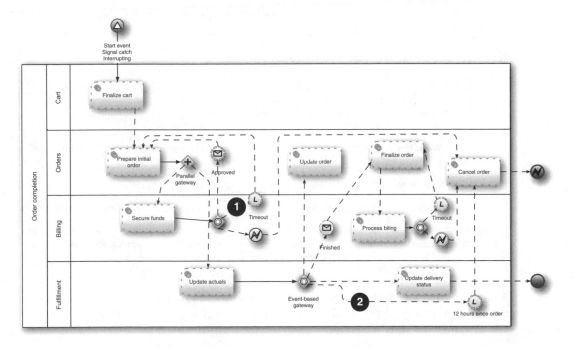

Figure 7.9 An updated workflow for processing produce orders. This flow is much more complex than the initial naïve version. When initializing the order, you need to secure the maximum order value with an external credit card processing company, and only when the order is finalized and you know the exact amounts do you calculate and bill the actual value.

and, depending on the capabilities of the services involved, it may not require any code changes. A timeout on delivery causes the whole process to be aborted ❷; this is a new requirement.

Used properly, the Orchestration pattern can add a lot of flexibility to SOA as well as keep you from losing sight of the forest for the trees—the many services you may have in your system. The main risk you run when using the Orchestration pattern is to overuse it, which can result in SOA antipatterns like Nanoservices (discussed in chapter 8). To help avoid this problem, you can partition the workflows between the external flow (Orchestration) and internal flows (the Workflodize pattern in chapter 2).

Orchestration also works well with the Service Bus pattern discussed in the previous section.

TECHNOLOGY MAPPING

Like the Service Bus pattern, you're most likely to implement the Orchestration pattern by choosing an off-the-shelf implementation rather than creating one from scratch. Orchestration is implemented by two classes of tools: ESB engines that also provide some orchestration capabilities, and business process management (BPM) systems that are built for handling orchestration and workflows.

The choice of one type of tool over the other depends on the complexity of your processes, the performance you need, and other factors. Table 7.4 provides some general guidelines for these two classes of tools (specific products can be more versatile than the table may indicate).

Table 7.4 ESB versus BPM tools as orchestration engines

	ESB	BPM
Main purpose	Integration and virtualization of services	Running and monitoring business processes
Workflow	Basic workflows	Extensive support including loops and rules
Performance	Built for high message flows	Built for complex processes
Human workflow	Not supported	Supported by some implementations
Saga support (long-running interactions)	Suitable for supporting sagas in event-based systems by providing store and forward services	Suitable for supporting sagas by keeping track of and following the state of long-running interactions

Note that you can combine both product types by having the ESB invoke processes that are managed by the BPM, as well as having the ESB virtualize the endpoints of the services used in the BPM processes.

Another option is to use more basic workflow engines and build your own service orchestration on top. In most cases that's not the best option, because it wastes a lot of effort. There are open source options (like jBPM) available at no cost.

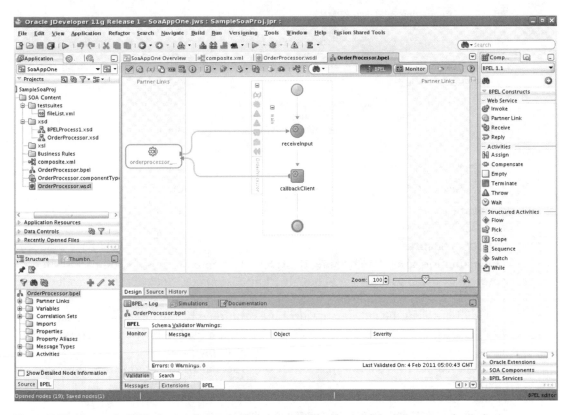

Figure 7.10   A sample BPEL diagram in Oracle JDeveloper. Notice the detail level here on a simple flow as compared to the high-level view in the BPMN diagram in figure 7.9.

There are two main notations used by the various workflow and BPM tools:

- Business Process Execution Language (BPEL)
- Business Process Model and Notation (BPMN)

An example of a BPMN diagram was shown in figure 7.9. BPEL is a more technical, developer-oriented approach to describing interactions. Figure 7.10 shows a simple BPEL process on a commercial designer (Oracle JDeveloper).

Both BPMN and BPEL are common notations. Some tools use one or the other and some tools support both. Table 7.5 provides a short comparison of the two formats.

When using tools that support both notations, you can combine the notations so that BPMN is used by business analysts to describe the process at high level, and these processes are then expanded by more technical people using BPEL.

Regardless of the specifics of the technology used, all Orchestration implementations externalize the process from the services and provide flexibility to a SOA. There are few other quality attributes that Orchestration promotes, and we'll examine them in the next section.

Table 7.5   Comparing BPEL and BPMN

	BPEL 2.0	BPMN 2.0
Notation characteristics	Developer oriented	Business oriented—more abstract
Strengths	– Includes low-level concepts like compensation, fault handling, and so on – Built for integration with WS-* standards	– Easy to model complex interactions (higher level of abstraction) – Greater readability
Human workflow	Not supported	Supported
Standard	WS-BPEL by OASIS	Visual notation defined by OMG
REST support	No—requires WSDL 1.1 contracts	Possible

QUALITY ATTRIBUTES

The main motivation for choosing the Orchestration pattern is flexibility, allowing the business to respond quickly to changing business needs, both at the macro level and at the practical technical level.

Flexibility isn't the only quality attribute promoted by the Orchestration pattern. It also permits increased runtime governance (by monitoring flows in progress), as well as increasing the chances to reuse services in multiple processes.

Table 7.6 identifies a few quality attributes scenarios to demonstrate these quality attributes.

Table 7.6   Orchestration pattern quality attributes and scenarios

Quality attribute	Concrete attribute	Sample scenario
Manageability	Understanding the system's health	Under error conditions, an administrator will be able to understand the problem and performance bottlenecks of different business flows.
Changeability	Replacing components (vendors)	During development, replacing a credit card processing gateway should take one week or less.
Flexibility	Business flows	During development and operations, adding timeouts to all ordering processes will take less than one week.
Flexibility	Composability	During development, a developer will be able to find and reuse services in multiple business processes.

The next pattern also deals with integration—it takes a look at how you can get an integrated view of the data needed for reporting, despite SOA encouraging each service to hold its own data internally.

7.3 Aggregated Reporting pattern

Getting an SOA system right is hard, not so much because of the technical problems but because it's hard to understand a business and figure out how to effectively partition it into services. Let's assume that you somehow have managed that and have your business logic neatly divided into services. You then develop your business logic and business processes, and you're almost done. All that's left is to produce a few reports.

Well, maybe more than a few. Perhaps dozens and dozens of reports. Assuming you did a good job of partitioning your business into services, many of these reports will fall within the boundaries of your services. But you'll need the Aggregated Reporting pattern to deal with the rest of the reports—those that require data from several services.

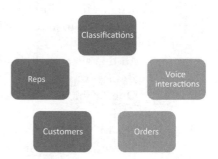

Figure 7.11 Services in a call center system. Customers make orders and then call a call center to complain and resolve problems. The customer's interactions with the call center representatives are recorded and analyzed.

PROBLEM

Let's try to visualize the problem. One project I worked on involved an analytics platform for call centers. The real-life system had a lot of services, but to illustrate this problem we'll examine just five of them.

These are the five services in figure 7.11:

- *Voice Interactions*—Stores all the past and current calls customers have made to the call center as well as data relating to calls, such as call transcripts (after speech-to-text processing), emotions detected, phone numbers, and so on.
- *Customer*—Provides access to all the data about a customer. Most of this data is imported from other systems, such as the CRM system. The Customer service also does identity resolution (for example, given a cell number, it can find the user ID).
- *Reps*—Provides access to information about the call center representatives. Data comes here from the operational system that the sales reps use when they interact with customers.
- *Orders*—Provides access to information about customer's orders.
- *Classifications*—Classifies calls according to business-driven criteria, such as calls by VIP customers that canceled their service. Classifications occur in real time (on incoming calls). It's task-driven, so any knowledge it has about customers or interactions is transient; it only stores the category definitions.

Management wants to know if there are any correlations between sales reps' performance and the loss of business in general and the loss of VIP customers specifically.

All the information you need is in the system. The Voice Interactions service contains all the calls' classifications as well as the customer and sales rep IDs—you can find out which representatives handled which customers from there. The Customer service has the information about which customers are VIPs and which aren't, plus it will allow you to access orders to find out how much business was generated by each customer.

All that's left to do is to build the SQL query that takes all this data and produces the desired report, right? Unfortunately, there are two problems with this approach.

One problem is the assumption that all services use an RDBMS as persistent storage. A few years ago, that might have been a reasonable assumption, but today with the rise of NoSQL databases, that may not be the case.

The other, more important, problem with the "use SQL to generate the report" approach is that it introduces a lot of coupling between the different services. By using a single SQL query to solve the problem, you need to know and understand the internal structures of each service. You constructed services with API-level integration to avoid this very problem.

The question, then, is how to generate reports in a way that doesn't violate SOA principles on the one hand, and that produces the reports efficiently on the other.

How can you get efficient business intelligence and summary reports spanning the business, when the data is scattered and isolated in autonomous services?

One possible solution would be to create the report at the consuming end (in the UI). The consumer would call each service to get its part of the data, and perform all the grouping, crosscuts, and so on in the UI. This solution is rarely a good idea. It puts the burden of understanding the data and of optimizing the query on the shoulders of each report consumer. In this case, the consumer would first need to go to the Customer service to find out which of them are VIPs and then go to get their total orders, but how would you connect that data to each rep's performance? Which order of performing these queries would run faster—should you call Customers or Reps first? And that's just a single report.

Another option is one we've already discussed—going straight to the data. For example, create an SQL query that will go into all the services' databases, join the data, and get all the relevant bits. You've seen why that's not a good idea.

Maybe the answer is "aggregation services," also known as "entity aggregation." This is a notion that appeared in the early days of SOA, and the idea is that when the granularity is such that the view of an entity is spread over multiple services (meaning the granularity was wrong), you can create a single service that creates a holistic view of that entity. The same idea can be applied to creating an aggregated entity for the purpose of each report type, and you can copy over some data from the relevant services (so you won't have the problem mentioned for the consumer-side reports). It turns out that aggregation services is a bad idea for its original purpose, and it isn't a great idea here either. Who would be the master of the data? Does each entity aggregate have its own copy of the data? Is the data federated from each service? What do you do when data changes? If you can make it work, how many of these entity aggregates will you need to properly provide reporting capabilities?

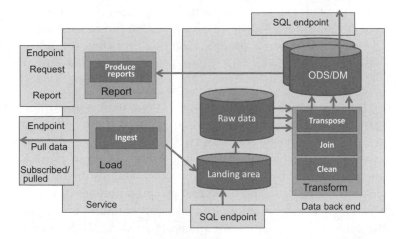

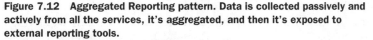

**Figure 7.12   Aggregated Reporting pattern. Data is collected passively and
actively from all the services, it's aggregated, and then it's exposed to
external reporting tools.**

The answer is that you can have one aggregated service, and to make it work it needs
to follow specific guidelines. I call this the Aggregated Reporting pattern.

SOLUTION

✓ Use the Aggregated Reporting pattern to create a service that gathers immutable
copies of data from multiple services for reporting purposes.

Before we delve into the differences between "aggregated reporting" and "entity
aggregation" and why aggregated reporting is a good idea, let's first look at exactly
what this pattern is. Unsurprisingly, the Aggregated Reporting pattern is about aggre-
gating data from the services and providing reporting facilities above the data to make
it useful.

As illustrated in figure 7.12, the pattern consists of two main components: a service
and a data back end.

The service component is the SOA endpoint of the Aggregated Reporting pattern,
and by "SOA," I mean it utilizes standard SOA technologies like web services or messaging. The service exposes two types of endpoints:

- An output endpoint that provides reports or queries that other services and service consumers can use
- An input endpoint that collects data from other services, either by subscribing
  to their events or by allowing other services to push data

The second component, the data back end, is the core component of the Aggregated
Reporting pattern. This component has three data stores:

- A landing area where data from external interfaces is temporarily stored. This is
  done mainly for security purposes and to isolate the SQL input endpoint from
  the raw data.

- A raw data store. This can be a temporary storage area to coordinate data that arrives asynchronously or a long-term data store that can be used as the basis for advanced analytics (answering questions you don't yet know you need to ask).
- A reporting data store where data is kept in a reporting friendly structure— most likely an RDBMS.

The main active functionality of the data back end component is the Transformation service (which you can think of as an implementation of the Active Service pattern discussed in chapter 2). The Transformation service's responsibility is to rearrange all the incoming data in a way that's useful for reporting. An Aggregated Reporting implementation will have extensive transformation components that will sift through the raw data, clean it, aggregate it, and build useful representations of it.

The data back end also has two endpoints: an input endpoint for importing data and a reporting endpoint that allows for querying of data. These endpoints are unique, because they use SQL and not technologies usually associated with service orientation. The main reason for this is that standard tools for both importing data and for business intelligence and reporting over data have been built on top of SQL for decades, and forcing them to use other technologies is usually not practical (in terms of effort versus benefit). You have to treat these endpoints as bona fide SOA endpoints, isolating them from internal data structures, providing contracts, and so on. We'll discuss this in more depth shortly.

There are a lot of components that play together here, so let's take a look at the pattern from another perspective. Figure 7.13 illustrates how data can flow into the Aggregated Reporting implementation.

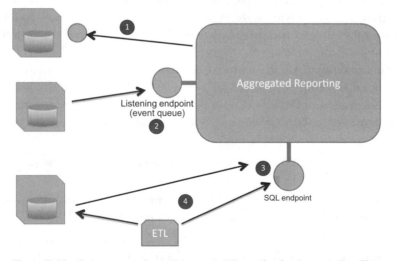

Figure 7.13 Data sources for an Aggregated Reporting implementation. The illustration shows four ways you can get data into an Aggregated Reporting implementation: actively going to the data ❶, listening to events ❷, SQL push by other services ❸, and SQL push by ETL tools ❹.

Essentially there are four ways to get data into an Aggregated Reporting implementation:

- *Actively calling other services*—The Aggregated Reporting implementation can use other services' contracts to sample them for new data. This is probably the worst way to go about getting data because the Aggregated Reporting implementation has to know about all the other services to be able to do that. Also, all the services' contracts should be expressive enough to export all the needed data.

- *Passively getting data from services*—There are two subtypes here. First, services can call the Aggregated Reporting server with data they wish to expose to reports, such as by submitting a CSV file with exported data to the Aggregated Reporting service API. The second variant is to have the Aggregated Reporting implementation subscribe to events published by other services.

- *Service SQL push*—Where services export a view of internal data, the services can establish a connection to the Aggregated Reporting landing area, create their own tables, and save data for reporting there.

- *ETL SQL push*—This is similar to the preceding option, but the responsibility of getting data from services and getting it to the Aggregated Reporting implementation is on an external tool. This isn't recommended because the ETL tool is likely to violate the services' autonomy to get the data. From the Aggregated Reporting side, though, it's still OK because the ETL tool doesn't know the internal implementation or representation of data within the service.

Once you have the data in, what happens next? Figure 7.14 illustrates the process that the data goes through once it arrives at the Aggregated Reporting service. In essence, what happens now is the transform and load process.

The first step is getting the data into the Aggregated Reporting implementation. It's recommended that the SQL endpoint use a landing area that's separate from the raw data store to provide a security buffer.

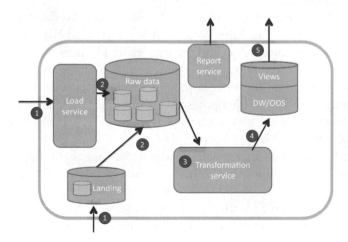

Figure 7.14   Data processing within the Aggregated Reporting pattern. First you accept the data from external sources ❶. Then you save it to a raw data store ❷, process it and prepare it for reporting ❸. The data is then saved into a data mart or an ODS ❹ and exposed ❺ via a reporting interface or views or both.

The next step is to get the data into the raw data store. There are two options here. Either you keep the files the way they arrived at the landing zone, or you can aggregate data from multiple files into entities. Both options hold data before transformation, but the second option makes the next step easier (at the cost of more complication in the raw data store)

The next step is to process, cleanse, aggregate, and prepare the data for reporting, creating star schemas, building cubes, and so on.

The fourth step is to store the data in a form ready for reporting. You can make a choice between longer-term and shorter-term solutions. If you opt for a shorter-term solution, you can make the reporting data store an operational data store (ODS)—a database that's structured like a data mart (containing denormalized data) but with short retention. The second option is to create a data mart for reporting. It's more common to store the raw data for the long term when choosing to use a data mart for reporting.

The last step is to expose the reports. This is done in two ways:

- Via a service interface for queries and predefined reports
- Via SQL endpoints that expose views that serve as a contracts and edge components to isolate the internal data mart structure from consumers

You should now have a better understanding of what Aggregated Reporting is, but there are still a few open questions we need to address:

- How is aggregated reporting SOA-friendly?
- How does aggregated reporting differ from direct access to each service's internal database?
- How is aggregated reporting different from entity aggregation?
- What are the drawbacks of using aggregated reporting?

Let's take these questions one at a time.

How is aggregated reporting SOA-friendly?
How can an Aggregated Reporting implementation get data from several, if not all, of the services and not violate SOA principles? What makes Aggregated Reporting a service is that the data it holds is immutable, and the Aggregated Reporting service isn't the owner of changes in the data. It holds a representation of unchanging data for use in its reporting service it provides. In this regard, it's recommended that data kept by an Aggregated Reporting service be idempotent (versioned) so that the relations it expresses will always be true (for the versions involved). In any event, the source of the "truths" is the original services whose data is mirrored.

On the structural level, the Aggregated Reporting service is SOA-compatible because it externalizes its capabilities via well-defined interfaces. The incoming SQL endpoint needs to be configurable via the regular service API—a service should contact the service API to request an allocation of space, and it will then be guaranteed connection credentials to its own landing area. The implementation specifics can vary, but the idea that the interaction with the incoming SQL endpoint is to be controlled via a contract should hold.

As for the output SQL endpoint, the separation of internal data structures and the notion of a contract should be implemented by a layer of views. The views represent the external agreement, and the internal implementation doesn't have to match and can vary from the external one.

How does aggregated reporting differ from direct access to each service's internal database?
First, as already mentioned, the internal structure of a service might not be an RDBMS.

Second, exposing SQL at each and every service increases the risk that this won't be done correctly—either by exposing internal data structures or mangling security, and so on.

The real benefit of using the Aggregated Reporting pattern (instead of directly accessing each service's internal database) is that the Aggregated Reporting service's internal structure is built for reporting. It will likely provide much better performance than accessing even a single service directly, because the service's internal data stores are transaction-oriented (OLTP) and not reporting-oriented. That's even more true for reports that need data from multiple services.

How is aggregated reporting different from entity aggregation?
They both have the word *aggregation* in their names, but the similarity ends there. The Aggregated Reporting pattern means building a service that keeps data ownership with the different services. It isn't focused on a single entity, it's built on immutable data, and it's geared only toward reporting. Entity aggregation has none of these traits, as was discussed in the problem section.

What are the drawbacks of using Aggregated Reporting?
I personally believe Aggregated Reporting is the best way to handle reporting in SOA. But like every design pattern, it comes with its own tradeoffs.

The main tradeoffs here are the relative complexity of the solution (as compared to reporting on the service consumer side and reaching out for data from other services as needed for each report). These tradeoffs translate to longer time to market, increased latency in terms of freshness of data (data has to be processed before it's available), and increased storage costs resulting from duplication of data.

The benefits, as I've already mentioned, are high performance of reports, a cohesive view of the data, the separation of responsibilities, and retaining SOA's flexibility benefits. Additional non-SOA benefits of the Aggregated Reporting pattern include the promotion of concepts such as command-query responsibility segregation (CQRS) and master data management (MDM); resources on both are pointed out in the further reading section.

TECHNOLOGY MAPPING
You've seen the structure of the Aggregated Reporting pattern in the previous section, and you've seen that it has a lot of functionality. That means there are plenty of ways to implement it and plenty of technologies that can play the various parts.

As usual, the point of this technology mapping section isn't to provide an exhaustive list of implementation option but rather to provide a taste of what's available. One of the interesting options, which has grown in popularity in recent years, is to implement Aggregated Reporting as a big data store. (Big data, as it relates to SOA, is discussed in chapter 10.)

Recent systems I worked on used Hadoop and a conventional data mart together as the Aggregated Reporting implementation. The Hadoop system was used as a data warehouse for the long term, never deleting any of the historic data coming from all the services. The data from the services was saved in almost raw form in Hadoop's distributed filesystem (HDFS) as it arrived, and it was processed at later intervals to provide data useful for reporting. An ETL process took recent months' data and exported it to a star schema in a conventional data mart (Oracle).

An interesting scenario in this regard is the case where the data exported to the data mart is summary data and not the detailed data. Returning to the example from the beginning of this chapter, you could have the sales reps' monthly performance data in the data mart and their call-by-call performance data remaining in the data warehouse. The benefit of this approach is that the data load on the data mart is reduced, which provides for better performance and reduced costs. (Hadoop uses commodity hardware and is a lot cheaper than traditional databases.)

Figure 7.15 illustrates how a drill-through from data mart data to Hadoop data can occur.

The first step in figure 7.15 occurs when the summary data is calculated ❶. The map/reduce job that calculates the summary and exports the data to the data mart also saves the source data for each calculation ❷ in HBase (HBase is a Hadoop-based NoSQL solution that supports high-throughput random read/write).

When a report is processed, it runs against the data mart ❸, ❹, ❺.

When a user asks to see how the summary data was calculated ❻, the reporting tool makes a REST call ❼ to a service (which would be part of the Aggregated Reporting

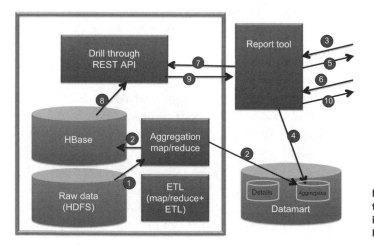

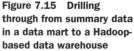

Figure 7.15   Drilling through from summary data in a data mart to a Hadoop-based data warehouse

implementation) that gets the details from HBase ❽ and provides it ❾ to the reporting tool, which in turn notifies the user ❿.

Note that the Aggregated Reporting implementation includes both the components on the Hadoop side as well as the data mart (which is the SQL endpoint for reporting). Also, the diagram doesn't include all the components of the solution (such as the landing zone).

The scenario in figure 7.15 is one possible implementation. In another, smaller project, we used an operational data store to hold the latest data in a start schema without retaining a long-term historic view of the data. The details change, but the architectural principles stay the same.

The last thing to discuss about the Aggregated Reporting pattern is quality attributes, where things are a little different from other patterns in this book.

QUALITY ATTRIBUTES

The Aggregated Reporting pattern is probably the only architectural pattern in this book whose main drivers are functional requirements rather than architectural qualities. The reason the Aggregated Reporting pattern is still architectural is that its implications are solution-wide (or system-wide) and not local. As mentioned previously, the Aggregated Reporting pattern provides a functional solution that still retains SOA's architectural benefits, and that's its strength.

> **NOTE** The Aggregated Reporting pattern does promote desirable quality attributes like flexibility and maintainability, but it isn't driven by them. Its motivation is functional, not nonfunctional.

7.4   Summary

This chapter's goal was to highlight the main integration patterns that enable services to work together and become a system, rather than a bunch of services or an unmaintainable knot (see the Knot antipattern in the next chapter).

The chapter covered the following patterns:

- *Service Bus*—Allows services to connect in a loosely coupled manner.
- *Orchestration*—Describes how to externalize business process flows from services to a centralized components. Orchestration promotes flexibility and governance.
- *Aggregated Reporting*—Provides an SOA-friendly way to solve the reporting conundrum.

That's the end of part 1 of this book. The next part takes a look at some aspects of implementing SOA in the real world. The next chapter will take a look at some of the common pitfalls, or antipatterns, that can ruin a fledgling SOA implementation at the start.

7.5   *Further reading*

SERVICE BUS

Gregor Hohpe and Bobby Woolf, "Message Bus," *Enterprise Integration Patterns*,
www.eaipatterns.com/MessageBus.html.

> This is a great book on communications patterns in general. I specifically suggest reading about the Message Bus pattern, which is the base pattern for the Service Bus pattern.

ORCHESTRATION

Arnon Rotem-Gal-Oz, "SOA—Contracts, Events and Ownership", *Cirrus Minor* (blog), http://
arnon.me/2010/09/soa-contracts-events-ownership/.

> This article discusses which party, the service consumer or the service, should own the messages and event contracts.

AGGREGATED REPORTING

Martin Fowler, "CQRS" (Command Query Responsibility Segregation), http://martinfowler
.com/bliki/CQRS.html.

> Martin Fowler's site provides a good explanation of the CQRS concept.
>
> CQRS is a complimentary approach for aggregated reporting, which, as its name implies, suggests that data for commands (such as updates) is sent to one source, whereas the data for queries arrives from a different source. Usually the context for CQRS should be within services, but if you implement the Aggregated Reporting pattern, you can use it as the source for queries in a CQRS system and even provide wider reporting capabilities (with data originating from multiple services.

"Master data management," *Wikipedia*, http://en.wikipedia.org/wiki/Master_data
_management.

> Master data management (MDM) is an important approach for managing multiple facets of entities. MDM can be used as a complementary approach for the Aggregated Reporting pattern.

Part 2

SOA in the real world

In part 1 we looked at patterns for solving SOA challenges. Patterns are a powerful medium for explaining solutions, at least in part because the discussion of each problem is focused and isolated. This is also a weakness, because the real world is rarely like that. Part 2 of this book takes a look at what happens in different aspects of SOA when you try to implement services and apply patterns.

Chapter 8 talks about antipatterns you may encounter when you implement a service. Like patterns, antipatterns discuss problems in context, with the difference being that antipatterns look at common mistakes and how to solve them, as opposed to patterns, which look at solutions.

Chapter 9 offers a case study and demonstrates how patterns can be used together to build a complete solution.

Chapter 10 takes a look at what other technologies mean for SOA. Specifically, it examines the relationships between SOA and REST, the cloud, and big data.

Service antipatterns

8

We've spent several chapters looking at SOA patterns. Antipatterns are the other side of the equation—instead of contexts and solutions, this chapter discusses common pitfalls you're likely to stumble upon and how to avoid or refactor them. This complementary view is important, because it's easy to make these mistakes when you're starting out with SOA, even if you follow guidance such as the patterns we've already looked at.

Antipatterns, like patterns, are about contextual wisdom. A discussion of antipatterns needs to talk both about when a behavior is a problem and when that behavior might be acceptable. The following sections will introduce each antipattern and then focus on the following topics:

- *Consequences*—Why the antipattern is a problem.
- *Causes*—Why the antipattern occurs.
- *Refactoring*—How you can change the design to avoid the problems the antipattern causes.

- *Known exceptions*—When using the antipattern might be acceptable.

The following antipatterns are discussed in this chapter:

- *Knot*—Where the services are tightly coupled by hardcoded point-to-point integration and context-specific interfaces
- *Nanoservice*—Where a service is too fine-grained, and its overhead (communications, maintenance, and so on) outweighs its utility
- *Transactional Integration*—Where transactions extend across services boundaries (instead of being isolated inside services)
- *Same Old Way*—Where you dress whatever you did before in SOA clothing

The first antipattern we'll take a look at is the Knot. It's an antipattern of SOA naiveté, but you must understand its root causes so that you don't repeat it, even as an SOA veteran.

8.1   *Knot antipattern*

Everything starts so well. You embark on a new SOA initiative, and the whole team feels as if it's pure green field development. The first service is designed—it's got all sorts of bells and whistles, and it's even using XML, so it must be good. Then you design the second service, and the two services talk to each other. Then comes a third service, and it has to talk to the other two. The fourth service only talks to a couple of the previous ones. The twelfth talks to nine of the others, and the fourteenth has to contact them all—yep, your services are tangling up together in an inflexible, rigid knot.

This scenario might sound wacky and improbable—why would anyone in their right mind do something like that? Let's take another look, with a concrete example this time, and see how the road to hell is paved with good intentions.

Figure 8.1 shows a vanilla ordering scenario. An Ordering service sends the order details to an Inventory service, where the items are identified in inventory and marked for delivery. Then the details are sent to a Delivery service, which talks to external shipping companies.

You'll see that when an item is missing from the inventory, you'll probably have to talk to external suppliers, order the missing items, and wait for their arrival, so the whole process isn't necessarily immediate. Because the process takes time, it seems reasonable to cancel the process if an order is canceled.

This means there are two options (see figure 8.2): either the Ordering service will ask the two other services to cancel processing related to the order, or the two services

Figure 8.1   An Ordering service sends the order to an Inventory service. When the goods are provisioned, the details pass to a Delivery service, which is responsible for coordinating with a shipping company that will send the products to the customer.

Figure 8.2 **A more realistic version of the ordering scenario from figure 8.1. Now you also need to handle missing items in the inventory, canceled orders, and paying external suppliers. In this scenario, the services are more coupled. The Ordering service is now aware of the Delivery service and not just the Inventory service.**

will call the Ordering service before they decide what to do next. Naturally, the system wouldn't stop here. You'd want to introduce more services and more connections, such as an Accounts Payable service that interacts with external suppliers, the Inventory service, and the Delivery service (because you also need to pay shipping companies).

With each new service, you end up drawing more lines from service to service, and with each new service you update the other services' business logic with the new business rules and knowledge of the other services' contracts.

CONSEQUENCES

Lines going from service to service are normal, aren't they? If the services won't talk to each other, they won't be very useful, will they? Isn't that the whole point of SOA?

Well, yes—and no. It's normal for services to connect to each other. Creating a system in an SOA is all about connecting services together. As for the "no" part, the problem lies in the way these integrations are developed. If you aren't careful, it's easy to get the integration lines into a big ugly mess—a Knot.

A Knot is an antipattern where the services are tightly coupled by hardcoded point-to-point integration and context-specific interfaces.

Consider what happens when you want to reuse the ordering service discussed earlier. The Knot prevents you from reusing it without hauling in the rest of the baggage—all the other services (Inventory, Delivery, and so on). If the new context isn't identical in its ordering processes, you can't use it without adding one-off interfaces (specific messages for the new context and all sort of `if` statements to distinguish between the old and new behavior). Another option might be to alter the messages in the existing contract of the Ordering service. Unfortunately, this is usually either not possible or it would force you to make sure the other services (Inventory, Delivery, and others) are still functioning. In any event, it's a big mess.

You moved to SOA to get flexibility, increase reuse within your systems, and prevent spaghetti point-to-point integration, but what we're looking at here isn't flexible, it's hard to maintain, and it looks like we're back at square one after having invested gazillions of dollars to get here.

CAUSES

How can a wonderful, open standard, distributed, flexible SOA solution deteriorate into an unmanageable knot?

It's tempting to dismiss the Knot as the result of inadequate planning. If you only planned everything in advance, you wouldn't be in this mess now, would you? Trying to plan everything ahead of time is an antipattern in itself (an organizational antipattern that isn't in the scope of this book). But even if you could plan everything, there's still a good chance you'd get to the Knot anyway, because the problems are inherent in the way businesses work.

In chapter 1 we looked at an integration spaghetti scenario (section 1.2.2, and shown again in figure 8.3). You can see that the Knot was there as well, when business processes evolved and you needed to interact with information from other parts of the system. The flow of a business process expands to supply that needed information or service, and thus the Knot grows.

From the technical perspective, there are two forces working here to push a system into a Knot. One is the granularity of the services, and the other is the business processes.

In terms of granularity, services are sized so that a business process requires several of them to work together, but they aren't small enough that they are end-nodes in the process, with other services only calling the service to obtain a result. This isn't a bad thing in itself; after all, if each process were implemented by a single service, you'd have silos not unlike the ones you're trying to escape by using SOA, and if you made

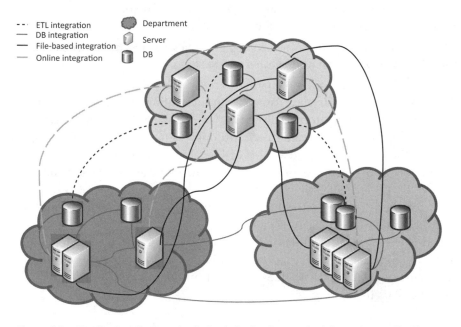

Figure 8.3   The Knot antipattern is similar in both effect and origin to the spaghetti integration in non-SOA environments.

the services too small, you'd fall into another trap (see the Nanoservice antipattern later in this chapter). The bottom line is that while the granularity is a force that drives us toward the Knot, there's not a lot we can do about it without getting ourselves into worse problems.

The second, stronger, force is the business process itself. Because the process flows through the services, the services need to be aware of the flow and call other services to complete the flow. In order for a service to call another service, it has to know about its contract and its endpoint. When another business flow goes through that service, you not only add new contracts and endpoints but also the contextual knowledge of which other services need to be called depending on the process. And that's where the trouble arises—as you implement more business processes and flows, the services start to tie themselves to each other more and more.

But SOA should have solved all that, shouldn't it? Surely there's something we can do about it—or isn't there?

REFACTORING

As you've seen, most of the problem is caused by having the services' code determine where to go next and what to do with the results of the services' processing. If there was only a way to pry these decisions away from the services' greedy hands.

As you've probably guessed, there is such away. In fact, there are several such ways.

One option is to be very mindful about the communication patterns of services, and make sure that services only care about their immediate connections, and not about any dependencies of services they interact with. Michael Poulin calls this "Knight Rules of Ownership."[1] Limiting dependencies and managing the scope of services' knowledge helps solve the knot by keeping the number of connections low. Sometimes, however, services do need to interact with lots of other services, so we need additional measures.

There are three other possibilities for refactoring the knot that I'll discuss in this book: the Workflodize pattern (chapter 2), Orchestration (chapter 7), and Inversion of Communications (chapter 5). Let's look at each of these patterns and see how they help.

The Workflodize pattern suggests adding a workflow engine inside the service to handle both sagas (long-running operations; the Saga pattern is discussed in chapter 5) and added flexibility. The "added flexibility" is the key point here. When you express the connections as steps in the workflow, they aren't part of your services' business logic. They're also easier to change in a configuration-like manner. Both of these points are big pluses.

Still, a better way to solve the service-to-service integration problem is to use an external orchestration engine. The idea of using the Orchestration pattern is to enable business process management—a way for business analysts and IT to control

---

[1] Michael Poulin, "Knight Rules of Ownership in Service-Oriented Ecosystem," *EBizQ* (June 2012), www.ebizq.net/blogs/service_oriented/2012/06/knight_rules_of_ownership_in_service-oriented _ecosystem.php.

and verify that the processes are carried out as intended (you don't have to use an orchestration engine for that, but it helps). In the context of solving or avoiding the Knot antipattern, the Orchestration pattern is better than the Workflodize pattern because it centralizes and externalizes all the interactions between services, effectively removing all the problematic code from the services themselves.

> **NOTE** There's a fine line between externalizing the flow and externalizing the logic itself. See the discussion of the Orchestration pattern in chapter 7.

The third pattern you can use to refactor the Knot is Inversion of Communications. Inversion of Communications means modeling the interactions between services as events rather than as calls. Inversion of Communications is, in my opinion, the strongest countermeasure to the Knot. The Workflodize and Orchestration patterns bring a lot of flexibility in routing the messages between the services, but the Inversion of Communications pattern also helps the message designers remove specific contexts from the messages, because when the service's status is raised as an event, it isn't addressed to any other service in particular. Note that using Inversion of Communications doesn't negate using either of the two other patterns; once the event is raised, you still need to route it to other services, and using a workflow engine is a good option for that. Another implementation option is to use an infrastructure that supports publish/subscribe (see Inversion of Communications pattern in chapter 5 for more details.)

Let's return again to the ordering scenario we discussed earlier in this section. When we left it, the services were growing with needless knowledge of specific business processes. The ordering service had to know both about the Inventory and the Delivery services. When it's refactored with the Inversion of Communications pattern, the same Ordering service doesn't have to know about any of the other services. In figure 8.4 you can see that the Ordering service sends two business events (new order, canceled order) and the routing of these messages is no longer the responsibility of the service.

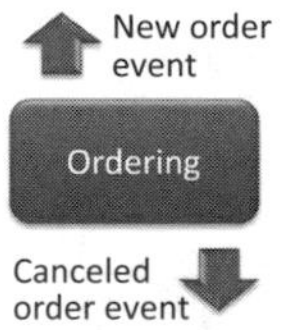

Refactorings aside, one question you still need to think about is whether there are any circumstances where having a Knot is acceptable.

Figure 8.4   The Ordering service using the Inversion of Communications pattern. Now the service doesn't know about or depend on other services directly. It's only aware of two business events—new order and canceled order—which are relevant to the business function that the service handles.

KNOWN EXCEPTIONS

In a sense, the Knot is a distributed version of an antipattern described by Brian Foote and Joseph Yoder as "Big Ball of Mud"—spaghetti code where different types of the system are tied to each other in unmanageable ways. My reason for mentioning this connection is that "Big Ball of Mud" might be considered a pattern rather than an antipattern. When "you need to deliver quality software on time, and under budget ... focus first on features and functionality, then focus on architecture and performance."[2]

Starting on a large project, such as moving an enterprise to SOA, is difficult. You can't figure out everything in advance, and you need to deliver something, so as the Nike slogan goes, you "just do it." Get something done. You need to be prepared to let go and redesign further down the road.

In the current system I'm working on—a visual recognition/search engine for mobile, we went with a Knot approach for the first release. The simplicity of the implementation—less investment in infrastructure, ad hoc integration, and so on—enabled us to deliver a first working version in less than six months. These six months also helped us understand the domain we're operating in much better, and more importantly allowed us to get to market with the features the business needed inside the schedule the business wanted. We spent the next six months rewriting the system, including applying the Inversion of Communications pattern.

To sum up, coding the integration code into services is likely to produce a Knot. It's acceptable to go down this path for a prototype or first version to show quick results. But you do need to plan for and take the time to refactor the solution so you don't get stuck down the road.

One of the forces that contributed to forming the Knot was the granularity of services. The next antipattern talks about another granularity-related problem: Nanoservice. Sometimes size does matter.

8.2   *Nanoservice antipattern*

Getting the granularity of services right is one of the toughest tasks involved in designing services. There's a lot to balance: the communications overhead, the flexibility of the system, the reuse potential, and so on. I can't give you an exact recipe to follow to get service granularity right, because what is "right" depends on the context, the environment, and other decisions the service designers take. It's easier to define what shouldn't be a service than what should. For instance, you should definitely not call all of your existing ERP system a single service. The Nanoservice antipattern talks about the other extreme—the smaller services.

Consider the Calculator service that appears in all sorts of code examples (I've seen examples in .NET, Java, PHP, C++, and a few more). A basic desk calculator, as we all know, supports several simple operations like add, subtract, multiply, and divide, and sometimes a few more.

Implementing a Calculator service isn't very complicated. The next listing comes from an Apache example. It shows part of a WSDL file for a Java Calculator service that accepts two numbers and adds them.

---

[2]   Brian Foote and Joseph Yoder, "Big Ball of Mud," www.laputan.org/mud/.

Listing 8.1   Excerpt from a WSDL file for a stateless Calculator service[3]

```
<wsdl:types>
      <xsd:schema xmlns:xsd="http://www.w3.org/2001/XMLSchema"
                  xmlns="http://jws.samples.geronimo.apache.org"
                  targetNamespace="http://jws.samples.geronimo.apache.org"
                  attributeFormDefault="unqualified"
➥  elementFormDefault="qualified">

            <xsd:element name="add">
                <xsd:complexType>
                    <xsd:sequence>
                        <xsd:element name="value1" type="xsd:int"/>
                        <xsd:element name="value2" type="xsd:int"/>
                    </xsd:sequence>
                </xsd:complexType>
            </xsd:element>

            <xsd:element name="addResponse">
                <xsd:complexType>
                    <xsd:sequence>
                        <xsd:element name="return" type="xsd:int"/>
                    </xsd:sequence>
                </xsd:complexType>
            </xsd:element>
      </xsd:schema>
</wsdl:types>

<wsdl:message name="add">
   <wsdl:part name="add" element="tns:add"/>
</wsdl:message>

<wsdl:message name="addResponse">
   <wsdl:part name="addResponse" element="tns:addResponse"/>
</wsdl:message>

<wsdl:portType name="CalculatorPortType">
   <wsdl:operation name="add">
     <wsdl:input name="add" message="tns:add"/>
     <wsdl:output name="addResponse" message="tns:addResponse"/>
   </wsdl:operation>
</wsdl:portType>

<wsdl:binding name="CalculatorSoapBinding" type="tns:CalculatorPortType">
    <soap:binding style="document"
➥  transport="http://schemas.xmlsoap.org/soap/http"/>

      <wsdl:operation name="add">
          <soap:operation soapAction="add" style="document"/>
          <wsdl:input name="add">
              <soap:body use="literal"/>
          </wsdl:input>
          <wsdl:output name="addResponse">
```

[3]. Apache Geronimo, "jaxws-calculator—Simple Web Service with JAX-WS," https://cwiki.apache.org/ GMOxDOC21/jaxws-calculator-simple-web-service-with-jax-ws.html. © 2003-2010, The Apache Software Foundation, licensed under ASL 2.0.

```
                <soap:body use="literal"/>
            </wsdl:output>
        </wsdl:operation>

    </wsdl:binding>

    <wsdl:service name="Calculator">
        <wsdl:port name="CalculatorPort" binding="tns:CalculatorSoapBinding">
            <soap:address location=
➥"http://localhost:8080/jaxws-calculator/calculator"/>
        </wsdl:port>
    </wsdl:service>
```

As you can see, that's a lot of code (and overhead) for a simple function.

Calculator services can be more advanced and have memory—the next listing is taken from an MSDN example, and it shows the interface definition for such a calculator in .NET. It's a WCF example that uses workflow services and accepts a single value at a time.

Listing 8.2 A service contract definition for a stateful calculator service[4]

```
[ServiceContract(Namespace = "http://Microsoft.WorkflowServices.Samples")]
public interface ICalculator
{
    [OperationContract()]
    int PowerOn();
    [OperationContract()]
    int Add(int value);
    [OperationContract()]
    int Subtract(int value);
    [OperationContract()]
    int Multiply(int value);
    [OperationContract()]
    int Divide(int value);
    [OperationContract()]
    void PowerOff();
}
```

Both versions of this calculator service are very fine-grained—all they can do is accept numbers and return the sum. Hopefully the Calculator examples are just oversimplified services designed to demonstrate SOA-related technologies (JAX-WS in the first excerpt and WCF and WF in the second). The problem is when you see this level of granularity in real-life services.

CONSEQUENCES

Why is fine granularity a problem? Isn't SOA all about breaking monolithic silos into smaller reusable services? The finer grained a service is, the less context it carries. The less context a service carries, the more reuse potential it has. And reuse is one of the holy grails of SOA, isn't it? The Calculator service seems like the epitome of a reusable service. There's no doubt you can reuse it over and over and over.

---

[4] MSDN, "Calculator Client Sample," http://msdn.microsoft.com/en-us/library/bb410782(v=vs.90).aspx. © 2007 Microsoft Corporation. All rights reserved.

Reuse is indeed a noble goal. The culprit of fine-grained services, however, is the network. Services are consumed over networks—both local (LANs) and remote (extranets, WANs, and the like). The result is that services are bound by the limitations and costs incurred by communicating over those networks (the time it takes to send messages, the bandwidth needed, and so on). Trying to disregard these costs is exactly what ailed most, if not all, RPC distributed system approaches that predated SOA (Corba, DCOM, and so on). The calculator service and other similarly sized services are nanoservices.

> **!** **Nanoservice is an antipattern where a service is too fine-grained. A nanoservice is a service whose overhead (communications, maintenance, and so on) outweighs its utility.**

So how can nanoservices harm your SOA? Nanoservices cause many problems, the major ones being poor performance, fragmented logic, and overhead. Let's look at them one by one.

Every time you send a request to a service, you incur a few costs, such as serialization on the caller, moving the caller process to the OS network service, converting the messages to the underlying network protocol, traveling on the network, moving from the OS network service to the called process, deserializing the message back on the called process—and that's before adding security (encryption, firewalls, and the like), routing, and retries. Modern networks and servers can make all this happen rather quickly, but if you have a lot of nanoservices running around, these numbers add up to a significant performance nightmare.

Nanoservices cause fragmented logic almost by definition. As you break what should have been a meaningful cohesive service into miniscule steps, your logic is scattered between the bits that are needed to complete the business service. The fact that you need to use a bunch of services to accomplish something meaningful also means increased chances of running into the Knot antipattern.

A proliferation of nanoservices also causes overhead. The initial upfront cost for developing a service of any size is relatively high—just look at the amount of WSDL code needed to define the Calculator service in listing 8.1, and for what? A service that adds a couple of numbers. Additionally, each service, regardless of size, incurs management overhead. This includes things like keeping track of the service in a service registry, making sure it adheres to policy, writing the cruft (things you have to write around the business logic) for configuring it, and so on. Having nanoservices around means you have to do this more often per service compared with having fewer coarser-grained services.

The point of overhead outweighing utility, mentioned in the Nanoservice antipattern definition, is subtle but important. Whether or not a service is a nanoservice isn't always obvious.

If a contract doesn't have a lot of operations, you should make sure you don't have a nanoservice, but it doesn't automatically mean that you do. A fraud-detection service contract might only accept transaction details and decide whether to authorize the transaction, deny it, or move on to further investigation. This may sound simple, but the innards of this service involve complex processes such as running the details through a rule engine checking for fraudulent behavior patterns, matching blacklists, and so on.

On the other side of things, a comprehensive contract doesn't guarantee that a service isn't a nanoservice. I once helped develop a resource management service. It supported some very nice operations like getting the status of all the services in the system, running sagas, and allocating services. Allocating services meant that whenever an event occurred that needed a new service instance to handle it, we had to call the resource manager to get one. This provided for centralized management and also created a performance bottleneck that slowed the whole system. The utility of the resource management (easy management of running sagas) was not worth the overhead associated with the service (the number of calls and the performance hit on the system). It was a nanoservice.

> **NOTE** To solve that performance bottleneck, we went with distributed resource management, but that's beyond the scope of this discussion.

CAUSES

From a more technical point of view, you get to nanoservices by not paying attention to at least a couple of the fallacies of distributed computing. Mentioned in chapter 1, the fallacies of distributed computing are a few false assumptions that are easy to make and that prove to be wrong and are costly down the road. Specifically, I'm talking here about two assumptions:

- *Bandwidth is infinite*—Even though bandwidth keeps getting better and better, it's still not infinite within a specific setup. In one project I worked on, we were sending images over the wire and distributing them to computational services (using map/reduce—the discussion of the Gridable Service pattern in chapter 3 covers such a scenario). Things were working OK when we sent small images, but when we sent larger images we saw that the system didn't work as expected. Further investigation showed we were sending the images as bitmaps, which is a wasteful format, and not as JPEGs or some other compressed format. This generated too much load on the backbone of our switches.
- *Transport cost is zero*—Every over-the-wire call incurs a lot of costs as compared to a local call (see figure 8.5). The cost of the transport can be considered in two ways: the amount of time it take to make each of these calls, or the real dollar value attached to making sure you have enough bandwidth (connection/routers, firewalls) to handle the traffic.

Another reason beginners might end up with nanoservices is poor examples. As noted earlier, the Calculator services in listings 8.1 and 8.2 are taken from real examples provided by vendors. SOA newcomers or people without a lot of distributed systems development experience can easily take these samples at face value and go about

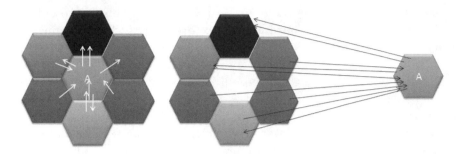

Figure 8.5 Local objects can "afford" to have intricate interactions with their surroundings. Similar functionality delivered over a network is more likely to cause poor performance because of the network-related overhead.

implementing services with similar granularity. The fact that web service frameworks mostly map service calls to object method calls makes this even more tempting.

Nanoservices are also an inherent risk when applying the Orchestration pattern. Adding an orchestration engine that's capable of controlling flow and is external to services tempts you to use it to drive all flow, as small as that flow may be. Couple this with the fact that the smaller the services are, the more reusable they are, and, again, you may end up with a lot of nanoservices on your hands.

Because the line between nanoservices and appropriately sized services is fuzzy, behaviors that may look promising at design time can prove to be nanoservices when they're implemented (like the resource manager example I mentioned). This can be acceptable if your SOA is developed iteratively (see the exceptions discussed in section 8.2.4) but it still means that you'll have to come up with ways to refactor nanoservices.

REFACTORING

There are two main ways to solve the Nanoservices antipattern problem. One, which is relatively easy, is to group related nanoservices into a larger service. The second option, which is more complicated, is to redistribute a nanoservice's functionality among other services. Let's take a look at these options in turn.

I worked on one project where we needed to send out notifications to users and admins via SMS messages. The software component that did the actual SMS dissemination was a third-party application, so we decided to create a simple service (not unlike an OO adapter) that accepted requests for SMS and talked to the third-party software. A nanoservice was born, and it even got a nice little name: Post Office Service.

Why is this a nanoservice? It really doesn't do much—it would be even simpler to package this as a library that other services can use. Also, as mentioned earlier, it has all the maintenance overhead of any other system service.

The way we redesigned it was to add similar functionality to the Post Office service to make it more meaningful. Thus, it learned to send emails, tweets, MMSs, and the like. A serendipitous effect of this approach was that instead of sending a request like

TweetMessage or SendSMS to the Post Office service, we could raise more meaningful events, such as SystemFailureEvent, and have the service make decisions about how to alert administrators based on the severity of the problem. By combining the related functionality, we made the Post Office service even more meaningful.

Unfortunately it isn't always possible to find another suitable services (nano- or right-sized) that can assimilate the functionality of a nanoservice. In those cases, getting rid of a nanoservice is more of an exercise in redesign than it is a refactoring. I worked on a project that had a services allocation service (SAS). The SAS's role was to know about other services' locations, health statuses, and utilization, and upon request to decide what service instances should be used (such as at the beginning of a saga—see chapter 5 for a discussion of the Saga pattern). The service also provided reporting capabilities for active sagas, service utilization, and so on. This might not sound like a nanoservice, and at first we thought it wasn't, but as the project progressed, we found that because the SAS was a central hub, as shown in figure 8.6, the SAS became a performance bottleneck. It incurred additional costs (in latency) on a lot of the calls and interactions made by other services. The utility of the SAS was being diminished by the cost. It was a nanoservice after all.

To solve the SAS problem, we had to put in quite a lot of work. The solution, essentially, was to move to distributed resource management, so that each service had some knowledge of what the world looks like, so that it could decide which service instance to talk to by itself.

To sum up this section, sometimes it's easy to notice that something is a nanoservice, and in those cases, chances are that it will also be easy to take the functionality and group it with related functionality in another service. Other times, the fact that a service provides too little benefit isn't as apparent, and that only becomes clear as you move along. In those cases it's also harder to fix the problem.

One question we still need to cover is whether there are any situations where you'd use a nanoservice even if you know it's one at the outset.

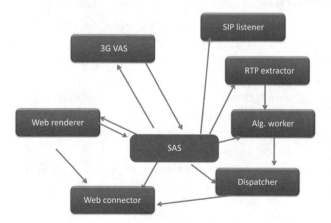

Figure 8.6 Sometime nanoservices can provide important services, but the cost of that functionality is more than their usefulness. This synchronization service became a bottleneck for performance because everything goes through it.

KNOWN EXCEPTIONS

When is it OK to have nanoservices? It's OK when you're starting out. When your approach to SOA is evolutionary, and you don't plan everything in advance, there's a good chance that the first versions of services you build won't show a lot of business benefit, but they will need the full overhead of a service. The Post Office service discussed earlier is a good example of that—when it started out, it only dealt with a single type of message, and it didn't do a whole lot with it either.

The Post Office service is also a good example of another reason you might want a nanoservice: when you want to build an adapter or bridge to other systems, whether they're legacy systems or third-party ones. In these cases, you need to weigh the advantage of using a service against building the same functionality as a library that can be used within services. In many cases, keeping the flexibility and composability of SOA is worth the overhead associated with having an additional service to manage.

Keep in mind that Nanoservice is a rather soft antipattern. The value of a small service can radically change from system to system or even within a system as time and requirements progress. It's worthwhile questioning your assumptions and looking at your services from time to time to ensure the usefulness of what you're building.

Now let's look at the Transactional Integration antipattern.

8.3   *Transactional Integration antipattern*

Suppose you have an ordering system (say the one from the Knot antipattern—figure 8.1) and the business representatives say they want to confirm an order with the user only if the item has been secured in the inventory. From the technical point of view, two separate services are involved—one handles the orders and the other handles inventory (figure 8.7). Now what?

This sounds like a textbook case for using transactions, but in reality it isn't. I'll explain why shortly, but before we go there let's recap transactions and distributed transactions.

Transactions build on four basic tenets:

- *Atomicity*—The transaction is "all or nothing," meaning that once a transaction ends, the state is either completely done (commit) or undone (abort).
- *Consistency*—The actions included in the transaction are done together so the state is kept consistent. If you were to remove an item from inventory and add it to a shipment in the same transaction, you won't have a situation where the item was removed from inventory and not added to a shipping list.
- *Isolation*—While the transaction is in progress, logic that isn't part of the transaction won't see the world in an inconsistent form.
- *Durability*—The consequences of the transaction are saved to persistent storage so that they're available after a system restart.

Figure 8.7   A vanilla ordering scenario. An Ordering service needs to confirm that the item is available before confirming the order with the customer.

The simplest way to create transactions is using "pessimistic locking." In this case, a writer can only write to a specific piece or block of data if no other resource is reading or writing from it, and a reader can only read if no other resource is writing. On top of that, to ensure ACIDness you need to write the data twice: once where you want it to end up, and then to a log file. This double bookkeeping ensures that if a crash occurs before the transaction is finalized (committed or aborted) you can check to see that both copies match, and if not either (re)apply the log data or roll back the data. (This is necessarily a simplistic overview. See the further reading section for more thorough explanations.)

Unfortunately pessimistic locks rarely work in real-life scenarios, so more advanced ways of locking and still maintaining ACIDness have been developed. But all the mechanisms hold resources for the transactions, and all locking mechanisms build on the assumption that the time spent inside the transaction is short.

The plot thickens further when it comes to distributed transactions. Now you have at least two transactional resources, and not only does each of them have to handle the transaction, but you also need to coordinate the state between them because if one commits the transaction and the other rolls it back, the overall transaction is incomplete. Still computer scientists were smart enough to come up with several solutions to achieving distributed consensus, and they gave us two-phase commits, three-phase commits, paxos commits, and so on. Case closed. You can use transactions in SOA, and life is beautiful.

Or is it?

CONSEQUENCES

Transactions, even distributed ones, aren't a problem in themselves. Chapter 2 introduced the Transactional Service pattern to allow the handling of incoming messages in a reliable manner. The problems begin when the transaction scope involves more than one service.

❗ Transactional Integration is an antipattern where transactions extend across service boundaries (they're not isolated inside services).

So what sorts of problems can Transactional Integration introduce into your SOA solution? Quite a few, with the main three being performance problems, security threats, and rigidity. Let's take a look at them one by one.

With all the goodness transactions offer, they also introduce temporal coupling—the need for all the involved actions to finalize on or about the same time. Even if the locks held while the transaction continues are permissive (optimistic), the coordination that's needed to ensure consistency needs to be synchronized. When you develop a solution, you may be able to take all the performance considerations into account at design time and make sure the system behaves. But I'd say distributed transactions aren't highly recommended even then, because the rigidity of the consistency needed to achieve a distributed consensus can still mean holding locks for a long time in cases of partial failures.

The situation is much worse in an SOA solution because each service can and will evolve independently, both in terms of deployment and functionality. What will happen when the Inventory service moves to another data center (for example, when it's ported to the cloud)? What if the designers of the Inventory service decide that when the inventory level hits a threshold, the service will automatically order new supplies in a transaction? Now you can't secure an item in the inventory until new supplies are ordered. All of a sudden, your transaction has expanded and now includes the Ordering service, the Inventory service, and a supplier's service. As you can see, one risk of Transactional Integration is that designers of services participating in your transaction will extend the transaction to handle business rules they need to comply with.

Another risk highlighted by the preceding scenario is related to security. If the supplier's services are added into your transaction, you now run the risk that external systems will hold locks on your system. This may happen maliciously or by neglect, but it can effectively create a denial of service scenario on your services. A service boundary—its edge—should also be a trust boundary. Externalizing transactions to third parties might be far-fetched, but externalizing them to other teams within the organization who work on their own services with their own priorities isn't, and the same risk applies there.

The last risk related to this example is connected directly to the Knot antipattern. Having transactions between services increases the coupling between them, and increased coupling increases the risk of ending up with a Knot, which effectively kills SOA.

You could argue that most or even all of these are hypothetical situations, and that when you design your SOA solution, you can take the real constraints into consideration and plan for them. Isn't that what you have enterprise architects for? Though the scenarios are oversimplified to illustrate the problems clearly, real-life scenarios manifest the same problems in subtler ways. The main point is that evolvability and flexibility are the hallmarks of SOA. That's why you want an SOA solution in the first place—so that you can evolve the IT of the organization to better match the *changing* needs of the business. The end result is that regardless of how you plan it at on the outset, it's hard to control who participates in the transactions in the long term, which means that adding distributed transactions to the mix is an accident waiting to happen.

CAUSES

The main reason Transactional Integration happens has been mentioned—when you start out and design your SOA, you have a relatively good grasp of the enterprise's business, and it's easy to build the system to suit that understanding.

When approaching a new project, you might think the best approach is setting up a multimonth (or multiyear) project to document and design the overall architecture and services, and only then to begin the transition to the new architecture. But an SOA solution isn't static, nor is your understanding of the business. Even if you do have a good initial understanding of the business flows, that understanding can change pretty quickly. It isn't just that business requirements change over time—

an even greater force of change is your increasing understanding as to exactly what is needed.

No, the more realistic and cost-effective approach is to do some upfront design but to also begin developing real services and work them into the existing software portfolio. This is somewhat like building a new intersection where you also have to build detours to keep some of the lanes open—anything to keep the traffic going. When you work on an SOA project in this manner, the rework, your growing understanding of the business, and the changing requirements mean you can expect a lot of evolution to happen, and the Transactional Integration will work against that evolution.

Other forces pushing you toward the Transactional Integration antipattern are the marketing organizations of technology vendors. Whenever there's a new buzzword, these marketing organizations take whatever technology they currently have and slap the buzzword on it. The end result is a lot of confusion regarding which products and features are really related to the buzzword (SOA, in our case) and which aren't.

Take Microsoft's Windows Communication Foundation (WCF), which is a unified infrastructure for remote communications between components. WCF offers message-based communications along with support for named pipes, it's built to replace RPC technologies like remoting, and it provides support for SOAP (WS-*) web services, some support for REST-style services, and so on. Yet WCF is by and large marketed as an "SOA foundation." This isn't to say you can't use WCF for SOA, but it does a lot more—it also does transactions. Other vendors follow the same path. The use of transactions for cross-service integration is, unfortunately, just one example of this effect.

If transactions aren't the way to go, what can you do instead?

REFACTORING

There are several ways to get around the problem, using the Orchestration, Saga, or Inversion of Communications pattern, or others, to achieve eventual consistency.

But what exactly is the problem we're trying to solve? We're trying to achieve distributed consensus and consistency in the data and business picture, as seen by several services. Let's look at the business scenario presented earlier. You have an ordering system, and the business only wants to confirm an order with the user if the item is already secured in the inventory for that order.

One way to solve this would be to externalize both the transaction scope and the business flow to an orchestration engine (see the Orchestration pattern in chapter 7). The advantage of using an orchestration engine over transactions directed from within the services is that the orchestration engine has the full picture of which services are involved (and their various trust levels) and of which services call to which services, so there's more control over who does what and when. Still, the participating services need to be transaction-aware and need to retain internal locks for external constraints, so use this approach with caution.

Another alternative is to use sagas (see the Saga pattern in chapter 5). Sagas are basically long-running interactions (where messages are related and belong to the same conversation), but they don't hold the same transactional guarantees as ACID transactions. In the case of an inventory problem, the ordering service will have to perform a compensating action to handle the problem. In order for this to work in a reasonable manner, the services may need to hold some data about the world, such as some data about inventory levels, so it can make a reasonable decision on its own.

Sagas can be augmented by the Inversion of Communications pattern to make the services send events based on their actions and subscribe to other events to create choreography scenarios (choreography is described in chapter 7 as part of the Orchestration pattern). In our ordering example, the Ordering service would publish that it has a new order that needs handling, and the Inventory service would listen to that. Once the Inventory service secures the items, it would publish an event stating that, and the Ordering service could notify the customer that the order is ready. (In a real-life scenario, there would be additional steps, like shipping the product.)

Both the Saga and Inversion of Communications patterns implement an eventually consistent system—you basically relax the temporal constraints on decision making by the various services. This can, and usually does, translate into how the business works in general. In the ordering example, it may mean that it would be better to send an additional notification to the customer stating that the order was received when the order service processes the order.

KNOWN EXCEPTIONS

I can't think of many SOA solutions that would benefit from cross-service transactions. Transactional Integration is usually a bad idea for most distributed systems for the reasons mentioned in the previous sections.

A rare exception to this rule might be for a closed solution (a system, not an organization) that's built on SOA principles. In a closed environment where everything is controlled, it might be possible to pull it off without suffering from the rigidity and performance problems induced by Transactional Integration. But even in these rare cases, it would still be preferable to control the transaction scope outside of the service by using an orchestration engine. Using Orchestration means that at least the scope of the transactions and the general flow of the business processes will be handled in the same place.

I would be wary of going down this path, because even closed systems tend to evolve over time, so be forewarned.

A related antipattern that bears some resemblance to Transactional Integration is the Same Old Way antipattern.

8.4   *Same Old Way antipattern*

Every time a new concept makes headway, technology vendors' marketing departments run amok rebranding their current offering with the shiny new buzzword. We've seen this phenomena occur over and over, with Agile, Cloud, Big Data, and even SOA. Savvy developers that we are, we're mostly smart enough to know that the first incarnation of a product on the hype cycle is just that. But it's harder for us to notice when we do pretty much the same thing with our designs.

The Same Old Way is probably the most generic antipattern. It can occur any time you want to apply a new technology or architecture and you struggle with what it means to implement it in the real world.

Let's look at a simple example. Figure 8.8 shows a sample "SOA"-based architecture. On the left hand is a data service—a database wrapped in web-service or RESTful clothing. In the middle are entities, where the business logic of handling customers and accounts happens. On the right is the CRUD service interface. What's missing is an additional tier, which would be a UI consuming these so-called services, though it would likely only see the service interface and not the other types.

The next thing to do is take a look at what's wrong with this picture. The problem is that figure 8.8 doesn't describe an SOA. It's an *n*-layer/*n*-tier architecture. Sure, the moniker "service" is thrown displayed over the place, but if you examine it more closely, you can identify the layers. There's the data layer, which is most likely a tier (layers are logical, tiers are physical). The entities and the service interface most likely reside on the application server tier and will be two layers within the business logic.

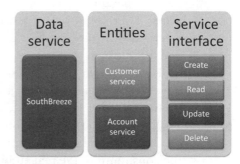

Figure 8.8 This isn't an SOA. There are several components that have "service" names (data service and customer service) but the distribution of logic and components doesn't follow SOA principles.

NOTE   You may think that I've just built a straw man here, so that it's easy for me to destroy it, but these examples are based on things I've actually seen in systems I've reviewed.

CONSEQUENCES

An *n*-tier architecture was called an SOA. What's the big deal?

If, indeed, the only thing wrong in the example was the wrong names, there's no harm done (except maybe to SOA's name). Unfortunately, these layers and tiers are often implemented as services—that is, they have separation between contracts and implementations, they may run as autonomous services, and so on.

The problem, then, can be summed up as follows:

Same Old Way is an antipattern where you implement non-SOA architectures with SOA tooling and overhead, paying the SOA tax without reaping the SOA benefits.

Let's clarify this. Not reaping SOA benefits means that because it isn't an SOA solution, you don't get the flexibility you wanted, or you didn't simplify your system by breaking the solution into smaller, more manageable, pieces.

The SOA tax refers to the fact that you have to invest more in both design time and runtime. SOA involves increased latency, for example, because there are additional layers like serialization and deserialization, communications, and so on. If instead of two services you could manage using objects that would talk to each other in the same memory space, you'd have none of that overhead. The SOA tax can also refer to the increase in local complexity of each component. The implementation for the data service as discussed previously was something like figure 8.9. You have a service hosted in a web server sporting a rich REST API that enables queries and the other CRUD operations, instead of just having the data access layer you'd have used otherwise. This service would also involve extra effort in testing, deploying, and monitoring.

For all the work the data service needed, the benefit you get from using it over a simple data access layer is nothing.

To look at all this from a broader perspective, when you have a Same Old Way antipattern on your hands,

Figure 8.9   Structure of a data service. A web-based service host, hosting a service exposing a rich REST API for querying and updating an underlying RDBMS.

the constraints of the real architecture hinder your ability to utilize SOA properly, and the constraints of SOA hinder your ability to use the real underlying architecture effectively. That's not a good place to find yourself in.

CAUSES

The Same Old Way antipattern is primarily caused by a lack of SOA understanding. This ignorance is aided by confusion that may have originated with a vendor pushing SOA-related technologies as SOA itself.

The most obvious misunderstanding about SOA is the wrong direct association between web services and SOA services. Sure, SOA services can be implemented using web services, but services can also be implemented with myriad other technologies—you can use a messaging API in conjunction with EDA (see the Inversion of Communications in chapter 5), or you can use a REST API, or use the Thrift API, and so on. Not only that—most, if not all, of these other ways are better than web services in many scenarios. Slapping a few web services on whatever architecture you have doesn't turn it into an SOA system.

You might also end up with the Same Old Way antipattern if you have a system in transition from another architectural style to SOA. In this case, it's probably not an occurrence of the antipattern so much as an interim state if the architects are aware of the situation.

REFACTORING

The main trick with refactoring this antipattern is noticing it in the first place and acknowledging that you're forcing whatever you used to do into SOA clothing. To help identify the problem, you can think about the fallacies of distributed computing (see section 1.1.3 of chapter 1). If you find that what you call "SOA" assumes one or more of them, that's a smell that what you have might not really be SOA.

Unfortunately, it isn't easy to refactor this antipattern. Not only will solving the problem most likely require a redesign rather than a refactoring, there's no straight recipe to get there. In essence, you need to get a better understanding of SOA, its principles, and its constraints, and redesign accordingly. Hopefully this book can help with that.

If we look back at our oversimplified scenario in figure 8.8, the data service could be OK if it's the API for your implementation of the Aggregated Reporting pattern (see chapter 7). As for the entities, they are probably right in the domain, but you'd want them to handle their own data, isolate the data from other services, and replace the CRUD API with domain-oriented messages such as "upgrade customer status" or "add address" for the customer service entity.

KNOWN EXCEPTIONS

Unlike the other antipatterns, I can't think of any situations where the Same Old Way antipattern would be acceptable.

The main symptom of the Same Old Way antipattern is a lot of friction in your development, resulting from the fact that you're not actually implementing SOA. If whatever architecture you are using is viable for your problem and serves you well, then use it. On the other hand, if you've turned to SOA because your original architecture was problematic, don't expect repeating it using new tooling and technologies to solve the problem.

It's important to note that the three-tiered architecture mentioned earlier is a viable architecture. There are many successful deployments of three-tiered solutions. If it's a good fit for your project, don't feel the need to call it SOA or to overload it with SOA-related technologies just for the heck of it. SOA has a lot of advantages, but it's not the solution for every problem.

8.5 Summary

This chapter introduced some of the common pitfalls you're likely to make when moving to SOA.

- *Knot*—Services are tightly coupled with point-to-point integration
- *Nanoservice*—Services are made too small, resulting in an unmanageable soup of services
- *Transactional Integration*—Transactions cross service boundaries and couple services together
- *Same Old Way*—You into using your previous architecture, mistakenly thinking it is SOA

I mentioned at the beginning of this chapter that this second part of the book takes a look at different aspects of SOA in the real world. Now that we've finished looking at antipatterns, next we'll look at another aspect of real-world SOA, which is that real problems are so big and complex that a single pattern can't solve them. We'll go over a case study of an end-to-end solution that integrates several patterns into a greater whole.

8.6   *Further reading*

KNOT

Brian Foote and Joseph Yoder, "Big Ball of Mud," www.laputan.org/mud/.
> This is a very good paper discussing pragmatic situations. Among them, it explains when it is valid to have a mess of an architecture ("a big ball of mud").

TRANSACTIONAL INTEGRATION

Leslie Lamport, Robert Shostak, and Marshall Pease, "The Byzantine Generals Problem," *ACM Transactions on Programming Languages and Systems*, vol. 4, no. 3 (July 1982), http://research.microsoft.com/en-us/um/people/lamport/pubs/byz.pdf.
> This is a seminal paper that explains the challenge of distributed consensus.

Roger Sessions, "Shootout at the Transaction Corral; BTP versus WS-T," *ObjectWatch Newsletter*, no. 41 (October 3, 2002), www.objectwatch.com/newsletters/issue_41.htm.
> This is a good paper by Roger Sessions from 2002(!) that explains why transactions between services are bad.

Christophe Bare, "Transactional Processing Cheat Sheet" (September 2005), www.cbare.org/writing/Transactions/transactions.html.
> Christophe's paper provides a thorough explanation of transactions (in general).

Putting it all together— a case study

This book details a lot of different patterns, and each pattern handles just one aspect of building a solution, like security, scalability, and integration. But real systems have lots and lots of different challenges that need to be resolved. It's interesting to see how the patterns can combine to provide a single cohesive solution— that's what this chapter is about.

The case study discussed in this chapter is divided into two parts: background presenting the problem, and a solution. The problem introduction describes the system that was developed as well as the quality attributes of that project. The second part, which takes up most of the chapter, presents the solution and the patterns that were used in it.

This chapter demonstrates how you can combine multiple patterns to create a larger whole. It also shows how patterns fit into the development lifecycle, demonstrating how to choose appropriate patterns based on the requirements, and

211

offering a glimpse into the implementation of the patterns in that project. (Note that the implementation here is one of many way you can implement this book's patterns.)

9.1   Problem

To present a real-world solution that integrates several patterns in a meaningful way, we need a good-sized project. To that end, I'm going to present a system I worked on a few years ago, where a lot of the patterns discussed in the book were implemented. It's also the system that delayed this book for three years (taking up all my time), so it seems fair it should serve as an example.

We'll start by looking at the general characteristics of the system, then at some of the architectural requirements, and finally at the mapping to relevant patterns.

SYSTEM REQUIREMENTS

The system we'll look at allows you to perform a visual search, which is an interesting way to explore the world. The idea is simple enough: you see something of interest, take a picture of it with your mobile phone's camera, send the photo to a service, and get back relevant information. Google Goggles is a public solution that performs this function. The system we're looking at does essentially the same thing with two key differences:

- The system supports multiple ways to send in images—via video phone call, SMS, email, and apps on various platforms. (Goggles can only be used via apps.)
- The system is an OEM white-label solution for content providers—it's a software as a service (SaaS) solution that provides visual search.

Figure 9.1 shows the main business services involved in the system. The system has four services for providing visual search, each of which is a different business offering. It also has a service for managing interactions, where the clients can design the experience users will get when a search yields a result; a service for managing advertising campaigns; and other standard services like billing and reporting.

The business services give us a high-level overview of the intended functionality of the system and provide hints toward partitioning the solution into services. When designing an SOA solution, the next step would usually be to understand and analyze the business processes in order to gain insights into what messages and contracts are needed. We'll look at some of the results of such an analysis when we get to the solution (the analysis itself isn't in the scope of the book).

Before that, we need to take a look at some of the system's quality attributes.

Figure 9.1   Some of the business services the image search system exposes. The services include several ways to perform a visual search (via email, app, video call, and SMS), billing, interactions management, and so on.

What's the difference between service orientation and SOA?

Differentiating between service orientation and SOA is beyond the scope of this book. But it's important to discuss it in the context of this case study for two main reasons:

- Service orientation is a stepping-stone toward deciding which services an SOA will include.

- SOA services and business-level services (services originating from service orientation analysis) are related but may not necessarily have a one-to-one relationship.

So, what is service orientation?

In a nutshell, service orientation is an approach to analyzing some of the aspects of enterprise architecture—specifically functional decomposition, business processes, and data architecture. Applying service orientation means focusing on breaking down business capabilities and functions into business-level services. The business level services are logical components whose composition and interactions provide the business's processes.

SOA, as explained in the first chapter, is an architectural style (a software concept) concerned with building interconnected coarse-grained components. SOA focuses on flexibility and composition. The resemblance between the "service oriented architecture" and "service orientation" names isn't accidental. SOA is a good fit for implementing service orientation.

In a sense, the business services and business processes identified at the service orientation level are the requirements that are fed into the architecture, technology mapping, and implementation at the software level, where SOA plays.

QUALITY ATTRIBUTES

Quality attribute scenarios help us understand how to design a solution. Quality attribute scenarios, as explained in appendix A and demonstrated throughout the book, provide a good way to describe architectural requirements.

Expressing quality attributes as scenarios carries many additional benefits: they can help you gain a better understanding of the requirement, allow you to build tests to demonstrate the quality, serve as a means to prioritize and evaluate an architecture, and so on.

Table 9.1 lists some of the system's quality attributes and scenarios, along with candidate patterns that could handle the scenarios.

Now that we have an understanding of the functionality and some of the quality attributes needed, we can move on to the more interesting part— the solution.

Table 9.1   A few of the case study's quality attributes and patterns used to tackle them

Concrete quality attribute	Scenario	Relevant patterns
Adaptability/changeability (add/remove feature)	During development and operations, a change in a component will only affect the direct components (for development and production). Once in production, a change in an interface will be compatible at least one version back.	Edge Component (chapter 2)
Unplanned downtime	Under normal conditions, a failure in a single component won't result in call termination.	Service Watchdog (chapter 3) Service Instance (chapter 2)
Time to repair/detect	Under normal conditions, the system will detect a failure in a component in less than 5 seconds.	Service Monitor (chapter 4)
Deployment	Under normal conditions, the system won't require manual configuration to work. Under normal conditions, deploying a new version will be done by xcopy.	Inversion of Communications, (chapter 5) Reservation (chapter 6)
Scalability	Under all conditions, adding additional hardware units (deployment units) will enable linear growth in image database capacity.	Gridable Service (chapter 3)
Cost	The cost of a deployment unit shall not exceed $1000.	Gridable Service (chapter 3)

9.2   *Solution*

The system that was constructed to handle the system's requirements evolved over time. Initially, the system only had to handle identification in 3G video calls and small numbers of links. Then the business added requirements for SMS and email, followed by a demand to handle large numbers of links and to open the platform for mobile apps and general internet use.

As you can probably guess, we decided to build the system based on SOA principles. That helped us meet the system's requirements, but more importantly it helped us constantly adapt the system to the changing requirements. SOA's flexibility allowed us to add more components (services) as well as evolve the internal structure of existing services while keeping the system working.

We'll look at a few of the SOA patterns that were used to make this happen. Let's start with a look at some of the services that the system contains (depicted in figure 9.2). These services will be used to demonstrate how the patterns were implemented:

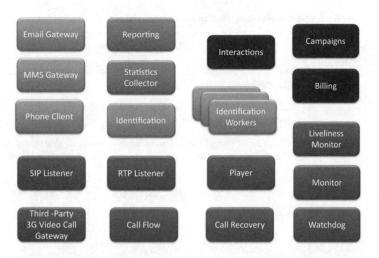

Figure 9.2 Some of the services in the system that implement business services. Providing identification by email involves several services: the Email Gateway, Identification (with its ID Workers), Watchdog, Statistics Collector, Monitor, and Billing. The discussion of the solution will use these services in different contexts to demonstrate different patterns.

- *Email Gateway, MMS Gateway, and Phone Client*—These are adaptor services that translated external protocols to internal ones (discussed in section 9.2.1).
- *SIP Listener, RTP Listener, Player, Call Recovery, and Third-Party (3G Video Call) Gateway*—These services handle different aspects of 3G video calls (discussed in sections 9.2.1 and 9.2.2).
- *Billing, Interactions, and Campaigns*—These are B2B-oriented services. One handles billing, one handles the interactions (what end users see when a link is identified), and the last handles advertising campaigns.
- *Liveliness Monitor, Monitor, and Watchdog*—These are technical services in charge of keeping the system running (discussed in section 9.2.3).
- *Statistics Collector, Reporting*—These services are responsible for collecting all the information passed through the system (from logs to what end users do while interacting with the system) and turning that into data for reports (not discussed in this chapter, but the discussion of the Aggregated Reporting pattern in chapter 7 covers some details).
- *Identification and ID Workers*—These services form the image identification subsystem (discussed in section 9.2.1).

I mentioned that identifiable business services can serve as a guide to partitioning of services in SOA, and that mapping isn't necessarily one to one. Table 9.2 shows the mapping of business services to the SOA services that enable them. Section 9.2.2 on the use of the Inversion of Communications pattern will expand more on how a sample business service is implemented by the interaction and coordination of several services.

Table 9.2   Business services and the services used to implement them

Business service	Services involved
App image search	Phone Client, Identification, Identification Workers, Watchdog, Billing, Statistics Collector, Campaigns
Email image search	Email Gateway, Identification, Identification Workers, Watchdog, Billing, Statistics Collector, Campaigns
MMS search	MMS Gateway, Identification, Identification Workers, Watchdog, Billing, Statistics Collector, Campaigns
3G video call search	SIP Listener, RTP Listener, Player, Call Recovery, Identification, Identification Workers, Watchdog, Billing, Statistics Collector, Campaigns
Billing	Billing, Reporting
Campaign management	Campaigns, Reporting
Interactions	Interactions, Reporting, Campaigns

We have a bunch of SOA services, but a bunch of services doesn't make a system. A system is created when components, or services in our case, cooperate and work together toward fulfilling a purpose. The following sections will look at how SOA patterns help weave the different services into a system.

STRUCTURE (EDGE COMPONENT, GRIDABLE SERVICE, PARALLEL PIPELINES)

We'll start off by looking at the structure of the system and at some of the patterns that were applied there.

The first pattern we'll look at is also the first pattern that appears in the book (chapter 2). Edge Component is a basic pattern, and as an architectural pattern it can be applied on many levels. As a reminder, here's how the Edge Component pattern is defined:

Add an edge component to the service implementation to add flexibility and separate the business logic from other concerns (such as contacts, protocols, technology choices, and additional cross-cutting features).

When working on the system, we implemented this pattern on multiple levels. First, you can see the Edge Component pattern at the architectural level where the different ways to send an image for identification and search (smartphone apps, MMS, and 3G video calls) are separated from the business logic performing the actual identification and search. Conceptually, this implementation can be thought of as a single service performing image search with the different gateways serving as edge components, as illustrated in figure 9.3.

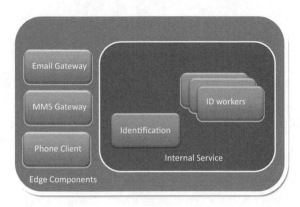

Figure 9.3 Application of the Edge Component pattern at the architectural level. Edge services translate external protocols into the system's internal protocols. The Email Gateway works with IMAP protocols to get emails, extract the images from them, and call the Identification service to perform a search.

Can an Email Gateway be considered a service?

An interesting consideration is whether the different gateways mentioned in this system can be considered services. We all know that SOAP web services are services, right? But email? MMS?

I'll first say that using SOAP and web services doesn't automatically mean you have an SOA and a service. You could take any object you have in the system, wrap it with a SOAP-enabling technology like WCF or JAX-WS, and you'd just get a fancy way to do RPC.

A component is a service if it adheres to the definition of a service. Let's take another look at the definition of SOA from chapter 1:

> Service-oriented architecture (SOA) is an architectural style for building systems based on interactions of loosely coupled, coarse-grained, and autonomous components called services. Each service exposes processes and behavior through contracts, which are composed of messages at discoverable addresses called endpoints. A service's behavior is governed by policies that are external to the service itself. The contracts and messages are used by external components called service consumers.

The different gateways do meet this definition. Let's take the Email Gateway as an example:

- *Course-grained and autonomous*—The component lives on its own. It can handle everything that's related to email, and it communicates with other services to provide business functions. If the image search service isn't available, the Email Gateway doesn't fail (it can still return an email reply that the system is unavailable)—it's the system as a whole that fails, in this case, to provide the business value.

- *Use of a contract and messages at a discoverable address*—The contract is based on a known protocol (IMAP) where the message structure is an email that must have an image attachment in one of supported formats and where the email is addressed to a specific mailbox (the endpoint).

(continued)

- *Governed by policies*—The policies that can be set include the origin of emails accepted, that the origin email address are verifiable (by using protocols such as DomainKeys Identified Mail (DKIM), that messages are signed or not, and so on.

Services can come in different shapes and sizes, and can use different protocols and technologies. What makes something a service is the way it's constructed and the way it interacts and is used within a system.

We also implemented the Edge Component pattern at the code level. The following listing shows simple WCF data and operation contracts, which define an external interface (something other services can use) for sending MMS messages.

Listing 9.1   Simple WCF contract for sending an MMS message

```
[ServiceContract]
public interface IHandleSendMms                          Declare
{                                                        IHandleSendMms
    [OperationContract]                                  as a contract
    int SendMms(SendMmsRequest eventOccurred);
}
                                                         Declare SendMms
[DataContract]                                           as a message
public class SendMmsRequest : ImEvent
{                                                        Specify SendMms
    /// <summary>                                        message structure
    /// end user's number. should be in international
    format: +[country-code]number. Example: +491737692260
    /// </summary>
    [DataMember]
      public string ToNumber { get; set; }
    /// <summary>
    /// service's number, usually a short-code. Example: 84343
    /// </summary>
    [DataMember]
    public string FromNumber { get; set; }
    /// <summary>
    /// Text, as byte array. Use Encoding classes to do it.
    /// </summary>
    [DataMember]
    public byte[] TextAsByteArray { get; set; }
    /// <summary>
    /// Image, as byte array. Can be: jpg, gif, png, bmp. (jpg rulez!!)
    /// </summary>
    [DataMember]
    public string ImageExtension { get; set; }
    /// <summary>
    /// the mms message should have a subject. just put something there.
    /// </summary>
    [DataMember]
    public string Subject { get; set; }
}
```

The following listing shows one of the methods of an Edge Component in the service that fulfills the preceding contract for sending out the MMS messages.

Listing 9.2   Converting external contract to an internal construct in an Edge component

```
public int SendMms(SendMmsRequest eventOccurred)                      ◁ Accepts
    {                                                                     external
        var eventContext = eventOccurred.ToString();                     message
        if (log.IsDebugEnabled)                                          from wire
            log.Debug("inside 'SendMms', event context = ["
    ➥ + eventContext + "]");
        var fromNumber = eventOccurred.FromNumber;
        var sender = mmsSenderFactory.Get(fromNumber);
        if (null == sender)
        {
            if (log.IsWarnEnabled)
                log.Warn("cannot get mms sender derived from '"
    ➥+ (fromNumber ?? "null") + "'");
            return 0;
        }
        IMmsSubmitResponse response;
        try                                                           ┐ Adds missing
        {                                                             │ information
            var extension= GetImageExtension                          ◁ used internally
    ➥(eventOccurred.ImageAsByteArray);
            var mmsMessageDetails = new MmsMessageDetails
    ➥        (eventOccurred.ToNumber,
                eventOccurred.TextAsByteArray,
                eventOccurred.ImageAsByteArray,                       ┐ Converts to
                extension),                                           │ internal
                    eventOccurred.Subject);                           ◁ structure
            response = sender.Submit(mmsMessageDetails);              ◁ Calls
        }                                                               internal
        catch (Exception ex)                                            service with
        {                                                               internal
            log.Error("cannot send mms message, context =              message
    ➥ [" + eventContext + "]", ex);                                    structure
            return -1;
        }
        if (log.IsInfoEnabled)
        {
            var responseMessage = (null == response) ?
    ➥ "null" : response.ToString();
            log.Info("sent mms with event context =
    ➥ [" + eventContext + "], response = [" + responseMessage + "]");
        }
        return 0;
    }
```

You can see that the method in this listing translates the external message into the internal data structure used within the service. You can also see that it adds missing information that doesn't appear in the external contract. In this example, the file extension (the type) of the image that's being sent via the MMS is needed internally.

The edge component looks at the image and infers its type so that the business logic can concentrate on sending messages and not on image parsing.

The Edge Component pattern helped us build individual services. We also needed a way to tie services together to fulfill the business services. This was especially challenging for video calls. Performing image search for video calls is a clientless service—the client-side application is the video call provider (a closed application developed by the phone manufacturer), and it creates a two-way video channel and passes DTMF tones (keystrokes). This means that a lot of the handling of video calls requires stateful services to handle the incoming video stream, generate the outgoing video stream, and maintain the state of the client.

To solve this problem we applied the Parallel Pipelines pattern, which was described in chapter 3 as follows:

> Implement the Parallel Pipelines pattern, where you break the process into subtasks, add a queue between them, and make each subtask an independent component.

Figure 9.4 shows an excerpt from the process of handling videos calls and demonstrates how the Parallel Pipelines pattern was put to use. Each service implements just one subtask related to handling the video call visual search, and the results are passed from service to service to complete the overall business process.

Specifically, the RTP Listener accepts an incoming RTP (Real-Time Transport Protocol) video in H.263 format and keystrokes from the user (each video call generates a distinct stream of video and keystrokes). Depending on what was decoded (image or keystroke) the RTP Listener sends the data to either the Identification service, which performs the image search, or the Call Flow service, which decides what needs to be shown to the user, such as instructions on what to do next or a result. The player takes care of displaying information to the user, based on the decisions of the Call Flow service.

Using the Edge Component and Parallel Pipelines patterns helped make the system tick, but to solve the core problem of the system—searching based on images—we needed another pattern: the Gridable Service pattern (see chapter 3):

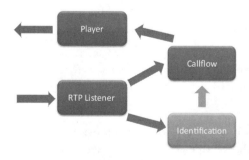

Figure 9.4   An implementation of the Parallel Pipelines pattern. The RTP listener takes on the subtask of decoding RTP and sends the results to the Call Flow and Identification services. Identification takes the subtask of performing the visual search, and Call Flow takes the subtask of understanding what's happening and deciding what the user needs to see (instructions, the results of the search, or something else). The Player service performs the subtask of providing video to the end user. All together they perform the business service of visual search over video call.

Introduce grid technology to the service, via the Gridable Service pattern, to handle computationally intense tasks.

You can take it from me that visual search is a "computationally intense task." In a nutshell, it involves building an identifier or signature for each image in the database (something done offline), and when you receive a new image, you build a signature for that image and compare the results. You can disqualify some of the results based on different aspects of the image; for example, application icons have different features from general images. On top of that, you can use all sorts of metadata to narrow the search; for example, if you have a client with a magazine in Germany and another with a newspaper in the United States, you can decide not to check some images based on the location where they were taken. All of this is rather complicated and involves math that's well beyond the scope of the book (and me, to be honest).

I do know a bit more about software architecture, so let's focus on that. Figure 9.5 illustrates how the Gridable Service pattern was utilized in the system. The Identification service is the grid root, and it distributes a search to different machines that register on the grid. Within each machine, there's an instance of the Identification Worker service, which contains a local database that contains part (a shard) of the overall database (we used Cassandra for that) and computational agents—the Identifier Node and Worker components, that work against the database to perform the image search.

You might argue that this is more of a computation cluster than a grid, but we did have some grid traits in the sense that nodes in the cluster were added and removed dynamically in various scenarios, such as in cases of node failure, and when we needed to cope with larger databases. On a later version of the product, we added the ability to grow and shrink the cluster elastically (when we worked on adding support to deploying the system to Amazon's cloud). Thus, one of the roles of the root node (the Identification service) is to periodically check whether new servers have joined the gird (crashed or failed servers are removed when a call to them fails). In listing 9.3, you can see the code that checks the current worker count. The HandlersRefresher ❶ accepts

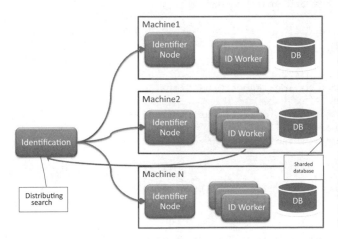

Figure 9.5 An application of the Gridable Service pattern. The Identification service is the grid's root, distributing the search to various machines. Each machine has an instance of the Identification Worker service, which is comprised of Identifier Node and Worker. The Identifier Node is a local manager that employs the Workers, which are the computation engines. The Workers perform the actual search on a fragment of the image database.

a thread (the `dispatcherFiber` parameter) of execution from Retlang (a .NET open source library for Erlang-style concurrency[1]) and uses it ❷ to schedule a timed event to recheck for new servers that are available within the grid.

> **Listing 9.3   A class to check for current workers (handlers) that are active in the grid**

```
public class HandlersRefresher
{
    private readonly IFiber dispatcherFiber;
    private const int HandlersUninitializedValue = -1;
    private int idealNumberOfHandlers = HandlersUninitializedValue;
    private static readonly ILog log =
        LogManager.GetLogger(MethodBase.GetCurrentMethod().DeclaringType);
    public const int RefreshIntervalInMs = 30*1000;
    public const int TimeToFirstCheckInMs = 10*1000;
    private readonly Action<bool> refreshMatchersAction;
    private ITimerControl timerControl = null;

    public HandlersRefresher(
        IFiber dispatcherFiber,
        Action<bool> refreshMatchersAction)
    {
        if (dispatcherFiber == null)
            throw new ArgumentNullException("dispatcherFiber");

        if (refreshMatchersAction == null)
            throw new ArgumentNullException("refreshMatchersAction");

        this.dispatcherFiber = dispatcherFiber;
        this.refreshMatchersAction = refreshMatchersAction;
    }

    public int CurrentIdealNumberOfHandlers
    {
        get { return this.idealNumberOfHandlers; }
    }

    public void InspectHandlers(IFrameHandler[] handlers)
    {
        var numberOfHandlers = handlers == null ? 0 : handlers.Length;

        ScheduleRefreshIfNotAlreadyScheduled();

        if (numberOfHandlers > 0
            && numberOfHandlers >= idealNumberOfHandlers)
        {
            log.DebugFormat("Setting the ideal number of handlers
                to {0}", numberOfHandlers);
            idealNumberOfHandlers = numberOfHandlers;
        }
    }

    private void CancelRefreshSchedulingIfExists()
    {
```

❶ **Get execution thread to check for new workers**

---

[1] Yes, Erlang and Scala actors are much better, but we didn't know that at the time.

```
        if (timerControl == null)
            return;

        log.Debug("Stopping scheduled handlers refresh");

        timerControl.Cancel();
        timerControl = null;
    }

    private void ScheduleRefreshIfNotAlreadyScheduled()
    {
        if (timerControl != null)
            return;

        log.DebugFormat("Scheduling handlers refresh every
{0} ms.", RefreshIntervalInMs);
        timerControl = dispatcherFiber.ScheduleOnInterval(
            () => refreshMatchersAction(false),
                TimeToFirstCheckInMs,
                RefreshIntervalInMs);
    }

}
}
```

❷ Schedule new check event

If you want to understand how the refreshMatchersAction ❶ does its magic, and how messages travelled between all the services, you need to take a deeper look at the communications mechanisms in the system and the patterns they use.

> **NOTE** In .NET an Action<T> type is a delegate (a pointer to a function or method) for a method that accepts a single parameter of type T and does not return a value.

COMMUNICATIONS (INVERSION OF COMMUNICATIONS, SERVICE BUS, SAGA, RESERVATION)

At the heart of the communications mechanism of the system lies a software component called eventBroker. As implied by the name, it implements the Inversion of Communications pattern (see chapter 5):

✓ **Implement the Inversion of Communications pattern by supplementing SOA with event-driven architecture (EDA)—you can allow services to publish streams of events that occur in them instead of calling other services explicitly.**

The system's use of event semantics extends both to events notifying that something happened (such as the Frame-Arrived event emitted when a new image is made available for identification in a video call) and to asynchronous requests (such as the Send-Coupon-Request event sent from the Call Flow service).

The following listing shows how the eventBroker is used from the consumer side. The SendCoupon method prepares a request with all the needed data and then calls the eventBroker's RaiseEvent method to dispatch the message to another (unknown) service that will send the actual SMS with the coupon inside.

Listing 9.4   Code from the Call Flow service raising an event

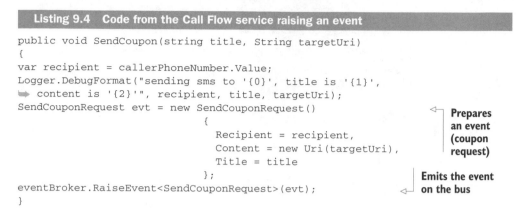

```
public void SendCoupon(string title, String targetUri)
{
var recipient = callerPhoneNumber.Value;
Logger.DebugFormat("sending sms to '{0}', title is '{1}',
⇒   content is '{2}'", recipient, title, targetUri);
SendCouponRequest evt = new SendCouponRequest()        ◁─── Prepares
                             {                               an event
                                 Recipient = recipient,      (coupon
                                 Content = new Uri(targetUri),  request)
                                 Title = title
                             };
eventBroker.RaiseEvent<SendCouponRequest>(evt);        ◁─── Emits the event
}                                                            on the bus
```

The `eventBroker` name is a bit misleading because the `eventBroker` is actually a bus (an agent on each server, and not a centralized node or broker). It implements the Service Bus pattern (discussed in chapter 7):

✓ **Implement the Service Bus pattern and use a unified messaging infrastructure for message transformation, mediation, routing, and invocation.**

The `eventBroker` isolates the business logic from any information related to the target or targets of the event, as well as from the implementation details of how messages are sent (the actual messages were sent over HTTP using WCF). Sometimes an event is sent to multiple subscribers, sometimes it's sent to different subscribers based on context (more on that later), sometime it's broadcast. The `eventBroker` also encapsulates failures, performing retries, ignoring cyclic messages if there's a timeout, skipping failed recipients if they are optional, and so on.

You can see another interesting capability of the `eventBroker` in the following listing. This code shows another method from the Call Flow service that sends a request to play a movie to a video-call end user.

Listing 9.5   A method from the Call Flow service raising a saga event

```
public void PlayMovie(
String mediaLocation,
bool loop,
string interactionID)
{
  var playMovReq = new PlayMovieRequest(SessionId, mediaLocation,
⇒ loop, interactionID);
  if (Logger.IsDebugEnabled)
  {
Logger.Debug("in saga [" + playMovReq.SessionID + "]
⇒    about to play movie '" + mediaLocation.ToString()
⇒    + "', loop = " + loop.ToString() +                    ❶ Raises
⇒    " interaction ID = '" + interactionID + "'");            saga
  eventBroker.RaiseSagaEvent(playMovReq);                ◁─── event
}
```

Overall, this method is very similar to the SendCoupon method in listing 9.4. The main difference lies in the last row of the code ❶. While the event in listing 9.4 isn't related to other events and stands completely alone, the event in snippet 9.5 is raised as part of a saga—the event is sent as part of a series of related events that are a part of a single business process.

Here's a reminder of the definition of the Saga pattern as it appears in chapter 5:

✓ **Implement the Saga pattern and break the service interaction (the business process) into multiple smaller business actions and counteractions. Coordinate the conversation and manage it based on messages and timeouts.**

Why did we need to use the Saga pattern? One reason is that we also used the Service Instance pattern, and we wanted to make sure related calls would be sent to the same instance (see section 9.2.3 for more details). Another reason is to take care of failure scenarios. You don't want to bill a client who didn't receive the product or service you're billing for. When there's a problem with one of the services involved in the saga (whether it's a communications or a business logic problem) it can throw a Saga-Fault event, and some other service or services will try to handle the failure.

Let's revisit the Parallel Pipelines scenario we discussed in figure 9.4 to demonstrate what happens in failure scenarios. In figure 9.6, you can see the RTL Listener raising an event that needs to go to the Call Flow service ❶, which in turn fails. Because this is a communications problem, the eventBroker will raise the Saga-Fault event without the business logic intervention. The Call Recovery service subscribes to the Saga-Fault event and will get the notification when it occurs ❷. The Call Recovery service will then try to handle the failure by allocating another Call Flow instance to the saga so calls can be completed.

The initiator of a saga sets the context for that saga, and the bus (the eventBroker) then routes events based on that context. To illustrate this, consider this simple scenario: All the different gateway services (Email Gateway, MMS Gateway, and Phone Gateway) send out the same event when they have a new image ready for identification, and the result of the search needs to go back to the right gateway. The Identification service will emit an Identification-Found event regardless of where the request

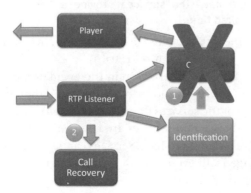

Figure 9.6   The eventBroker in the RTP Listener tries to send an event to the Call Flow service ❶. When it fails, the RTP Listener raises a Saga-Fault event, and the Call Recovery service ❷ listens to it and tries to contain the failure.

originated. You don't want the service to know about the recipient—that's the whole point of having a bus. Similarly, you don't want to broadcast the result because it's not scalable and creates needless load. Instead, we employed context-based routing.

Each service contract includes a list of the events that the service listens to, as well as a list of contexts where these messages are applicable. The following listing shows the list of contexts—the different `Participate` attributes (or annotations in Java speak)—that the Identification service listens to. In this case, these contexts are the different ways to perform an image search.

Listing 9.6   Contract listing the events and contexts where these messages are relevant

```
[ServiceContract]
[BroadcastStatus]
[Participate(Contexts.3rdParty)]                    ◁  Identifies contexts the
[Participate(Contexts.VidCall)]                         service participates in
[Participate(Contexts.Client)]
[Participate(Contexts.Mms)]
[Participate(Contexts.Email)]
public interface ImIdentifier : ImContract,
                                IHandleNewImageInSequence,
                                IHandleCallStarted,
                                IHandleCallEnded,
                                IHandleCallAborted,           ◁  Identifies
                                IHandleSearchStarted,            events
                                IHandleInteractionStarted,       handled by
                                IHandleReadyForSearch,           the service
                                IHandleImageIdentification,
                                IHandleReshardingOccurred

    {}
```

When a new event is raised, the `eventBroker` needs to find out what types of services are subscribed and notify them, and it needs to notify other members of the saga (because each member holds its own instance of the `eventBroker`). Because some of the services had limited capacity and needed to be verified as participants, we also implemented the Reservation pattern (discussed in chapter 6):

✔ **Implement the Reservation pattern and have the services provide a level of guarantee on internal resources for a limited time.**

The `eventBroker` basically tries to connect to what it thinks is a free service and retries until it secures all the services it needs (or maxes out on retries).

Listing 9.7 shows the code for handling the reservation in the `eventBroker`. It basically sets a time limit (a timeout) for all the reservations to be done, and then it tries to reserve each of the candidates. If some of the services deny the reservation, the process tries to find new candidates. Once all the needed services are reserved, the `eventBroker` tries to commit the reservations with all the services. Services can fail during a commit or after the saga is in use—the Saga-Fault event handles these situations.

> **Listing 9.7 Code used to reserve instances when new members are added to the saga**

```
private IEnumerable<Uri> Reserve(IEnumerable<ProxyWrapper> wrappers)
{
 var timeToComplete = DateTimeOffset.Now + TIMEOUT;
    var uris=Reserve(wrappers,                          Initiate reservations
                     MAX_RETRIES,
                     new List<Uri>(),                        Return
                     timeToComplete);                        reservations
    return FinalizeReservation(uris)                         for saga
}

private IEnumerable<Uri> Reserve(IEnumerable<ProxyWrapper> wrappers,
                                 int retries,
                                 ICollection<Uri> failedUris,
                                 DateTimeOffset timeToComplete)
{
   var success = true;                                  Get URIs of
var newUris = GetCandidateUris(wrappers, failedUris);   services for saga
if (null == newUris) return null;
if (newUris.Count == 0) return newUris;
failedUris = TryReserveNewMembers( newUris);           Try to reserve
if (failedUris.Count>0)                                 services
    success = false;
if (DateTimeOffset.Now>timeToComplete)
    success = false;
if (!success && retries==0)
    return null;
if (!success && retries > 0)
    return Reserve(wrappers,
                   retries - 1,                         Retry
                   failedUris,                          reserving
                   timeToComplete);                     failed URIs
return newUris;
}

private ICollection<Uri> TryReserveNewMembers( IEnumerable<Uri> newUris)
{
    var notifier = new SagaNotifier(Id,
                                    Route,
                     newUris,
                     OptionalMembers,
                     LocalUri,
                     Allocator);
    var failedUris = notifier.ReserveAll();
    return failedUris;
}
```

The instances of the ProxyWrapper class encapsulate the communications to specific services (one wrapper per service). In order for the eventBroker to be able to allocate services to a saga, it has to know where to find these services so it can create valid proxy wrappers for them. It needs to know where the active service endpoints are.

To understand how we did this, let's take a look at a couple of other patterns implemented in the system: Service Watchdog and Service Instance.

AVAILABILITY (SERVICE INSTANCE, SERVICE WATCHDOG)

While most of the services, like Billing and the different gateways, are stateless, some aren't, especially the different services that provide visual search over 3G video calls. In that setup, a user calling the system doesn't install any client, which means that the system has to maintain state on behalf of the user. It also needs to constantly stream relevant videos to the user (instructions, results of searches, and so on). We chose to implement these stateful services using the Service Instance pattern (chapter 3):

✓ **Implement the Service Instance pattern by deploying multiple instances of the service business logic.**

The main reason for this choice was availability and failure-handling concerns. Figure 9.7 illustrates the problem solved by using Service Instance.

Video calls are carried on E1 lines, each of which can handle up to 30 concurrent calls. Let's say we have one such line, and it's connected to a single Call Flow service. The service in stateful (hydrating/dehydrating state takes too much time), so a failure in one call may cause the whole Call Flow service to fail and take with it all 30 calls, resulting in dissatisfied customers and a loss of business. Using one Call Flow per caller provides better isolation—a failure affects only one caller. It also makes the service much simpler to program, as there are fewer multithreading and multitenancy issues to worry about.

We also implemented the Service Instance pattern for the individual computation instances (Identification Worker service), as part of the identification grid (shown earlier in figure 9.5). This was done to provide better isolation in cases of failure as well as to bring computations closer to the data for greater speed.

We've already talked about two components that were used to handle failures: the Saga-Fault event that services can raise when something is wrong, and the Service Instance pattern. The third measure taken against service failure that we're going to discuss is the implementation of the Service Watchdog pattern in the system.

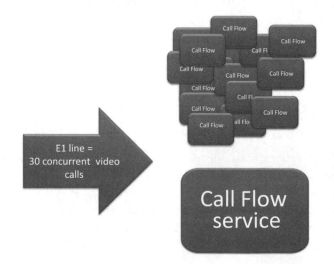

Figure 9.7 Using the Service Instance pattern to minimize the effect of failure. An E1 line can transfer 30 concurrent video calls. When you connect them to a single Call Flow service, a problem with one call may bring down the whole service, cutting off 30 users. If each Call Flow service handles only one call at a time, a failure will affect only a single caller.

The Service Watchdog pattern is defined (in chapter 3) as follows:

✓ **Implement the Service Watchdog pattern, where the service actively monitors its internal state, acts on potential trouble, tries to heal itself, and continuously publishes its status.**

Let's take another look at the failure scenario we discussed earlier in regard to the Saga-Fault event (see figure 9.8).

The RTP Listener service raises a saga event that is supposed to get to the Call Flow service, which it can't raise. The RTP Listener then tries to raise a Saga-Fault event, but how do you know what the problem is? Here are few options:

Figure 9.8 The advantage of using the Service Watchdog pattern. When the RTP Listener can't raise an event ❶ to the Call Flow service, an external observer (the watchdog) can figure out if the problem is with the publisher, the subscriber, the network, or any combination of the three.

- The Call Flow service is down.
- The RTP Listener (actually, the `eventBroker` within it, in this case) is failing somehow.
- The network is down.
- The whole computer that hosts the Call Flow service (and most likely other services) is down.
- There is a combination of the preceding problems.

The Service Watchdog, as an external observer, is able to discern what the states of the local machine and services are and expose those states to other components (services and service instances). In order for the watchdog to understand what's happening, it uses small agents that run inside each service. The following listing shows the watchdog class that manages the agents (there was one instance per agent). We deployed one watchdog instance per logical (virtualized or real) server.

Listing 9.8 Watchdog's proxy class used to manage its agents running in services

```
public class WatchedServiceAgentProxy : IWatchedServiceAgent, IDisposable
{
    internal readonly Uri agentAddress;
    private IWatchedServiceAgent agentProxy = null;
    private int failures = 0;
private static readonly ILog log =
➥ LogManager.GetLogger(MethodBase.GetCurrentMethod().DeclaringType);
private const int MAX_FAILURES = 3;
private readonly ResourceContractInfo resourceContractInfo;

public WatchedServiceAgentProxy(
            ResourceContractInfo resourceContractInfo,
            int instanceIdentifier)
{
    this.resourceContractInfo = resourceContractInfo;
```

```
     agentAddress = AgentAddressProvider.GetAddress(
     resourceContractInfo, instanceIdentifier);
}
public Uri Address
{
    get { return agentAddress; }
}

    public void Dispose()
{
    if(this.agentProxy != null)
        ((ICommunicationObject)agentProxy).Abort();
}

void EnsureAgentProxy()
{
    if (agentProxy == null)
      agentProxy =
      ChannelFactory<IWatchedServiceAgent>.CreateChannel(
                     new NetNamedPipeBinding(),
                     new EndpointAddress(agentAddress));
                     }
}
void RenewFaultedAgentProxy()
{
    if(agentProxy != null)
        ((ICommunicationObject)agentProxy).Abort();

    agentProxy = null;
    EnsureAgentProxy();
 }

 public LivelinessResult IsAlive()
 {
     try
     {
         EnsureAgentProxy();
         var isAlive = agentProxy.IsAlive();
         return isAlive;
     }
     catch(CommunicationException ex)
     {
         throw new ServiceCommunicationException
     ("Call to IsAlive failed", ex);
     }
 }

 public string GetName()
 {
     EnsureAgentProxy();
     return agentProxy.GetName();
 }

 public void Shutdown()
 {
      EnsureAgentProxy();
      agentProxy.Shutdown();
    }
```

Create named pipe to communicate with agent ⟵

Check liveliness of service ⟵

Request services to exit on shutdown ⟵

```
public void AcceptResourcesStatusBroadcast
(ServiceStatus[]
    resourcesStatus)
{
    try
    {
        EnsureAgentProxy();
        agentProxy.AcceptResourcesStatusBroadcast(resourcesStatus);
        Interlocked.Exchange(ref failures, 0);
    }
    catch(CommunicationException ex)
    {
        if (resourceContractInfo.IsOptional)
        {
            log.Info(string.Format("optional resource '{0}'
cannot be reached, ignored",
resourceContractInfo.ContractName));
            return;
        }
        if (failures > MAX_FAILURES)
        {
            log.WarnFormat("Could not reach the watch
 dog agent on pipe '{0}' for {1} times in a row.
 Renewing the agent proxy,
exception={2}", agentAddress, MAX_FAILURES + 1,ex);
        RenewFaultedAgentProxy();
            Interlocked.Exchange(ref failures, 0);
        }
        Interlocked.Increment(ref failures);
    }
  }
}
```

> **Update services
> with current
> status info**

As you can see, the agent proxy creates a named pipe channel to the service, through which it periodically asks about the health of the service and provides a liveliness report about other services. It also uses the channel to ask services to shut down when there is an orderly shutdown of the logical machine.

The service watchdogs also form a network between themselves and discover new servers waking up and going down. This enables you to use the watchdog as a poor man's service registry, in the sense that it provides endpoint management capabilities—a way to discover and locate available service endpoint across the whole system and provide some reporting capabilities. But it was far from a real service registry because it lacked governance capabilities, such as the ability to manage versioning, SLAs, assets, and so on.

9.3 *Summary*

In this chapter, you've seen that in order to achieve a desirable architecture, you need to use several patterns together. This is also true when you're building a whole system.

Let's take another look at the patterns we've looked at in this case study:

- *Edge Component (chapter 2)*—Separates business logic from technical concerns
- *Parallel Pipelines (chapter 3)*—Increases throughput of handling requests by breaking the process into steps
- *Gridable Service (chapter 3)*—Solves a computationally intensive problem
- *Inversion of Communications (chapter 5)*—Adds flexibility in changing the way a system behaves
- *Service Bus (chapter 7)*—Provides location transparency and communications
- *Saga (chapter 5)*—Ties together related events
- *Reservation (chapter 6)*—Secures instances to a saga
- *Service Instance (chapter 3)*—Breaks a service into multiple instances to increase overall availability
- *Service Watchdog (chapter 3)*—Monitors health of local resources and reporting to a central monitor

We also used a few other patterns when we built the system, such as these:

- *Aggregated Reporting (chapter 7)*—Builds reports by listening to events already being raised in the system
- *Active Service (chapter 2)*—Allows some services to have their own thread of control (and not just react to requests)
- *Service Host (chapter 2)*—Shares code to ensure that services have some standard facilities (such as the watchdog agent)

The point of this chapter isn't to show off how many patterns I know, or how many we implemented in this case study. The point of this chapter is to provide you with a glimpse into how the patterns in this book can be implemented. The patterns in this book are architectural, and as such they can be interpreted in different ways. The technology mapping section for each pattern only touched on implementations briefly; this chapter has shown a little more detail about what's involved.

This chapter has also demonstrated how you can move from requirements to services. I've just touched on the process, but I hope it has given you some insight into what's involved. I think it's also important to show the differences and relations between business services and the architecture that's built to support them.

Finally, this chapter has demonstrated how using multiple services together increases their overall usefulness and enables you to create a system. The system illustrated here is just one example of how you could compose the services. Other requirements will require a different set of patterns with a different set of relations and ultimately different architectures and designs. The important point is that patterns can work together to provide a cohesive whole.

The next, and final, chapter takes a look at another aspect of SOA meeting the real world—how SOA works with other important and common architectures and technologies (REST, the cloud, and big data).

SOA vs. the world 10

In this part of the book, we've looked at antipatterns, discussing some of the things that can go wrong, and we've looked at a case study, exploring how different patterns can interact with and complement each other. This chapter takes a look at the impact of other architectural styles and trends on SOA. We're going to cover:

- *REST*—What is the relationship between REST and SOA? Are they friends? Foes? Can they work together?
- *Cloud*—Is SOA a good fit for cloud-based deployments? How does the cloud affect SOA?
- *Big data*—NoSQL is starting to mature, with offerings from the big vendors both in the advanced analytics front (IBM and EMC offer distributions of Hadoop; Microsoft, Oracle, and others provide Hadoop integration) as well as solutions for big data in real time (such as IBM InfoSphere Streams and SAP HANA). How does SOA fit in?

Let's start by looking at the REST architectural style, which many see as an alternative to SOA.

10.1 *REST vs. SOA*

In recent years, the REST architectural style has become very popular, with a lot of companies building RESTful APIs (such as Twitter and Facebook) and a lot of other companies building value-added services, called mashups, by using these APIs.

Wikipedia defines mashups as:

> In *Web development*, a *mashup* is a *Web page* or application that uses and combines data, presentation or functionality from two or more sources to create new services. The term implies easy, fast integration, frequently using *open APIs* and data sources to produce enriched results that were not necessarily the original reason for producing the raw source data.
>
> The main characteristics of the mashup are combination, visualization, and aggregation. It is important to make existing data more useful, moreover for personal and professional use.[1]

This makes mashups sound a little like SOA, so to help clarify things I'll explain the differences between REST and SOA and what a RESTful SOA is. But first, let's look at what exactly REST is.

10.1.1 *What is REST anyway?*

REST is short for REpresentational State Transfer, and it's an architectural style defined by Roy T. Fielding in 2000 to describe the architectural style of the web. REST's basic component is the *resource*, which is addressable at an endpoint called a *URI*. Figure 10.1 illustrates the constraints the REST style defines.

Let's look at the constraints one by one:

- *Layered system*—The layered architectural style defines a hierarchy of components (layers) so that each layer can only know one level down. This promotes simplicity and the ability to enhance capabilities by adding middle layers (such as a firewall for added security).

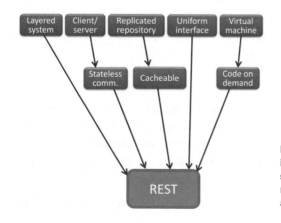

Figure 10.1   The REST architectural style is derived from five base architectural styles: layered system, client/server, replicated repository, uniform interface, and virtual machine

---

[1] Wikipedia mashup definition: http://en.wikipedia.org/wiki/Mashup_(web_application_hybrid).

- *Client/server*—The client/server architectural style introduces a separation of concerns between consumers and the providers.
- *Stateless communications*—This constraint means that each request made from the client to the server should have enough context (state) for the server to figure out what to do with it. This is why there are cookies that carry the session state from browser to server.
- *Replicated repository*—The idea behind this constraint is that it is OK to have more than one process provide a particular service in order to achieve scalability and availability of data.
- *Cacheable*—The cacheable constraint means that messages can specify whether it is OK to cache them and for how long. This constraint is an application of the replicated repository constraint to the message level, and it helps save on server round-trips, improves performance, and decreases server loads.
- *Uniform interface*—Probably the most distinct characteristic of REST is the use of a limited vocabulary. HTTP, the most prevalent REST implementation, offers just eight methods (GET, POST, PUT, DELETE, and the lesser known OPTIONS, HEAD, TRACE, and CONNECT). The uniform interface makes it relatively easy to integrate with RESTful services, and it also has a lot of impact on how you model RESTful services (as compared to non-RESTful services).
- *Virtual machine*—Virtual machine or interpreter is the ability to run scripted code. This is a prerequisite to the next constraint, "code on demand."
- *Code on demand*—This is an optional constraint that allows you to download code to the client for execution (such as JavaScript that runs in a browser). Code on demand makes integration easier, because clients can get code to handle the data they need instead of having to write code to handle the data themselves.

Another important aspect of REST is the use of Hypermedia as the Engine of Application State (HATEOAS). HATEOAS means that replies from a REST service should provide links (URIs) to the available options, which are based on the server's state, for moving forward from the current point. If a request to place an order was made, the reply can contain a URI for tracking the order, a URI for canceling the order, a URI for paying for it, and so on. HATEOAS is an outcome of using a uniform interface, and provides a map of the way to fulfill business goals when working with REST.

That's a view of REST from 50,000 feet, but even so, we can see some similarities to and differences from SOA.

10.1.2 How REST and SOA are different

REST shares a couple of constraints and components with SOA. Client/server and the notion of a layered system are basic building blocks of SOA, as they are for REST. On the other hand, constraints like uniform interface and virtual machine are very foreign to SOA.

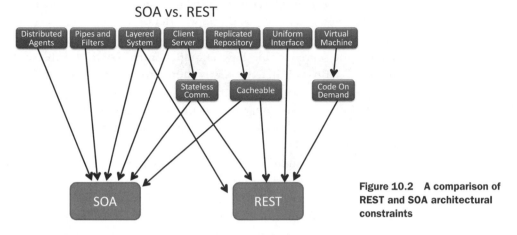

Figure 10.2   A comparison of REST and SOA architectural constraints

You can see the whole picture in figure 10.2, which illustrates SOA's influences as compared to REST's.

In addition to the layered system and client/server constraints, you can see two other REST constraints that are optional in SOA: stateless communications and cacheable. One of the optional constraints in SOA is the cacheable style.

In terms of the latter, we talked in chapter 5 about message exchange patterns and the benefits of sending immutable (versioned) data in messages. Immutable messages are SOA's way to specify cacheable messages; explicitly specifying cacheabilty, like in REST, is also an option.

The Service Instance pattern from chapter 3 is supportive of the replicated repository constraint. Similarly, while stateless communication is not a must in SOA, it is highly recommended (see the discussion on document-centric messaging in the Request-Reply pattern in chapter 5).

SOA's benefits over REST include governance and planned reuse as well as high security standards and a wealth of supporting components and message patterns (such as publish/subscribe). REST's advantages (especially REST over HTTP) include the ubiquity of the browser and the serendipity of reuse.[2]

The virtual machine constraint is very foreign to SOA, and fortunately it and its derived constraint (code on demand) are optional for REST. This means you can combine REST and SOA to enhance SOAs reuse with REST reuse serendipity.

10.1.3 *RESTful SOA*

I find that RESTful SOA is beneficial when you want to have a dual API. In most other cases, it's usually better to choose either SOA or REST (based on your specific needs) and stick with it.

---

[2] Steve Vinoski, "Serendipitous Reuse," *IEEE Internet Computing*, volume 12, issue 1 (January 2008), 84–87, http://steve.vinoski.net/pdf/IEEE-Serendipitous_Reuse.pdf.

How can you enrich SOA with REST? There are basically two approaches:

- Build a RESTful service and extend it to be an SOA one
- Take an SOA service and extend it to be a RESTful one

I recommend the latter approach, because SOA offers more flexible ways to connect services and has better tooling support. Also, it's likely that in enterprise environments SOA-related APIs will be more prevalent. That said, you'll often want to add REST to allow third-party integration and to allow mobile clients to interact and consume services directly (somewhat like the Composite Front End pattern in chapter 6).

NOTE The Edge Component pattern (discussed in chapter 2) is a good approach for adding a REST API on top of, or in addition to, an existing SOA API. You can even use technologies like Apache Camel, which enable flexible routing from external interfaces to internal ones.

The REST and SOA APIs will look radically different. REST comes with a hierarchical noun-oriented API, and SOA has a shallow verb-oriented API (both for event-oriented and web service-oriented APIs). Nevertheless, I find that mapping between the two is more straightforward than you might expect.

Mapping REST to SOA

Mapping REST to SOA is not an automatic task. But while you will have to put some thought into it, it's more than doable. The following list contains a few tips or things to remember when building a REST-to-SOA mapping:

- Different resources can map to a single service. If you have Order and Product resources, the Order resource may have a `GET /orders/<order id>` URI to see order details, and a `GET /products/orders/` URI to see the different orders a product participates in. Both might be mapped to an Order service with two messages in its contract, such as `ListOrderDetails` and `GetProductOrders`.

- Different REST URIs can point to the same message in a service. Both `POST /orders/`, which creates an order where the server allocated the key, and `PUT /orders/<order id>`, which creates an order where the client sets the order, ID can map to the same `CreateOrder` message, which accepts an XML message that may or may not have an order ID.

- As REST is new to most SOA practitioners, it is important to avoid common REST mistakes, like forgetting all the HTTP verbs and building a GETful architecture (where only the `GET` method is used), neglecting to use hypermedia, the error of using verbs as URIs (such as `/createOrder/`), and so on.

- If you have a proper REST API that utilizes HATEOAS and properly implements the `OPTIONS` verb to allow checking for next steps, a contract for the REST API isn't needed. Remember that the SOA API already has a more formal contract (event list or WSDL) and that the REST API is supplementary.

SOA and REST can be made to work together, and this combination can be beneficial, especially if you plan to expose an API for consumption by UI applications directly, and not limit it to being consumed by other applications. If you build your services properly and employ REST practices, using stateless communication and making results cacheable, you can add REST as an additional API (or as the only API for new services) and still get SOA's benefits.

That's enough about REST. Let's see how SOA matches up with another hot trend—the cloud.

10.2   SOA and the cloud

Cloud computing is an important IT trend, taking virtualization to the next level by using a large pool of virtualized hardware to provide utility computing capabilities. It provides an electricity-like model, where computational resources are available on demand (usually with pay-as-you-go billing) and with the ability to elastically grow and shrink your resource use as needed.

We'll take a look at how this relatively new playground affects SOA, but let's first try to make sense of the different cloud-related terms out there.

10.2.1   The cloud terminology soup

Cloud computing sounds a lot like many other virtualization and hosting solutions that have come around before. But while cloud technologies share concepts with previous solutions, there are several characteristics that differentiate cloud computing.

The U.S. National Institute of Standards and Technology published a formal definition of cloud computing (see the further reading section) in which it defined five essential characteristics:

- *On-demand self service*—The ability for cloud users to add capabilities (such as virtual machine instances or storage, and so on).
- *Rapid elasticity*—The ability to add or remove resources on demand.
- *Measured service*—The cloud service provider collects, controls, reports on, and optimizes resources (bandwidth, CPU usage, and so on). Users' consumption of these resources is usually the basis for service charges.
- *Resource pooling*—Resources are shared by multiple consumers transparently. Users do not know where the resources are located or what other tenants may be using them.
- *Ubiquitous network access*—Capabilities are accessed via heterogeneous networks.[3]

Cloud computing can be delivered as a "public cloud" where anyone can register and use the resources. Examples include Amazon Web Services (AWS) and Windows Azure. There are pros and cons to public cloud computing:

---

[3] NIST, *The NIST Definition of Cloud Computing*, Special Publication 800-145, http://csrc.nist.gov/publications/nistpubs/800-145/SP800-145.pdf.

Pros	Cons
▪ Low barrier to entry Increased latency	▪ Increased latency
▪ No up-front investment	▪ Can be costly for steady-state usage
▪ A convenient pay-as-you-go model	▪ Vendor lock-in (though this might be a temporary issue)
▪ Virtually infinite scalability	

An alternative to public clouds is the "private cloud," which involves deploying a cloud onsite for internal use by a single company. This can be done by building a solution based on OpenStack or using VMware vFabric. The pros of this approach include improved performance and latency, familiarity of tools and technologies (for the cluster managers), and privacy and security. The cons include greater up-front investment, limited resources, and reduced scalability.

There's also the option of "hybrid clouds"—using both a public and private cloud as a single solution. Hybrid clouds have the advantage of providing a good balance between flexibility and performance. On the other hand, hybrid clouds mean more complexity and security challenges, and the costs savings are there only if you optimize the cloud usage; otherwise it can prove to be more costly than the other options.

Cloud capabilities are delivered over the network "as a service." There are three main types of service delivery:

- *Infrastructure as a Service (IaaS)*—This type of service is usually provided by companies such as Amazon (AWS). The cloud capabilities are basic building blocks like virtual machines, storage, network bandwidth, and so on.
- *Platform as a Service (PaaS)*—In this type of cloud computing service, the provider delivers infrastructure software components such as databases, queues, and monitoring. Windows Azure is an example of this type of service.
- *Software as a Service (SaaS)*—These services are usually provided by smaller companies that deliver complete business capabilities. An example is Salesforce.com, which delivers a CRM solution as a service.

Now that we've got the vocabulary sorted out, let's take a look at the architectural implications of the cloud.

10.2.2 *The cloud and the fallacies of distributed computing*

I mentioned Peter Deutsch's fallacies of distributed computing several times in this book, and for a good reason. The fallacies are base architectural requirements that you have to account for when designing distributed systems. The cloud does not get a free ticket here.

Table 10.1 shows that cloud computing doesn't solve distributed computing problems, but it helps in making some of the fallacies more apparent, so you're less likely to assume they're not there.

Table 10.1   Fallacies of distributed computing and their relevance in cloud setups

Fallacy	What does it mean in the cloud
The network is reliable	No change—this is still a problem, especially in hybrid cloud solutions. If you have a real mission-critical app, you still need a disaster recovery plan (a backup in a secondary cloud provider).
Latency is zero	Latency has not decreased in the cloud, but by deploying in data centers near your end users, you can lower it. The cloud introduces another latency-related problem.
Bandwidth is infinite	In private clouds, this hasn't changed from traditional systems. In public clouds, it depends. For internal communications between deployed servers, bandwidth has been transformed into a cost problem. For clients connecting to your cloud application, bandwidth is same old problem.
Topology doesn't change	If you assume this in a cloud solution, you'll have a real problem. The whole notion of elasticity means there's no way the topology stays the same.
There's one administrator	This is still a fallacy in the cloud—just one that it's hard to believe someone would make.
Transport cost is zero	Transport cost is still a problem. The dollar costs of moving data in and out of the cloud are more apparent than in noncloud environments because cloud services come with a price list. The additional costs (performance, latency) on transforming data structures, encryption, and so on, can still be hidden.
The network is homogeneous	The network is not homogenous, but you don't need to care as much because you can define the types of machines you need and get virtualized copies that match your needs.

The flip side is that the cloud brings with it a couple of new fallacies to watch out for:

- *Nodes are fixed*—This point builds on the "topology doesn't change" fallacy, and it means you can't assume too much about the node you are running on. Not its IP address, not that items you copied to it will be there on the next boot, and so on. Don't assume anything. Any meaningful state should be persisted elsewhere on attached or connected storage.
- *Latency is constant*—This point builds on the "latency is zero" fallacy. The fact that latency isn't constant means that if you send messages asynchronously, you can't assume they'll arrive in order. If you connect with UIs, you need to understand the variance and plan for it so that users will get an appropriate experience. For instance, in the visual search service mentioned in chapter 9, we sometimes saw 5 to 15 seconds of latency when establishing communications with the server. To get a reasonable identification time, we had to think about sending images and videos in the background, before the user chose which image to identify.

Fine, but how does all this relate to SOA?

Nodes are fixed? A real-world example

On one project I worked on, we had a service hosted in Windows Azure in two distinct setups: staging and production. We used a Windows Azure feature that allows you to do a virtual IP switch to move the staging servers to production and it worked great—except the new production (former staging) service was still pointing to the staging data store and using the staging certificate store.

We solved this by orchestrating the switch from another service that also sent events to synchronize the whole move. But we learned our lesson: in the cloud, nodes aren't fixed and you can't assume anything.

10.2.3 The cloud and SOA

SOA is probably the best architectural style to enable a transition to cloud computing, especially for hybrid and public cloud scenarios.[4] Table 10.2 shows SOA's traits and how they're a good fit for the cloud.

Table 10.2 SOA traits that are good fit for the cloud

SOA trait	How is good for the cloud
Partitioning of the enterprise/ system into business components	A service is a good-sized unit to move to the cloud (as it is for moving to an external vendor). An SOA component presents a complete business function. Service boundaries already take into account the fallacies of distributed computing and already internalize the handling of messages.
Using standards-based message and contract communications	Encapsulating internal representations rather than relying on shared data means that services moved to the cloud will be able to operate in isolation from the rest of the world, communicating only via the messages defined in their contracts.
Treating service boundaries as trust boundaries	When you want to move functionality to a public cloud, it greatly helps if your software already assumes that anything foreign is hostile and should be authenticated, validated, and so on.
Keeping services autonomous	Autonomy better equips services to survive on their own. It also helps them to keep operating when other services go out.

A lot of the patterns in this book are very relevant to cloud deployments and even more so for the transition to the cloud:

---

[4] See the following articles: Andrew Oliver, "Long Live SOA in the Cloud Era", *InfoWorld* (June 2012), www.infoworld.com/t/application-development/long-live-soa-in-the-cloud-era-196053; Joe McKendrick, "SOA, Cloud: It's the Architecture that Matters," *ZDNet* (Oct. 2011), www.zdnet.com/blog/service-oriented/soa-cloud-its-the-architecture-that-matters/7908; and David Rubinstein, "SOA (the Term) is Dead, but SOA (the Architecture) Lives On," *SD Times* (April 2012), www.sdtimes.com/content/article.aspx?ArticleID =36566&page=3, (see particularly the "Without SOA, There Is No Cloud" section).

- *Service Bus (chapter 7)*—Helps in providing location transparency and service registration (so services will know where to find other services). Location transparency is very beneficial in the cloud because new services might be spawned in a new node with new IP address or be consolidated to a single node based on load.

- *Identity Provider (chapter 4)*—An identity provider is a crucial component when services are spread across the enterprise and a cloud, and users expect a single sign-on experience. This is even more important if you add REST to the mix, and you need to interleave WS-Trust and OAuth services.

- *Request/Reaction and Inversion of Communications (chapter 5)*—Asynchronous communication is more resilient than plain RPC, and that's a big plus in hybrid cloud setups.

- *Service Monitor and Service Watchdog (chapters 4 and 3 respectively)*—These patterns are always relevant, but they're even more important when you don't control the hardware.

- *Service Instance (chapter 3)*—This is another pattern that can help with elasticity and scaling out.

- *Virtual Endpoint (chapter 3)*—When running in the cloud, the endpoint in which services are delivered will most likely be a virtual endpoint, whether or not you like it.

In summary, SOA principles and patterns are a very good match for the cloud. The division of business capabilities into autonomous components fits well both for gradual transitioning to public clouds as well to hybrid cloud setups.

10.3 SOA and big data

There's an interesting video called "Shift Happens" (or sometimes "Did You Know?") that includes all sorts of interesting trivia on the rate at which the world is changing in the digital age.[5] Version 6 of this video includes an estimation that 40 exabytes (4.0 * 10^19) of unique information will be generated in 2012 (which is more than in the previous 5000 years combined). Most of us don't have to deal with these amounts of data, but there's no denying that the amount of data enterprises have to process and amass every year continuously grows. A TDWI research report from September 2011 states that a third of the organizations surveyed had more than 10 terabytes of data and that the number of larger sets (100s of terabytes) will triple in 2012.[6]

---

[5] Karl Fisch, Scott McLeod, and Jeff Brenman, *Shift Happens 3.0*, www.youtube.com/watch?v=cL9Wu2kWwSY. For more information on versions of the video, see the *shifthappens* web page: http://shifthappens.wikispaces .com/.

[6] Phillip Russom "Big data analytics, Fourth Quarter 2011," TDWI Research, http://tdwi.org/research/2011/ 09/best-practices-report-q4-big-data-analytics.aspx.

Most research organizations (like TDWI or Forrester Research) agree that big data evolves around different Vs, like velocity, volume, variety, and variability. Personally, I think the major drivers are just the first two Vs—the velocity at which you have to ingest data, along with the latency until it's usable, and the total volume of data you have to store and do something with. If you have a high peak load of messages for a couple of hours a day, and you don't need to see that data until a day later—that's not a big data problem. The same goes for terabytes of archival data you don't need to analyze, and are just storing for some regulatory reason.

Big data has a lot of implications, starting with changing the way we think about data and producing new professions like data science. It also has technical implications, which is what we'll take a look at next.

10.3.1 *The big data technology mix*

According to Gil Press, the first big data problem occurred in the 1880s (yes, you read that right).[7] In the late 1800s, the processing of the U.S. census was beginning to take close to 10 years. Crossing this mark was meaningful, as the census runs every 10 years and the population, and thus the amount of information, was increasing—the outlook wasn't very good. In 1886, Herman Hollerith started a business to rent machines that could read and tabulate census data on punch cards. The 1890 census took less than 2 years to complete and handled both a larger population (62 million people) and more data points than the 1880 census. (Hollerith's business merged with three others to form what became IBM.)

Today we find ourselves in a similar position when we try to solve big data problems with the traditional tools we have at hand, like our trusty RDBMSs or OLAP cubes. Those tools aren't going away, but we need additional tools—our own Hollerith machines to cope with the scale. The good news is that a lot of these new tools are emerging. The bad news is that a lot of these new tools are emerging.

Figure 10.3 shows some of the main categories of solutions for big data storage that have emerged in the market, and a few examples of tools in each category. For instance, there's the relational category, which is divided between NewSQL solutions (sharding solutions over regular RDBMSs) and massively parallel solutions. The massively parallel solutions are then divided into column-oriented solutions and row-oriented ones. On the other side of things are key-value stores, which are divided between in-memory and column-oriented solutions. The diagram is not exhaustive, but it does demonstrate the wide range of options and suboptions available. It also indicates that there's no single good solution—otherwise there'd be fewer options and everyone would standardize around the best solutions (as happened with RDBMSs 30 years ago).

---

[7] Gil Press, "The Birth of Big Data," *The Story of Information* (June 15, 2011), http://infostory.wordpress.com/2011/06/15/the-birth-of-big-data/.

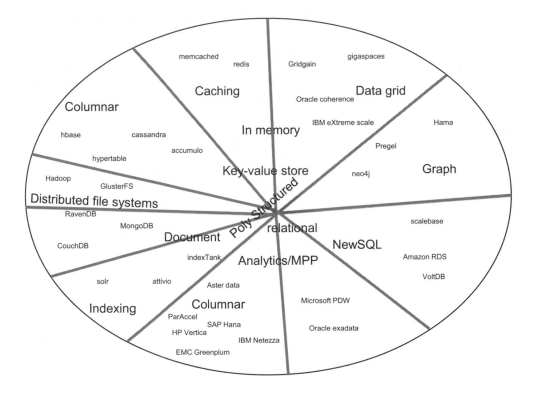

Figure 10.3   The big data storage space. There are several classes of solutions; some based on the relational paradigm and others remove database capabilities to get massive scale at cheap prices.

With this almost endless list of options to choose from, we need selection criteria in order to pick the best solution for a given project. Here are some of the criteria I find useful:

- *Type of organization*—Enterprises will likely be drawn to the more established vendors (for support, regulatory compliance, and so on). Startups will most likely gravitate toward the cheap, open source options.

- *Data access patterns*—Will you have mostly reads versus mostly writes, access based on the primary key or a lot of ad hoc queries. If you need to traverse relations back and forth (like walking a social graph), graph databases can be a good option.

- *Type of data stored*—Structured data is a good fit for relational models, semistructured data (XML/JSON) is a good fit for document and column stores, and unstructured data is good for file-based options like Hadoop.

- *Data schema change frequency*—Is your schema mostly fixed or constantly changing? Relational options are better with fixed schemas; document and name-value solutions handle open schemas better.

- *Required latency*—The faster you need the data, the more you'll want (or need) an in-memory solution.

> ### Apache Hadoop
>
> There are a lot of interesting technologies in the big data space, but one that stands out is Apache Hadoop. Hadoop is an open source implementation of Google's filesystem and map/reduce paradigm. Hadoop is interesting, not because it's necessarily the best solution for big data, but because it has gained massive backing from many of the major IT vendors. Oracle, IBM, EMC, Microsoft, and Amazon all offer a Hadoop distribution or service.
>
> I've included a few sources about Apache Hadoop in the further reading section of this chapter. Or you can go straight to the Hadoop web page: http://hadoop .apache.org/.

At this point, you might be thinking that big data sounds interesting, but where's the place for SOA in all this. How can you fit SOA into all of this?

10.3.2 *How SOA works with big data*

How can SOA work with big data? If we accept the premise that more and more enterprises are finding that they need to handle big data, SOA should be able to work with big data, or it should be replaced with a more appropriate architecture.

One way to deal with big data within SOA is for services to use big data-related technologies within the services. A service that needs to handle semistructured data can use a document database store, and a service that needs to handle event data in near real time can use a data grid or an event-stream processing solution. Like with cloud technology, the advantage of SOA is the separation and isolation of the various services from one another. The isolation allows for gradual adoption in the enterprise, where only services that need these technologies adopt them, and other services can stay with their current technologies.

One related pattern here is the Gridable Service (discussed in chapter 3), which describes taking a computationally intensive task and dividing it between multiple services—something you can achieve with both data-grid solutions as well as big data stores that support map/reduce.

When it comes to the analysis of big data, we should distinguish between situations where the analysis can be made within the boundaries of the service and those where the analysis requires data from multiple services.

For the second type of big data analysis, where a cross-service view is needed, the ideas described in the Aggregated Reporting pattern (see chapter 7) still apply. You can get the data from all the services in a way that does not violate SOA principles as long as you make the data immutable and you know where the ownership lies. The processes that perform the actual analysis can sometimes be considered services themselves, such as a recommendation service for e-commerce solutions.

When the analysis can be handled within the boundaries of a specific service, the implementation is a matter of utilizing big data-related technologies as part of the service.

In a system I recently worked on, we had to categorize multichannel interactions (voice, email, chat, and so on). The categorization service had a subscription for incoming interactions, which arrived both in batches and in real time. The same business logic that categorized data in real time was also used in the batch. The real-time categorization had a web service and messaging endpoints, and the batch processing used map/reduce on top of Hadoop—two parts of the same business service using the same business logic to do their work. Figure 10.4 provides an illustration of this service.

In addition to the specifics around big data, you can see the application of some of the patterns described in this book within the illustration. An implementation of the Service Host pattern (chapter 2) hosts the service with its two endpoints, each of implements the Edge Component pattern (chapter 2). Note that one of the endpoints is a RESTful one, as discussed earlier in this chapter. Additionally, you can see the Service Watchdog pattern (chapter 3) in use, and that the service is deployed multiple times (the Service Instance pattern from chapter 3).

In summary, you've seen that services can be used with big data. Big data emphasizes the need to make services coarse-grained (see also the discussion of the Nanoservices

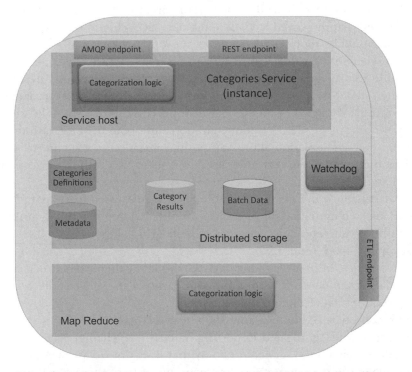

Figure 10.4   A categorization service that incorporates big data map/reduce handling with online handling. The service has three endpoints: an ETL endpoint that ingests large batches of updates, a REST endpoint that accepts small batches and online requests, and an AMQP endpoint for low-latency requests. The same categorization logic is used in the map/reduce batch processes and the online/ real-time processes.

antipattern in chapter 8), and what you learned about building services is still applicable. Nevertheless, big data is changing the way enterprises handle and think about data. For SOA to stay relevant as an architectural style, it should, and can, adapt and utilize the new technologies that solve big data problems.

10.4 Summary

There are, of course, other architectural styles and technologies that are related to SOA. We discussed event-driven architecture (EDA) and SOA as part of the Inversion of Communications pattern in chapter 5. Another relevant style is domain-driven design, which isn't as popular as the three trends discussed in this chapter, but it can complement SOA as a way to design individual services.

These are the three styles we did cover in this chapter:

- *REST*—An alternative architectural style that can be merged with SOA. If you build RESTful SOA, you can benefit from both and use either SOA-style or REST-style APIs for your services (or both).
- *Cloud*—A complementary IT trend that shares its principles with SOA, and for which SOA is a very good fit.
- *Big data*—An increasingly common reality in a lot of enterprises, and to which SOA has to adapt.

Congratulations on finishing the book. You should now be able to understand the main challenges and common pitfalls of building distributed systems in general and service-oriented ones in particular. You should also have an arsenal of architectural concepts that will help you cope with these challenges and build solid systems.

The focus of this book, is on using SOA as a way to solve distributed systems challenges, so naturally this chapter's coverage of other architectural styles only scratched the surface. You can take a look at the next section for resources that will expand on the topics mentioned here.

10.5 Further reading

REST

Roy Thomas Fielding, "Architectural Styles and the Design of Network-Based Software Architectures," (PhD thesis, 2000), www.ics.uci.edu/~fielding/pubs/dissertation/top.htm.
Roy Fielding's dissertation is where the REST architectural style was defined, and it's still one of the best sources for learning about it.

Jim Webber, Savas Parastatidis, and Ian Robinson, "How to GET a Cup of Coffee," *InfoQ*, www.infoq.com/articles/webber-rest-workflow.
Jim, Savas, and Ian take a simple, down-to-earth example (ordering a coffee) and use that to provide a good explanation of REST principles, including HATEOAS.

Leonard Richardson and Sam Ruby, *RESTful web services* (O'Reilly, 2007).
This is probably the best book on REST.

THE CLOUD

Jothy Rosenberg and Arthur Mateos, *The Cloud at Your Service: The When, How, and Why of Enterprise Cloud Computing* (Manning, 2010).
   Jothy's and Arthur's book provides a good all-round introduction to cloud concepts and technologies.

Peter Deutsch, "The Eight Fallacies of Distributed Computing," http://blogs.oracle.com/jag/resource/Fallacies.html.
   James Gosling (the father of Java) concisely lists Peter Deutsch's eight fallacies on his blog.

Arnon Rotem-Gal-Oz, "Fallacies of Distributed Computing Explained," www.rgoarchitects.com/Files/fallacies.pdf.
   This paper explains the fallacies in some detail.

OpenStack, http://openstack.org/.
   OpenStack is an open source cloud implementation that's trying to provide an alternative to closed source implementations like Amazon's and Microsoft's.

ReaderWriterCloud, www.readwriteweb.com/cloud/.
   ReadWriterWeb is a news and information site on internet-related technologies. ReaderWriterCloud is its channel dedicated to cloud computing.

BIG DATA

Alex Holmes, *Hadoop in Practice* (Manning, 2011).
   This book provides a relatively up-to-date view of Hadoop and related technologies.

Lars George, *HBase: The Definitive Guide* (O'Reilly, 2011)
   Lars is one of the contributors to HBase, and his book is currently the best one on HBase.

Phillip Russom, "Big data analytics, Fourth Quarter 2011," TDWI Research, http://tdwi.org/research/2011/09/best-practices-report-q4-big-data-analytics.aspx.
   This is TDWI research group report and overview of the big data landscape.

NoSQL Databases, http://nosql-database.org/.
   This site links to a lot of NoSQL databases (segmented by type). The site also provides links to articles related to NoSQL.

Curt Monash, DBMS2 (blog), www.dbms2.com/.
   Curt Monash's site provides good information and insights on databases (SQL and NoSQL) and related technologies.

Alex Popescu, myNoSQL (blog), http://nosql.mypopescu.com/.
   Alex's blog rounds up articles and news related to NoSQL.

Marco Seiriö, Marco on CEP (blog), http://rulecore.com/CEPblog/.
   Marco on CEP is a good blog covering complex event processing technologies.

appendix
From quality attributes
to patterns

This appendix provides a cross-reference from quality attributes and sample scenarios to individual patterns discussed in this book. As mentioned in chapter 1, quality attributes and quality attribute scenarios provide a good way to describe architectural requirements. In order to help you make better use of the mapping from quality attributes to patterns, I'll begin by introducing quality attributes in general.

A.1 Introduction to quality attributes

There are two types of requirements for software projects: functional and nonfunctional.

Functional requirements describe what the solution must do (usually expressed as use cases or stories). The functional requirements are what the users (or systems) that interact with the system do with the system (fill in an order, update customer details, authorize a loan, and so on).

Nonfunctional requirements are attributes the system is expected to have or manifest. These usually include requirements in areas such as performance, security, availability, and the like. A better name for nonfunctional requirements is "quality attributes."

The following are formal definitions for quality attributes and related concepts from the IEEE 1061 standard, "Standard for a Software Quality Metrics Methodology":[1]

- *Quality attribute*—A characteristic of software, or a generic term applying to quality factors, quality subfactors, or metric values.

- *Quality factor*—A management-oriented attribute of software that contributes to its quality. In this book, the term "quality attribute" is used instead of "quality factor," as it is a more common way to refer to it.

- *Quality subfactor*—A decomposition of a quality factor or quality subfactor to its technical components. I refer to "quality subfactors" as "concrete attributes" throughout this book, as I think it conveys the meaning better.

---

[1] IEEE, 1061-1998 *IEEE Standard for a Software Quality Metrics Methodology.*

- *Metric value*—A metric output or an element that is from the range of a metric.
- *Software quality metric*—A function whose inputs are software data and whose output is a single numerical value that can be interpreted as the degree to which software possesses a given attribute that affects its quality.

Most of the requirements that drive the design of a software architecture come from a system's quality attributes. That's because the effect of quality attributes is usually system-wide. (You wouldn't want your system to have good performance only in the UI—you want the system to perform well no matter what). This is exactly what software architecture is concerned with. Note that a few requirements might still come from functional requirements. The question is how do we find out what those requirements are?

The answer to that is also in the software architecture definition. The source for quality attributes is the stakeholders. So what or who are these "stakeholders"? A stakeholder is just about anyone who has a vested interest in the project. A typical system has a lot of stakeholders, starting with the (obvious) customer, the end users (those people in the customer's organization who will actually use the software), and going on to the operations personnel who will have to keep the solution running, the development team, testers, maintainers, and management. In some systems, the stakeholders can even be the shareholders or even the general public (imagine that you're building a new dispatch system for a 911 center).

One of the architect's roles is to analyze the quality attributes and define an architecture that will deliver all the functional requirements while supporting the quality attributes. As you might expect, sometimes quality attributes are in conflict with each other—the most obvious examples are performance versus security or flexibility versus simplicity, and the architect's role is to strike a balance between the different quality attributes (and the stakeholders) to make sure the overall quality of the system is maximized.

Contextual solutions (patterns) can be devised to solve specific quality attributes' needs. But saying that a system needs to have "good performance" or that it needs to be "testable" doesn't really tell you what to do. In order to be able to discern which patterns apply to specific quality attributes, you need a better understanding of what the formal definition of the quality attributes means; you need something that is more concrete.

The way to get that concrete understanding of the effect of quality attributes is to use scenarios. Scenarios are short, story-like statements that demonstrate how a quality attribute is manifested in the system using a functional situation.

Quality attribute scenarios originated as a way to evaluate software architectures. The Software Engineering Institute developed several evaluation methodologies, like Architecture Tradeoff Analysis Method (ATAM),[2] which builds on scenarios to contrast and compare how the different quality attributes are met by candidate architectures.

---

[2] Paul Clements, Rick Kazman, and Mark Klein, *Evaluating Software Architectures: Methods and Case Studies* (Addison-Wesley Professional, 2002).

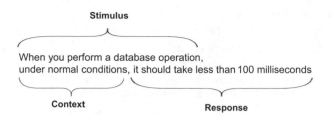

Figure A.1 Components of a quality attribute scenario

The scenarios can be used as inputs to make sure the quality attributes are actually met. Furthermore, you can identify which strategies or patterns will make the scenarios possible (and thus ensure the quality attributes are met) within the system.

ATAM (and similar evaluation methods like LAAAM, which is part of MSF 4.0) suggests building a utility tree that represents the overall usefulness of the system. The scenarios serve as the leaves of the utility tree, and the architecture is evaluated by considering how the architecture makes the scenarios possible.

I've found that using scenarios and the utility tree approach early in the design of the architecture can greatly enhance the quality of the architecture that is produced. When you examine the scenarios, you can also prioritize them and better balance conflicting attributes.

The tree representation helps present the whole picture, but the important bits are the scenarios. Scenarios are expressed as three-part statements containing a stimulus, a context, and a response. The *stimulus* is the action taken (by the system, user, other system, or any other person); the *response* identifies how the system is expected to behave when the stimulus occurs; and the *context* specifies the environment or conditions under which you expect to get the response. Figure A.1 identifies the three parts of a scenario.

It's usually best to use this sort of three-part statement to describe quality attribute scenarios because it makes the scenarios more verifiable and complete. But structuring scenarios this way is a guideline, not a commandment, and if a scenario feels more natural in another form, don't feel obligated to force it into this template.

Now that you know the importance of quality attributes to software architecture and how to write them up, you can think again about the architectural requirements in your projects. Once you do that, you can use the table in the next section to look for patterns that are relevant to the challenges you need to solve.

A.2 From quality attributes to patterns

When you're looking at the architectural requirements of your project, you can use table A.1 as a reference for finding applicable patterns.

Please keep in mind that the list is not exhaustive. There are additional uses for each pattern. Nevertheless, the table still provides a good starting point.

NOTE One pattern is missing from this table—the Aggregated Reporting pattern from chapter 7. That pattern is derived from functional requirements and not quality attributes.

Table A.1   Quality attributes to patterns cross-reference

Quality attribute	Concrete attribute	Sample scenario	Relevant pattern	Chapter
Availability	Uptime	Even disconnected from the WAN, the service can still produce internal results.	Active Service	2
Availability	Reduced system downtime	Upon a server crash, the system will remain operational.	Service Instance	3
Availability	Hardware failure resiliency	Upon a server crash, the system will remain operational.	Gridable Service	3
Availability	Hardware failure resiliency	When only one server crashes, the system will continue to operate with no less than 50 percent of its original capacity.	Service Instance	3
Availability	Hardware failure resiliency	Upon a server crash, the system will resume operations within two minutes.	Virtual Endpoint	3
Availability	Improved failure detection	Upon a failure or degraded performance, the system will alert the administrator (via SMS) within a well-defined amount of time.	Service Watchdog	3
Availability	Effort to change (deployment)	Under normal conditions, adding a server for scaling purposes should take no longer than four hours (including installation, configuration, and so on).	Service Bus	7
Budget	Contain hardware costs (TCO)	The grid allows you to spread load over less-expensive hardware.	Gridable Service	3
Business drivers	Time to market	The time to market of new changes should be less than six months.	Client/Server/ Service	6
Changeability	Add feature	Integrate a new capability into the system in three calendar weeks or less.	Inversion of Communications	5
Changeability	Replace component (vendors)	During development, replacing the credit card processing gateway should take one week or less.	Service Bus	7
Changeability	Replace component (vendors)	During development, replacing the credit card processing gateway should take one week or less.	Orchestration	7
Flexibility	Extension points	It is expected that the system will require SOX compliance within the next year and it will need auditing for all services.	Edge Component	2
Flexibility	Reduced assumptions	For normal interactions, services are invoked in a fire-and-forget manner.	Decoupled Invocation	3

Table A.1 Quality attributes to patterns cross-reference *(continued)*

Quality attribute	Concrete attribute	Sample scenario	Relevant pattern	Chapter
Flexibility	Temporal coupling	Under normal conditions, the ordering party will be notified about order shipments within two hours of shipping the package.	Request/ Reaction	5
Flexibility	Decoupling	Services should know as little as possible about each other.	Inversion of Communications	5
Flexibility	Interfaces	During development, adding a REST API to the system should be supported.	Service Bus	7
Flexibility	Business flows	During development and operations, adding timeouts to all ordering processes will take less than one week.	Orchestration	7
Flexibility	Composability	During development, a developer will be able to find and reuse services in multiple business processes.	Orchestration	7
Flexibility	Add new business processes	Under normal conditions, adding a new prepaid plan to the system and moving it to production will take less than two days.	Workflodize	2
Flexibility	Changeability	Under normal conditions, changing the billing process to support a new credit card clearance provider should take less than one week.	Composite Front End	6
Integrity	Correctness	Under all conditions, an order processed by the system will be billed.	Saga	5
Integrity	Predictability	Under normal conditions, the chances of a customer getting billed for a canceled order shall be less than 5 percent.	Saga	5
Integrity	Correctness	Under all conditions, failure to receive payment within five business days will cancel the order and shipping.	Reservation	6
Integrity	Predictability	Under normal conditions, the chances of a customer getting billed for a canceled order shall be less than 5 percent.	Reservation	6
Interoperability	Integration	During operations, integrating a new subsystem should take less than two calendar months.	Service Bus	7
Maintainability	Backwards compatibility	As contracts evolve, the services should be able to support consumers using older versions of the contract.	Edge Component	2

Table A.1   Quality attributes to patterns cross-reference *(continued)*

Quality attribute	Concrete attribute	Sample scenario	Relevant pattern	Chapter
Maintainability	Add service	Configuring the security for a new service will take less than half a day's work for a single developer.	Identity Provider	4
Maintainability	Easier upgrades	Individual service instances can be upgraded without disrupting service availability.	Virtual Endpoint	3
Manageability	Reporting	At all times, managers will be able to gain an overall view of the status and problems in handling business requests.	Service Monitor	4
Manageability	Understand system's health	Under error conditions, an administrator will be able to understand any problems and performance bottlenecks in the different business flows.	Orchestration	7
Performance	Latency	Evaluating the profitability of an offer suffers no delay from external service calls.	Active Service	2
Performance	Eliminate data loss	No message acknowledged by the system will be lost.	Decoupled Invocation	3
Performance	Decrease latency	Handle incoming requests without degrading latency, even under peak loads.	Decoupled Invocation	3
Performance	Higher message throughput	Under stress conditions, the system handles more than 10,000 requests per second.	Parallel Pipelines	3
Performance	Latency	Under normal conditions, service requests should complete in less than a second for 99 percent of the cases and less than two seconds for 100 percent of the cases.	Gridable Service	3
Performance	Latency	The cost of authenticating any request will not exceed 100 milliseconds.	Identity Provider	4
Performance	Responsiveness	Under normal conditions, the UI will not hang while long operations are performed (such as searches, course recalculations, and so on).	Request/ Reaction	5
Performance	Deadline	Under load and normal conditions, the system can continue to update stock prices at regular intervals.	Active Service	2
Portability	Installation	During installation, switching from one environment to another should take little to no time.	Service Host	2

Table A.1   Quality attributes to patterns cross-reference *(continued)*

Quality attribute	Concrete attribute	Sample scenario	Relevant pattern	Chapter
Reliability	Handle failure	When resuming from a communications disconnection, all the processes that were interrupted shall remain consistent.	Saga	5
Reliability	Reduce data loss	A message acknowledged by the system will not be lost.	Transactional Service	2
Reliability	Increase autonomy	During normal operations, the system will clear all its temporary resources continuously.	Service Watchdog	3
Reliability	Mean time to repair (MTTR)	Under normal operations, the time required to discover a faulty service will be less than two minutes.	Service Monitor	4
Reusability	Core module set definition	Reuse 90 percent or more of the common sales process activities for most new plans.	Workflodize	2
Reusability	Reduce development time	During development, the environment for a new service will be set up within minutes.	Service Host	2
Reusability	Interfaces	All services should support common service APIs in addition to any specific requests they may serve.	Inversion of Communications	5
Scalability	Handle increased loads	To handle increased loads, solve the problem with additional servers with no software changes.	Parallel Pipelines	3
Scalability	Scale out	It should be possible to deal with increased service loads with more hardware.	Gridable Service	3
Scalability	Ability to scale out	It should be possible to deal with increased service loads with more hardware.	Service Instance	3
Security	Spoofing	When receiving messages before handling a message, the system should verify signatures using the sender's public key to prevent impersonation.	Secured Infrastructure, Secured Message	4
Security	Spoofing	Under all conditions, when sending and receiving messages, the system should add timestamps, sequence numbers, or expiration times to messages (to cope with replay attacks).	Secured Infrastructure, Secured Message	4

Table A.1   Quality attributes to patterns cross-reference *(continued)*

Quality attribute	Concrete attribute	Sample scenario	Relevant pattern	Chapter
Security	Repudiation	During all communications, when sending messages the system should add timestamps and require signatures on messages (to prevent senders from claiming they didn't send a message).	Secured Infrastructure, Secured Message	4
Security	Information disclosure	When sending sensitive information, under all conditions, the system should encrypt important information (or the whole message) to prevent others from reading sensitive data.	Secured Infrastructure, Secured Message	4
Security	Tampering	During all communications, the system should verify signatures and to make sure no one changed the content of request or a reaction. If a signature is damaged, the system should log and discard the messages.	Service Firewall	4
Security	Tampering	During all communications, the systems should validate that messages are not malformed, and discard and log bad messages.	Service Firewall	4
Security	Information disclosure	During all communications, the system should scan outgoing messages for sensitive content and prevent sending it out.	Service Firewall	4
Security	Information disclosure	When sending out messages, if a reply message is targeted outside of the known group, log and alert the administrator.	Service Firewall	4
Security	Information disclosure, Elevation of privileges	Under all conditions, before processing a message, the system should inspect incoming messages for XPath, SQL injection attacks, and viruses, and notify an administrator if a problem is identified.	Service Firewall	4
Security	Denial of service	Under normal operations, when an attacker tries to bombard the system with requests, the system should identify the attack, blocking known attackers, ignore their requests, and notify an administrator.	Service Firewall	4
Security	Elevation of privilege	Under all conditions, before processing an incoming message, the system should validate contracts and sizes of elements and alert an administrator of any problems.	Service Firewall	4

Table A.1   Quality attributes to patterns cross-reference *(continued)*

Quality attribute	Concrete attribute	Sample scenario	Relevant pattern	Chapter
Security	Authentication	During normal operations, a revoked right will be updated in the system within five minutes.	Identity Provider	4
Security	Elevation of privilege	Under all conditions, when authorizing a user, the system should ensure that a service consumer doesn't assert any privileges it doesn't have.	Identity Provider	4
Security	Governance	During development and operations, the enterprise architecture team will be able to ensure that all services use secured channels.	Service Monitor	4
Security	Single sign-on (SSO)	Under normal operations, when a user has already authenticated with the system, the system should not require that user to enter credentials again.	Identity Provider	4
Security	Federated identity	Under normal operations, the system should be able to support authenticating external services (services managed by third parties).	Identity Provider	4
Security	Auditing	At all times, the system should keep track of any changes to authentication or authorization rules.	Identity Provider	4
Security	Spoofing	At all times, when handling a message, the system should verify that messages arrived with security tokens and authorize access according to privileges.	Identity Provider	4
Security	Auditing	At all times, the system should keep an audit trail for requesters and their requests.	Service Monitor	4
Security	Information disclosure	During normal operations, the system should look at message logs and try to identify man-in-the-middle attacks by comparing message traffic routes against known and configured routes.	Service Monitor	4
Testability	Test coverage rate	During development, for all critical requirements, achieve 100 percent test coverage.	Transactional Service	2
Testability	Performance	During stress tests, it should be possible to time the performance of each service in the system.	Service Monitor	4
Testability	Increase isolation	A service can be tested in isolation from the services it interacts with.	Decoupled Invocation	3

Table A.1 Quality attributes to patterns cross-reference *(continued)*

Quality attribute	Concrete attribute	Sample scenario	Relevant pattern	Chapter
Testability	Increase component isolation	Testing small, individual components helps to ensure their success when connected in a pipeline.	Parallel Pipelines	3
Testability	Coverage	During development, each capability of a service should have 100 percent test coverage.	Request/Reply	5
Time to market	Development ease	During development, exposing a new capability (already developed) in a service will take less than half a day to implement and test.	Request/ Reply	5
Usability	Operability	Under normal system use, the system should reuse entered data (like personal details) between different tasks so that end users can achieve business tasks fluently.	Composite Front End	6
Usability	Efficiency	When users need to learn new features, the experience should be streamlined to ensure a minimal learning curve.	Client/Server/ Service	6

index

RELATED MANNING TITLES

SOA Governance in Action
REST and WS-* Architectures
by Jos Dirksen

> ISBN: 978-1-617290-27-5
> 456 pages, $49.99
> August 2012

Activiti in Action
Executable business processes in BPMN 2.0
by Tijs Rademakers

> ISBN: 978-1-617290-12-1
> 456 pages, $49.99
> July 2012

Spring Integration in Action
by Mark Fisher, Jonas Partner,
   Marius Bogoevici, and Iwein Fuld

> ISBN: 978-1-935182-43-6
> 400 pages, $49.99
> September 2012

RabbitMQ in Action
Distributed messaging for everyone
by Alvaro Videla and Jason J.W. Williams

> ISBN: 978-1-935182-97-9
> 312 pages, $44.99
> April 2012

For ordering information go to www.manning.com

Camel in Action

by Claus Ibsen and Jonathan Anstey

    ISBN: 978-1-935182-36-8
    552 pages, $49.99
    December 2010

Mule in Action

by David Dossot and John D'Emic

    ISBN: 978-1-933988-96-2
    432 pages, $44.99
    July 2009

Open Source SOA

by Jeff Davis

    ISBN: 978-1-933988-54-2
    448 pages, $49.99
    May 2009

Open-Source ESBs in Action
Example Implementations in Mule and ServiceMix

by Tijs Rademakers and Jos Dirksen

    ISBN: 978-1-933988-21-4
    528 pages, $44.99
    September 2008

For ordering information go to www.manning.com

YOU MAY ALSO BE INTERESTED IN

Scala in Depth

by Joshua D. Suereth

ISBN: 978-1-935182-70-2
304 pages, $49.99
May 2012

Erlang and OTP in Action

by Martin Logan, Eric Merritt,
and Richard Carlsson

ISBN: 978-1-933988-78-8
432 pages, $49.99
November 2010

The Well-Grounded Java Developer
Vital techniques of Java 7 and polyglot programming
by Benjamin J. Evans and Martijn Verburg

ISBN: 978-1-617290-06-0
496 pages, $49.99
July 2012

Spring in Action, Third Edition
by Craig Walls

ISBN: 978-1-935182-35-1
424 pages, $49.99
June 2011

For ordering information go to www.manning.com